Drug Information for Teens

Second Edition

TEEN HEALTH SERIES

Second Edition

Drug Information for Teens

Health Tips about the Physical and Mental Effects of Substance Abuse

Including Information about Marijuana, Inhalants, Club Drugs, Stimulants, Hallucinogens, Opiates, Prescription and Over-the-Counter Drugs, Herbal Products, Tobacco, Alcohol, and More

◆

Edited by Sandra Augustyn Lawton

615 Griswold Street • Detroit, MI 48226

Bibliographic Note

Because this page cannot legibly accommodate all the copyright notices, the Bibliographic Note portion of the Preface constitutes an extension of the copyright notice.

Edited by Sandra Augustyn Lawton

Teen Health Series

Karen Bellenir, *Managing Editor*
David A. Cooke, M.D., *Medical Consultant*
Elizabeth Barbour, *Research and Permissions Coordinator*
Cherry Stockdale, *Permissions Assistant*
Laura Pleva Nielsen, *Index Editor*
EdIndex, Services for Publishers, *Indexers*

* * *

Omnigraphics, Inc.

Matthew P. Barbour, *Senior Vice President*
Kay Gill, *Vice President—Directories*
Kevin Hayes, *Operations Manager*
Leif Gruenberg, *Development Manager*
David P. Bianco, *Marketing Director*

* * *

Peter E. Ruffner, *Publisher*
Frederick G. Ruffner, Jr., *Chairman*
Copyright © 2006 Omnigraphics, Inc.
ISBN 0-7808-0862-2

Library of Congress Cataloging-in-Publication Data

Drug information for teens : health tips about the physical and mental effects of substance abuse / edited by Sandra Augustyn Lawton. -- 2nd ed.
   p. cm. -- (Teen health series)
   "Including Information About Marijuana, Inhalants, Club Drugs, Stimulants, Hallucinogens, Opiates, Prescription And Over-The-Counter Drugs, Herbal Products, Tobacco, Alcohol, And More."
   Includes bibliographical references and index.
   ISBN 0-7808-0862-2 (hardcover : alk. paper) 1. Teenagers--Drug use--United States. 2. Teenagers--Alcohol use--United States. 3. Teenagers--Health and hygiene--United States. 4. Drugs--Physiological effect. 5. Drug abuse--United States--Prevention. 6. Alcoholism--United States--Prevention. I. Lawton, Sandra Augustyn. II. Series.
   HV5824.Y68D774 2006
   613.8--dc22
                          2006012181

The information in this publication was compiled from the sources cited and from other sources considered reliable. While every possible effort has been made to ensure reliability, the publisher will not assume liability for damages caused by inaccuracies in the data, and makes no warranty, express or implied, on the accuracy of the information contained herein.

This book is printed on acid-free paper meeting the ANSI Z39.48 Standard. The infinity symbol that appears above indicates that the paper in this book meets that standard.

Printed in the United States

Table of Contents

Part III: Alcohol

Part IV: Tobacco

Part V: Other Drug-Related Health Concerns

Part VI: Treatment For Substance Abusers

Part VII: Drug Policy Controversies

Part VIII: If You Need More Information

Preface

About This Book

There are many reasons why some teens choose to use drugs, alcohol, or tobacco. The substances may make them feel grown up, provide entrance into a particular social circle, or be perceived as opening the door to fun and excitement, and some teens try drugs, alcohol, or tobacco out of simple curiosity. A recent survey found that 51% of high school seniors had tried an illicit drug at least once, 77% had used alcohol, and 53% had smoked cigarettes.

Adolescent substance use is a major health concern. It puts millions of teens at increased risk for traffic accidents, risky sexual practices, poor academic performance, juvenile delinquency, and developmental problems. It can lead to addiction—a chronic condition caused by changes in brain chemistry—and it can lead to health challenges during adulthood, including infectious diseases, organ damage, and cancer.

Drug Information For Teens, Second Edition provides updated facts about drug use, abuse, and addiction. It describes the physical and psychological effects of alcohol, tobacco, marijuana, inhalants, ecstasy, and many other drugs and chemicals that are commonly abused. It includes information about drug-related health concerns, such as HIV infection, risky sexual behavior, and drug-facilitated rape. A section on substance abuse treatment describes the types of treatment available and explains how to help a friend or parent with a substance abuse problem. Resource directories provide contact information for national organizations, hotlines and helplines, and other sources of support.

How To Use This Book

This book is divided into parts and chapters. Parts focus on broad areas of interest; chapters are devoted to single topics within a part.

Part I: What You Should Know About Substance Abuse And Addiction begins with a discussion of the difference between substance abuse and addiction and the two components of addiction—physical and psychological dependence. It provides statistics about teen substance abuse and gives tips on how to avoid drug use, including how to handle peer pressure.

Part II: Abused Drugs And Chemicals offers basic information about some of the most commonly abused substances, including marijuana, inhalants, ecstasy, cocaine, LSD, heroin, and anabolic steroids. Also included are facts about legally available substances of concern, such as prescription and over-the-counter drugs, herbal supplements, and caffeine and energy drinks.

Part III: Alcohol provides facts about alcohol use, abuse, and addiction in teens and their family members. It also discusses alcohol poisoning, statistics on alcohol consumption, and related health concerns.

Part IV: Tobacco presents facts on several forms of tobacco use, including cigarettes, cigars, pipes, smokeless tobacco, and secondhand smoke. Health risks associated with smoking are discussed, including cancer, emphysema, asthma, and bronchitis. Information on how to quit smoking is also provided.

Part V: Other Drug-Related Health Concerns covers some important topics that are associated with drug use but not necessarily related to the direct effects of the substances themselves. These include drug-facilitated rape, risky sexual behavior, the spread of infectious diseases via drug paraphernalia, drugged driving, violence, and the relationship between drugs and suicide.

Part VI: Treatment For Substance Abusers discusses the principles of treatment, the various types of treatments that are used, and the process of recovery. It offers encouragement for teens who need to seek help themselves and provides tips for helping friends and parents who may have a substance abuse problem.

Part VII: Drug Policy Controversies explains the Controlled Substances Act and offers information about some controversial drug policy issues, including drug testing in schools, drug legalization, and the medical use of marijuana.

Part VIII: If You Need More Information includes a directory of national organizations able to provide drug-related information and a directory of places able to provide support services, including hotline and helpline phone numbers and organizations that sponsor support groups. A state-by-state list of referral services will help readers find local information, and a chapter of additional reading presents lists of books, magazines and journals, and web pages that can be used as a starting point for further research.

Bibliographic Note

This volume contains documents and excerpts from publications issued by the following government agencies: Bureau of Justice Statistics; Centers for Disease Control and Prevention (CDC); National Cancer Institute (NCI); National Clearinghouse for Alcohol and Drug Information (NCADI); National Drug Intelligence Center (NDIC); National Highway Traffic Safety Administration (NHTSA); National Institute of Diabetes and Digestive and Kidney Diseases (NIDDK); National Institute on Alcohol Abuse and Alcoholism (NIAAA); National Institute on Drug Abuse (NIDA); National Institutes of Health (NIH); The National Women's Health Information Center (NWHIC); National Youth Violence Prevention Resource Center; Office of National Drug Control Policy; Office of the Surgeon General; Substance Abuse and Mental Health Services Administration (SAMHSA); U.S. Department of Labor; U.S. Drug Enforcement Administration (DEA); and the U.S. Food and Drug Administration (FDA).

In addition, this volume contains copyrighted documents and articles produced by the following organizations: American Academy of Allergy Asthma and Immunology; American Lung Association; Asthma UK; Community Counseling and Crisis Center; Drug Reform Coordination Network; Harvard School of Public Health; Hazelden Foundation; Health Day/Scout News; Henry J. Kaiser Family Foundation; Marijuana Policy

Project; Massachusetts Medical Society; National Association for Children of Alcoholics; National Campaign to Prevent Teen Pregnancy; Nemours Foundation; New Hampshire Civil Liberties Union; Partnership for a Drug-Free America; Quit Victoria, Australia; and the University of Michigan Health System.

The photograph on the front cover is from Tiburon Studios/shuter stock.com.

Full citation information is provided on the first page of each chapter. Every effort has been made to secure all necessary rights to reprint the copyrighted material. If any omissions have been made, please contact Omnigraphics to make corrections for future editions.

Acknowledgements

In addition to the organizations listed above, special thanks are due to research and permissions coordinator Elizabeth Barbour and to managing editor Karen Bellenir.

About the *Teen Health Series*

At the request of librarians serving today's young adults, the *Teen Health Series* was developed as a specially focused set of volumes within Omnigraphics' *Health Reference Series*. Each volume deals comprehensively with a topic selected according to the needs and interests of people in middle school and high school.

Teens seeking preventive guidance, information about disease warning signs, medical statistics, and risk factors for health problems will find answers to their questions in the *Teen Health Series*. The *Series*, however, is not intended to serve as a tool for diagnosing illness, in prescribing treatments, or as a substitute for the physician/patient relationship. All people concerned about medical symptoms or the possibility of disease are encouraged to seek professional care from an appropriate health care provider.

If there is a topic you would like to see addressed in a future volume of the *Teen Health Series*, please write to:

Editor
Teen Health Series
Omnigraphics, Inc.
615 Griswold Street
Detroit, MI 48226

Locating Information within the *Teen Health Series*

The *Teen Health Series* contains a wealth of information about a wide variety of medical topics. As the *Series* continues to grow in size and scope, locating the precise information needed by a specific student may become more challenging. To address this concern, information about books within the *Teen Health Series* is included in *A Contents Guide to the Health Reference Series*. The *Contents Guide* presents an extensive list of more than 12,000 diseases, treatments, and other topics of general interest compiled from the Tables of Contents and major index headings from the books of the *Teen Health Series* and *Health Reference Series*. To access *A Contents Guide to the Health Reference Series*, visit www.healthreference series.com.

Our Advisory Board

We would like to thank the following advisory board members for providing guidance to the development of this *Series*:

Dr. Lynda Baker, Associate Professor of Library and Information Science, Wayne State University, Detroit, MI

Nancy Bulgarelli, William Beaumont Hospital Library, Royal Oak, MI

Karen Imarisio, Bloomfield Township Public Library, Bloomfield Township, MI

Karen Morgan, Mardigian Library, University of Michigan-Dearborn, Dearborn, MI

Rosemary Orlando, St. Clair Shores Public Library, St. Clair Shores, MI

Medical Consultant

Medical consultation services are provided to the *Teen Health Series* editors by David A. Cooke, M.D. Dr. Cooke is a graduate of Brandeis University, and he received his M.D. degree from the University of Michigan. He completed residency training at the University of Wisconsin Hospital and Clinics. He is board-certified in internal medicine. Dr. Cooke currently works as part of the University of Michigan Health System and practices in Ann Arbor, MI. In his free time, he enjoys writing, science fiction, and spending time with his family.

Part One

What You Should Know About Substance Abuse And Addiction

Chapter 1

What Are Substance Abuse And Addiction?

Jason and Brent have been best friends since kindergarten. Now that they're in high school, they're drifting apart. It's not because they're in different classes; it's because Brent has noticed some changes in Jason. His grades have slipped, he's moody, he doesn't talk to his old friends, and he rarely shows up for practice. Brent is aware that Jason has been doing drugs and he's worried that Jason has become addicted.

Defining an addiction is tricky, and knowing how to handle one is even harder—keep reading to find out more about addiction.

What Are Substance Abuse And Addiction?

The difference between substance abuse and addiction is very slight. Addiction begins as abuse, or using a substance like marijuana or cocaine. You can abuse a drug (or alcohol) without having an addiction. For example, just because Sara smoked weed a few times doesn't mean that she has an addiction, but it does mean that she's abusing a drug—and that could lead to an addiction.

About This Chapter: Information in this chapter is from "Dealing With Addiction." This information was provided by TeensHealth, one of the largest resources online for medically reviewed health information written for parents, kids, and teens. For more articles like this one, visit www.TeensHealth.org, or www.KidsHealth.org. © 2004 The Nemours Center for Children's Health Media, a division of The Nemours Foundation.

People can get addicted to all sorts of substances. When we think of addiction, we usually think of alcohol or illegal drugs. But people become addicted to medications, cigarettes, and even glue! And some substances are more addictive than others. Drugs like crack or heroin are so addictive that they may only be used once or twice before the user loses control.

Addiction means a person has no control over whether he or she uses a drug or drinks. A person who's addicted to cocaine has grown so used to the drug that he or she has to have it. Addiction can be physical, psychological, or both.

Physical addiction is when a person's body actually becomes dependent on a particular substance (even smoking is physically addictive). It also means that a person builds tolerance to that substance, so that person needs a larger dose than ever before to get the same effects. When a person who is physically addicted stops using a substance like drugs, alcohol, or cigarettes, he or she may experience withdrawal symptoms. Withdrawal can be like having the flu—common symptoms are diarrhea, shaking, and generally feeling awful.

Psychological addiction happens when the cravings for a drug are psychological or emotional. People who are psychologically addicted feel overcome by the desire to have a drug. They may lie or steal to get it.

Signs Of Addiction

The most obvious sign of an addiction is the need to have a particular drug or substance. However, there are many other signs that can suggest a possible addiction, such as changes in mood or weight loss or gain. (These are also signs of other conditions, too, though, such as depression or eating disorders.)

Signs that you or someone you know may have a drug or alcohol addiction include these signals:

♣ It's A Fact!!
A person crosses the line between abuse and addiction when he or she is no longer trying the drug to have fun or get high, but because he or she has come to depend on it. His or her whole life centers on the need for the drug. An addicted person—whether it's a physical or psychological addiction or both—no longer has a choice in taking a substance.

Psychological Signals

- Use of drugs or alcohol as a way to forget problems or to relax

- Withdrawal or keeping secrets from family and friends

- Loss of interest in activities that used to be important

- Problems with schoolwork, such as slipping grades or absences

- Changes in friendships, such as hanging out only with friends who use drugs

- Spending a lot of time figuring out how to get drugs

- Stealing or selling belongings to be able to afford drugs

- Failed attempts to stop taking drugs or drinking

- Anxiety, anger, or depression

- Mood swings

Physical Signals

- Changes in sleeping habits

- Feeling shaky or sick when trying to stop

- Needing to take more of the substance to get the same effect

- Changes in eating habits, including weight loss or gain

Getting Help

If you think you are addicted to drugs or alcohol, recognizing that you have a problem is the first step in getting help.

A lot of people think they can kick the problem on their own, but that doesn't work for most people. Find someone you trust to talk to. It may help to talk to a friend or someone your own age at first, but a supportive and understanding adult is your best option for getting help. If you can't talk to your parents, you may want to approach a school counselor, relative, doctor, favorite teacher, or religious leader.

✔ Quick Tip

Once you start a treatment program, try these tips to make the road to recovery less bumpy:

- Tell your friends about your decision to stop using drugs. Your true friends will respect your decision. This may mean that you need to find a new group of friends who will be 100% supportive. Unless everyone decides to kick their drug habit at once, you probably won't be able to hang out with the friends you did drugs with before.

- Ask your friends or family to be available when you need them. You may need to call someone in the middle of the night just to talk. If you're going through a tough time, don't try to handle things on your own—accept the help your family and friends offer.

- Accept only invitations to events that you know won't involve drugs or alcohol. Going to the movies is probably safe, but you may want to skip a Friday night party until you're feeling more secure. Plan activities that don't involve drugs. Go to the movies, try bowling, or take an art class with a friend.

- Have a plan about what you'll do if you find yourself in a place with drugs or alcohol. The temptation will be there sometimes, but if you know how you're going to handle it, you'll be OK. Establish a plan with your parents or siblings so that if you call home using a code, they'll know that your call is a signal you need a ride out of there.

- Remind yourself that having an addiction doesn't make you bad or weak. If you backslide a bit, talk to an adult as soon as possible. There's nothing to be ashamed about, but it's important to get help soon so that all of the hard work you put into your recovery is not lost.

If you're worried about a friend who has an addiction, use these tips to help him or her, too. For example, let your friend know that you are available to talk or offer your support. If you notice a friend backsliding, talk about it openly and ask what you can do to help. If your friend is going back to drugs or drinking and won't accept your help, don't be afraid to talk to a non-threatening, understanding adult, like your parent or school counselor. It may seem like you're ratting your friend out, but it's the best support you can offer.

Above all, offer a friend who's battling an addiction lots of encouragement and praise. It may seem corny, but hearing that you care is just the kind of motivation your friend needs.

Unfortunately, overcoming addiction is not easy. Quitting drugs or drinking is probably going to be the hardest thing you've ever done. It's not a sign of weakness if you need professional help from a trained drug counselor or therapist. Most people who try to kick a drug or alcohol program need professional assistance or treatment programs to do so.

Staying Clean

Recovering from a drug or alcohol addiction doesn't end with a 6-week treatment program. It's a lifelong process. Many people find that joining a support group can help them stay clean. There are support groups specifically for teens and younger people. You'll meet people who have gone through the same experiences you have, and you'll be able to participate in real-life discussions about drugs that you won't hear in your school's health class.

Many people find that helping others is also the best way to help themselves. Your understanding of how difficult the recovery process can be will help you to support others—both teens and adults—who are battling an addiction.

If you do have a relapse, recognizing the problem as soon as possible is critical. Get help right away so that you don't undo all the hard work you put into your initial recovery. And don't ever be afraid to ask for help!

Chapter 2

Two Components Of Addiction: Physical And Psychological Dependence

Addiction is a chronic, progressive, relapsing disorder characterized by compulsive use of one or more substances that result in physical, psychological, or social harm to the individual and continued use of the substance or substances despite this harm. Addiction has two possible components, physical dependence and psychological dependence:

Physical Dependence: A state of becoming physically adapted to alcohol or other drugs. There are two important aspects to physical dependence:

- *Tolerance:* The need for higher and higher doses to achieve the same effects

- *Withdrawal:* The appearance of physical symptoms (for example, nausea, chills, and vomiting) when someone stops taking a drug too quickly

Psychological Dependence: A subjective sense of need for alcohol or other drug, either for its positive effects or to avoid negative effects associated with no use.

About This Chapter: Information in this chapter is from "Addiction (Dependence)," United States Department of Labor, available online at http://www.dol.gov/asp/programs/drugs/workingpartners/sab/addiction.asp; cited August 2005.

Is everyone who tries alcohol or drugs destined for addiction?

No. Not everyone who uses alcohol or experiments with illegal drugs ends up addicted. In fact, alcohol can be enjoyed by many adults without serious negative consequences. Unfortunately, it is not possible to tell early on whose use may lead to addiction. The following are different ways that adults use alcohol and drugs:

Social/Recreational Use: For adults, drinking alcoholic beverages is permitted in American society. If use does not cause problems for the user, or cause problems for others, most people consider such use to be social or recreational.

♣ **It's A Fact!!**

Examples Of Substance Abuse

- Use of alcohol or drugs in spite of a drug-free workplace policy
- Taking prescription drugs without a prescription or taking drugs in a way that are not prescribed
- Use of over-the-counter drugs to the point of impairment

Abuse: Abuse is a condition in which the use of alcohol or other drugs has become such a central part of an individual's life that he or she is willing to let go of important activities in order to use the drug. Drug abuse involves the intake of a drug (alcohol is considered a drug) under circumstances that significantly increase the hazard potential.

What is the nature of addiction?

Although addiction unquestionably begins with a voluntary act of using a drug, continued use often becomes involuntary, ultimately to the point that a compulsive craving drives the behavior. The compulsion results from a number of factors, including dramatic changes in brain function produced by prolonged exposure to the drug. This is why addiction is considered a brain disease. It is this compulsion that causes most of the problems surrounding addiction and what requires multidimensional regimens of treatment. Once addicted, it is almost impossible for most people to stop the spiraling cycle of addiction on their own without treatment. Furthermore, addiction often becomes a chronic recurring disorder for which repeated treatment episodes are required before an individual achieves long-term abstinence.

What are the characteristics of addiction?

Addiction to alcohol or other drugs may be as follows:

Chronic: Once an addiction is developed, it will always have to be addressed. An addict may manage to stop using alcohol or other drugs for significant periods of time, but the disease typically does not disappear. Rather, it goes into remission. Should "normal" drug use be attempted, "out of control" use will return rapidly.

Progressive: Addiction gets worse over time. With some drugs, the decline is rapid. With others, like alcohol, it can be more gradual.

Primary: Addiction is not just a symptom of some underlying psychological problem. Once the use of alcohol or drugs becomes an addiction, the addiction itself needs to be treated as the primary illness.

Terminal: Addiction to alcohol or other drugs often leads to death through damage to major organs of the body. Also, the risks of contracting hepatitis C and HIV rise with use.

Is addiction a brain disease?

Yes. Research by the National Institute on Drug Abuse (NIDA) suggests that long-term exposure to drugs produces addiction—that is, the compulsion to take drugs—by eliciting changes in specific neurons in the central nervous system.

Does addiction result from moral weakness or overindulgence?

No. Addiction can be a life-threatening condition, like adult diabetes or hypertension, with roots in genetic susceptibility, social circumstance, and personal behavior.

If an addicted person has enough will power, can he or she stop using alcohol or other drugs?

Most people addicted to alcohol and other drugs cannot simply stop using them, no matter how strong their resolve. Most need one or more courses of structured treatment to reduce or end their dependence on alcohol and/or other drugs.

What is denial?

One of the most disturbing and confusing aspects of addiction is that it is characterized by denial. The user rejects the notion that his or her use is out of control or that it is causing any problems at home or on the job. There are effective strategies employed by professionals for helping break through this denial, which must be overcome before treatment can take place.

What is enabling?

Any action by another person or an institution that intentionally or unintentionally has the effect of facilitating the continuation of an individual's addictive process. Examples of enabling behavior include the following:

Covering Up: Providing alibis, making excuses, or doing an impaired person's work rather than allowing it to be known that he or she is not meeting his or her responsibilities.

Rationalizing: Developing reasons why the person's continued use is understandable or acceptable.

Withdrawing: Avoiding contact with the person with the problem.

Blaming: Getting angry at the individual for not trying hard enough to control his or her use.

Controlling: Trying to take responsibility for the person's use by throwing out his or her drugs or cutting off the supply.

Threatening: Saying that you will take action (for example, turning the person in) if he or she does not control his or her use, but not following through when he or she continues to use.

What are the typical signs of addiction?

Emotional: Aggression, anxiety, burnout, denial, depression, and paranoia.

Behavioral: Excessive talking, impaired coordination, inability to sit still, irritability, lack of energy, limited attention span, poor motivation, slow reaction time, and slowed or slurred speech.

Physical: Chills, the smell of alcohol, sweating, and weight loss.

How can I know if I am at risk for addiction?

Many factors can lead to developing a problem with alcohol and other drugs. Unfortunately, accurate prediction is difficult. There is, however, some evidence that suggests certain behaviors or histories can increase the likelihood of addiction.

Addiction Is A Family Disease: People with a history of drug abuse in their family are more susceptible to developing problems with addiction. Children of alcoholics or addicts are three times more likely to develop problems. If both parents are addicts or alcoholics, the risk increases five-fold. This is due to heredity as well as learned behavior. It is important for parents to realize that children learn much from watching the behaviors of others.

Prior Abuse Of Alcohol And Other Drugs Has A Great Impact On Developing Future Problems: A pattern of abuse develops and can lead to addiction and psychological reliance on drugs or alcohol. Research demonstrates that the later in life an individual first drinks alcohol or uses other drugs, the less likely he or she will progress to drug abuse or addiction.

Other Contributing Factors: Some people use alcohol or drugs as part of a self-destructive lifestyle. Other people start to use drugs to seek relief from depression or crisis in their lives. Although some fortunate individuals never develop serious problems, and use diminishes or ceases once the precipitating events change, others develop a serious problem before they even realize it.

What is drug addiction treatment?

There are a number of science-based treatment approaches that can be used as part of a comprehensive treatment program. The general approach to addiction treatment can be described as breaking a big task into manageable bits, each tailored to the needs of the individual patient. Regardless of approach, there are core components, such as assessment, support groups, and drug abuse monitoring programs that are critical to the treatment regimen.

Can addiction be treated successfully?

Yes. Addiction is a treatable disease. The National Institute on Drug Abuse (NIDA) recently published *Principles of Drug Addiction Treatment*, the first-ever science-based guide to drug treatment. It provides a context by which both health professionals and the general public can begin to understand and evaluate addiction treatment approaches. The guide addresses some of the essential characteristics of addiction and its treatment and lays out the principles derived from over two decades of scientific research.

Chapter 3

How Addiction Affects Your Brain

The brain is the command center of your body. It weighs about three pounds and has different centers or systems that process different kinds of information.

The brainstem is the most primitive structure at the base of your brain. The brainstem controls your heart rate, breathing, and sleeping. It does the things you never think about.

Various parts or lobes of the brain process information from your sense organs. The occipital lobe receives information from your eyes, for example. And the cerebral cortex, on top of the whole brain, is the "thinking" part of you. That's where you store and process language, math, and strategies. It's the thinking center. Buried deep within the cerebral cortex is the limbic system, which is responsible for survival. It remembers and creates an appetite for the things that keep you alive, such as good food and the company of other human beings.

The cerebellum is responsible for things you learn once and never have to think about, such as balance when walking or how to throw a ball.

About This Chapter: Information in this chapter is from "The Brain and Addiction," NIDA for Teens, National Institute on Drug Abuse, a component of the United States Department of Health and Human Services, June 2005.

How does your brain communicate?

The brain's job is to process information. Brain cells called neurons receive and send messages to and from other neurons. There are billions of neurons in the human brain, each with as many as a thousand threadlike branches that reach out to other neurons.

In a neuron, a message is an electrical impulse. The electrical message travels along the sending branch, or axon, of the neuron. When the message reaches the end of the axon, it causes the release of a chemical called a neurotransmitter. The chemical travels across a tiny gap, or synapse, to other neurons.

Specialized molecules called receptors on the receiving neuron pick up the chemical. The branches on the receiving end of a neuron are called dendrites. Receptors there have special shapes so they can only collect one kind of neurotransmitter.

In the dendrite, the neurotransmitter starts an electrical impulse. Its work done, the chemical is released back into the synapse. The neurotransmitter then is broken down or is reabsorbed into the sending neuron.

Neurons in your brain release many different neurotransmitters as you go about your day thinking, feeling, reacting, breathing, and digesting. When you learn new information or a new skill, your brain builds more axons and dendrites first, as a tree grows roots and branches. With more branches, neurons can communicate and send their messages more efficiently.

What do drugs do to the brain?

Some drugs work in the brain because they have a similar size and shape as natural neurotransmitters. In the brain in the right amount or dose, these drugs lock into receptors and start an unnatural chain reaction of electrical charges, causing neurons to release large amounts of their own neurotransmitter.

Some drugs lock onto the neuron and act like a pump, so the neuron releases more neurotransmitter. Other drugs block reabsorption or reuptake and cause unnatural floods of neurotransmitter.

All drugs of abuse, such as nicotine, cocaine, and marijuana, primarily affect the brain's limbic system. Scientists call this the "reward" system. Normally, the limbic system responds to pleasurable experiences by releasing the neurotransmitter dopamine, which creates feelings of pleasure.

What happens if someone keeps using drugs?

Think about how you feel when something good happens—maybe your team wins a game, you're praised for something you've done well, or you drink a cold lemonade on a hot day—that's your limbic system at work. Because natural pleasures in our lives are necessary for survival, the limbic system creates an appetite that drives you to seek those things.

The first time someone uses a drug of abuse, he or she experiences unnaturally intense feelings of pleasure. The limbic system is flooded with dopamine. Of course, drugs have other effects, too. A first-time smoker may also cough and feel nauseous from toxic chemicals in a tobacco or marijuana cigarette.

> ## ✎ What's It Mean?
>
> Neurons: Brain cells that receive and send messages to and from other neurons.
>
> Neurotransmitter: A chemical produced by neurons, which carry messages to other neurons.
>
> Dopamine: A chemical in the brain, which creates feelings of pleasure.

But the brain starts changing right away as a result of the unnatural flood of neurotransmitters. Because they sense more than enough dopamine, for example, neurons begin to reduce the number of dopamine receptors. Neurons may also make less dopamine. The result is less dopamine in the brain: This is called down regulation. Because some drugs are toxic, some neurons may also die.

How many times does someone have to take a drug to become an addict?

No one knows how many times a person can use a drug without changing his or her brain and becoming addicted.

A person's genetic makeup probably plays a role. But after enough doses, an addicted teen's limbic system craves the drug as it craves food, water, or friends. Drug craving is made worse because of down regulation.

Without a dose of the drug, dopamine levels in the drug abuser's brain are low. The abuser feels flat, lifeless, depressed. Without drugs, an abuser's life seems joyless. Now the abuser needs drugs just to bring dopamine levels up to normal levels. Larger amounts of the drug are needed to create a dopamine flood or high, an effect known as tolerance.

By abusing drugs, the addicted teen has changed the way his or her brain works. Drug abuse and addiction lead to long-term changes in the brain. These changes cause addicted drug users to lose the ability to control their drug use. Drug addiction is a disease.

If drug addiction is a disease, is there a cure?

There is no cure for drug addiction, but it is a treatable disease. Drug addicts can recover. Drug addiction therapy is a program of behavior change or modification that slowly re-trains the brain. Like people with diabetes or heart disease, people in treatment for drug addiction learn behavioral changes and often take medications as part of their treatment regimen.

Chapter 4

Who's At Risk For Substance Abuse?

What are risk factors and protective factors?

Research over the past two decades has tried to determine how drug abuse begins and how it progresses. Many factors can add to a person's risk for drug abuse. Risk factors can increase a person's chances for drug abuse, while protective factors can reduce the risk. Please note, however, that most individuals at risk for drug abuse do not start using drugs or become addicted. Also, a risk factor for one person may not be for another.

Risk and protective factors can affect children at different stages of their lives. At each stage, risks occur that can be changed through prevention intervention. Early childhood risks, such as aggressive behavior, can be changed or prevented with family, school, and community interventions that focus on helping children develop appropriate, positive behaviors. If not addressed, negative behaviors can lead to more risks, such as academic failure and social difficulties, which put children at further risk for later drug abuse.

Research-based prevention programs focus on intervening early in a child's development to strengthen protective factors before problem behaviors develop.

About This Chapter: Information in this chapter is from "Risk Factors and Protective Factors," National Institute on Drug Abuse, a component of the United States Department of Health and Human Services, February 2005.

Table 4.1 describes how risk and protective factors affect people in five domains, or settings, where interventions can take place.

Table 4.1. Risk Factors and Protective Factors

Risk Factors	Domain	Protective Factors
Early Aggressive Behavior	Individual	Self-Control
Lack of Parental Supervision	Family	Parental Monitoring
Substance Abuse	Peer	Academic Competence
Drug Availability	School	Anti-drug Use Policies
Poverty	Community	Strong Neighborhood Attachment

Risk factors can influence drug abuse in several ways. The more risks a child is exposed to, the more likely the child will abuse drugs. Some risk factors may be more powerful than others at certain stages in development, such as peer pressure during the teenage years; just as some protective factors, such as a strong parent-child bond, can have a greater impact on reducing risks during the early years. An important goal of prevention is to change the balance between risk and protective factors so that protective factors outweigh risk factors.

What are the early signs of risk that may predict later drug abuse?

Some signs of risk can be seen as early as infancy or early childhood, such as aggressive behavior, lack of self-control, or difficult temperament. As the child gets older, interactions with family, at school, and within the community can affect that child's risk for later drug abuse.

Children's earliest interactions occur in the family. Sometimes family situations heighten a child's risk for later drug abuse, for example, when there is:

- a lack of attachment and nurturing by parents or caregivers;
- ineffective parenting; and
- a caregiver who abuses drugs.

But families can provide protection from later drug abuse when there is:

• a strong bond between children and parents;

• parental involvement in the child's life; and

• clear limits and consistent enforcement of discipline.

Interactions outside the family can involve risks for both children and adolescents, such as:

• poor classroom behavior or social skills;

• academic failure; and

• association with drug abusing peers.

♣ **It's A Fact!!**
Association with drug-abusing peers is often the most immediate risk for exposing adolescents to drug abuse and delinquent behavior.

Other factors—such as drug availability, trafficking patterns, and beliefs that drug abuse is generally tolerated—are risks that can influence young people to start abusing drugs.

What are the highest risk periods for drug abuse among youth?

Research has shown that the key risk periods for drug abuse are during major transitions in children's lives. The first big transition for children is when they leave the security of the family and enter school. Later, when they advance from elementary school to middle school, they often experience new academic and social situations, such as learning to get along with a wider group of peers. It is at this stage—early adolescence—that children are likely to encounter drugs for the first time.

When they enter high school, adolescents face additional social, emotional, and educational challenges. At the same time, they may be exposed to greater availability of drugs, drug abusers, and social activities involving drugs. These challenges can increase the risk that they will abuse alcohol, tobacco, and other substances.

When young adults leave home for college or work and are on their own for the first time, their risk for drug and alcohol abuse is very high. Consequently, young adult interventions are needed as well.

When and how does drug abuse start and progress?

Studies such as the National Survey on Drug Use and Health, formally called the National Household Survey on Drug Abuse, reported by the Substance Abuse and Mental Health Services Administration, indicate that some children are already abusing drugs at age 12 or 13, which likely means that some begin even earlier. Early abuse often includes such substances as tobacco, alcohol, inhalants, marijuana, and prescription drugs such as sleeping pills and anti-anxiety medicines. If drug abuse persists into later adolescence, abusers typically become more heavily involved with marijuana and then advance to other drugs, while continuing their abuse of tobacco and alcohol. Studies have also shown that abuse of drugs in late childhood and early adolescence is associated with greater drug involvement. It is important to note that most youth, however, do not progress to abusing other drugs.

Scientists have proposed various explanations of why some individuals become involved with drugs and then escalate to abuse. One explanation points to a biological cause, such as having a family history of drug or alcohol abuse. Another explanation is that abusing drugs can lead to affiliation with drug-abusing peers, which, in turn, exposes the individual to other drugs.

Researchers have found that youth who rapidly increase their substance abuse have high levels of risk factors with low levels of protective factors. Gender, race, and geographic location can also play a role in how and when children begin abusing drugs.

Chapter 5

Statistics On Teen Substance Abuse

Use

The Monitoring the Future Study asked high school seniors, "On how many occasions, if any, have you used drugs or alcohol during the last 12 months or month?"

Self-reports of drug use among high school seniors may under represent drug use among youth of that age because high school dropouts and truants are not included, and these groups may have more involvement with drugs than those who stay in school.

Of high school seniors in 2004:

• 45.7% reported having ever used marijuana/hashish;

• 8.1% reported having ever used cocaine; and

• 1.5% reported having ever used heroin.

The increase in the use of marijuana has been especially pronounced. Between 1992 and 2004 past-month use of marijuana increased from:

• 12% to 20% among high school seniors;

About This Chapter: Information in this chapter is excerpted from "Drugs and Crime Facts, Drug Use," Bureau of Justice Statistics, Office of Justice Programs, U.S. Department of Justice, January 2005.

- 8% to 16% among 10th graders; and

- 4% to 6% among 8th graders.

Reported use of marijuana by high school seniors during the past month peaked in 1978 at 37% and declined to its lowest level in 1992 at 12%.

The use of cocaine within the past month of the survey by high school seniors peaked in 1985 at 6.7%, up from 1.9% in 1975 at the survey's inception. Cocaine use declined to a low of 1.3% in 1992 and 1993. In 2004, 2.3% of high school seniors reported past-month cocaine use.

Cocaine use among high school seniors peaked in 1985.

Table 5.1. Reported Drug and Alcohol Use by High School Seniors, 2004

Used within the last:

Drugs	12 Months	30 Days
Alcohol	70.6%	48.0%
Marijuana	34.3	19.9
Stimulants	10.0	4.6
Other opiates	9.5	4.3
Tranquilizers	7.3	3.1
Sedatives	6.5	2.9
Hallucinogens	6.2	1.9
Cocaine	5.3	2.3
Inhalants	4.2	1.5
Steroids	2.5	1.6
Heroin	0.9	0.5

Perceived Risk

From 1987 to 2004 the percentage of high school seniors that were asked, "How much do you think people risk harming themselves?" remained virtually stable.

Student Reports of Availability of Drugs

In 2003, 29% of all students in grades 9 through 12 reported someone had offered, sold, or given them an illegal drug on school property. This was an increase from 1993 when 24% of such students reported that illegal drugs were available to them on school property.

Between 1993 and 2003, males and females reported that illegal drugs made available to them on school property increased. Males were more likely than females to report that drugs were offered, sold, or given to them on school property. In 2003, 32% of males and 25% of females reported availability of drugs.

In 1999, 37% of students ages 12 through 18 reported that marijuana, cocaine, crack, or upper/downers were available at school. In previous School Crime Supplement (SCS) data indicated that 63.2% of students ages 12 through 18 in 1989, and 65.3 in 1995 reported drugs were available at school.

Table 5.2. Percent of High School Seniors Reporting They Could Obtain Drugs Fairly Easily or Very Easily, 2004	
Marijuana	85.8 %
Amphetamines	55.4
Cocaine	47.8
Barbiturate	46.3
Crack	39.2
LSD	33.1
Tranquilizers	30.1
Heroin	29.6
Crystal methamphetamine	26.7
PCP	24.2
Amyl/butyl nitrites	20.0

In 1999, the availability of drugs was reported more often by:

• public school students (38.4%) than by private school students (22.4%);

• students in upper grades (57.0%) than by students in lower grades (9.6%); and

• students reporting that street gangs (62.9%) were present than by other students (31.6%).

Similar rates of drug availability were reported by:

• white students (39.5%) and black students (33.6%).

• students residing in suburban areas (39.5%), urban areas (33.7%), and rural areas (34.3%).

Chapter 6

High School And Youth Trends

Trends In Use

Since 1975, the Monitoring the Future Survey (MTF) has annually studied the extent of drug abuse among high school 12th-graders. The survey was expanded in 1991 to include 8th- and 10th-graders. It is funded by National Institute on Drug Abuse (NIDA) and is conducted by the University of Michigan's Institute for Social Research. The goal of the survey is to collect data on 30-day, annual, and lifetime (refers to use at least once during a respondent's lifetime) drug use among students in these grade levels. This, the 30th annual study, was conducted during 2004.

Decreases or stability in use patterns were noted for the most part from 2003 to 2004. However, for the second year significant increases in inhalant abuse were seen among 8th-graders. Even a single session of repeated inhalant abuse can disrupt heart rhythms and cause death from cardiac arrest or lower oxygen levels enough to cause suffocation. Regular abuse of inhalants can result in serious damage to vital organs, including the brain, heart, kidneys, and liver.

About This Chapter: Information in this chapter is excerpted from "High School and Youth Trends," National Institute on Drug Abuse, a component of the United States Department of Health and Human Services, April 2005; available online at http://www.drugabuse.gov/Infofacts/HSYouthtrends.html.

Key Findings From The 2004 MTF

- **Any Illicit Drug:** 30-day use of any illicit drug decreased significantly among 8th-graders, from 9.7 percent in 2003 to 8.4 percent in 2004.

- **Inhalants:** Lifetime use of inhalants increased significantly among 8th-graders, from 15.8 percent in 2003 to 17.3 percent in 2004, continuing an upward trend in use noted among 8th-graders, after several years of decline. Since 2001, there appears to be a gradual decline among 8th-graders in the perceived risk of using inhalants.

- **Prescription Drugs:** Annual use of Ritalin and Rohypnol remained statistically unchanged for all grades from 2003 to 2004. Annual use of Vicodin and OxyContin remained stable among all grades, but at somewhat high levels. Annual use of Vicodin was at 2.5 percent for 8th-graders, 6.2 percent for 10-graders, and 9.3 percent for 12th-graders. Annual use of OxyContin was at 1.7 percent for 8th-graders, 3.5 percent for 10th-graders, and 5.0 percent for 12th-graders.

- **Marijuana:** 30-day use of marijuana was down significantly among 8th-graders, from 7.5 percent in 2003 to 6.4 percent in 2004. Some strengthening of attitudes against marijuana use also occurred among 8th- and 10th-graders.

- **MDMA (Ecstasy):** Lifetime use of MDMA decreased significantly for 10th-graders, from 5.4 percent in 2003 to 4.3 percent in 2004. Some strengthening of attitudes against use was seen among 10th- and 12th-graders. All grades had decreases in the perception of the availability of MDMA.

- **Methamphetamine:** Use decreased significantly among 8th-graders, from 3.9 percent in 2003 to 2.5 percent in 2004 for lifetime use; from 2.5 percent in 2003 to 1.5 percent in 2004 for annual use; and from 1.2 percent in 2003 to 0.6 percent in 2004 for 30-day use.

- **GHB And Ketamine:** Significant decreases in annual use were seen among 10th-graders for GHB, from 1.4 percent in 2003 to 0.8 percent in 2004, and Ketamine, from 1.9 percent in 2003 to 1.3 percent in 2004.

- **LSD:** Lifetime use of LSD decreased significantly among 12th-graders, from 5.9 percent in 2003 to 4.6 percent in 2004, continuing the pattern of decreases in LSD use noted in 2002 and 2003.

- **Anabolic Steroids:** Use of steroids decreased significantly among 8th-graders, from 2.5 percent in 2003 to 1.9 percent in 2004 for lifetime use and from 1.4 percent in 2003 to 1.1 percent in 2004 for annual use. Among 10th-graders, lifetime use decreased significantly, from 3.0 percent in 2003 to 2.4 percent in 2004, continuing the decrease in use among 10th-graders seen in 2003. Steroid use among 12th-graders, however, remained stable at peak levels.

- **Cocaine, Other Than Crack:** A significant increase in use of cocaine other than crack was seen among 10th-graders, from 1.1 percent in 2003 to 1.5 percent in 2004, for 30-day use. An increase in the perception of availability of all forms of cocaine was seen among 12th-graders.

- **Cigarettes/Nicotine:** Cigarette smoking decreased significantly among 10th-graders, from 43.0 percent in 2003 to 40.7 percent in 2004 for lifetime use and from 4.1 percent in 2003 to 3.3 percent in 2004 for those smoking one-half pack or more per day. The perception of harm from smoking one or more packs per day increased significantly among 8th- and 10th-graders from 2003 to 2004.

- **Alcohol, Heroin, Crack Cocaine, Hallucinogens Other Than LSD, PCP, Amphetamines, Tranquilizers, Sedatives, And Methaqualone:** Use remained stable among all grades from 2003 to 2004.

Perceived Risk Of Harm, Disapproval, And Perceived Availability

In addition to studying drug use among 8th-, 10th-, and 12th-graders, MTF collects information on three attitudinal indicators related to drug use. These are perceived risk of harm in taking a drug, disapproval of others who take drugs, and perceived availability of drugs.

The following POSITIVE attitudinal changes are from 2003 to 2004:

- **Marijuana:** Significant increases occurred among 8th-graders in perceived risk for regular marijuana use and for trying it once or twice. Additionally, disapproval of trying marijuana once or twice or smoking it occasionally increased significantly among 8th-graders. Among 10th-graders, disapproval of smoking marijuana occasionally or regularly increased significantly. Perceived availability of marijuana decreased significantly among 8th-graders.

- **Cigarettes/Nicotine:** The perceived risk associated with smoking one or more packs of cigarettes per day increased significantly among 8th- and 10th-graders. Perceived availability of cigarettes decreased significantly among 8th-graders.

♣ It's A Fact!!
Decline In Drug Use By Students

Overall, the 2005 Monitoring the Future (MTF) survey showed good news. While there was no substantive change in any illicit drug use between 2004 and 2005, analysis of the survey revealed an almost 19 percent decline in past month use of any illicit drug by 8th, 10th, and 12th graders between 2001 and 2005. This trend is driven largely by decreasing rates of marijuana use among these students. For example, since 2001, past month use of marijuana has fallen by 28 percent among 8th graders and by 23 percent among 10th graders.

Since 1975 the MTF survey has measured drug, alcohol, and cigarette use and related attitudes among adolescent students nationwide. Survey participants report their drug use behaviors across three time periods: lifetime, past year, and past month. Overall, 49,347 students in the 8th, 10th, and 12th grades from 402 public and private schools participated in this year's survey. The survey is funded by the National Institute on Drug Abuse (NIDA), a component of the National Institutes of Health (NIH), and conducted by the University of Michigan.

While the 2005 survey showed a continuing general decline in drug use, there are continued high rates of non-medical use of prescription medications, especially opioid painkillers. For example, in 2005, 9.5 percent of 12th graders reported using Vicodin in the past year, and 5.5 percent of these students reported using OxyContin in the past year. Long-term trends show a significant increase in the abuse of OxyContin from 2002 to 2005 among 12th graders. Also of concern is the significant increase in the use of sedatives/barbiturates among 12th graders since 2001.

- **MDMA (Ecstasy):** Among 10th-graders, the perceived risk of taking MDMA occasionally increased significantly, as did their disapproval of trying MDMA once or twice. Among 12th-graders, disapproval of taking MDMA once or twice increased significantly. Perceived availability of MDMA significantly decreased for all three grades.

- **Heroin:** A significant increase was noted in the percentage of 12th-graders who perceive risk in using heroin occasionally without a needle. Among 8th-graders, the perceived availability of heroin decreased significantly.

- **Alcohol:** Among 12th-graders, a significant increase was seen in the percentage perceiving risk in taking one or two drinks nearly every day.

"While cigarette smoking is at lowest levels in the history of the survey and overall drug use among teens and adolescents is continuing to decline, there remain areas of concern with specific drugs of abuse such as prescription painkillers," says Dr. Nora D. Volkow, director of the National Institute on Drug Abuse (NIDA), National Institutes of Health. "Prescription drugs are very powerful medicines that are effective when used properly and with a doctor's supervision. Using these drugs without a prescription is dangerous. It's imperative that teens get this message."

Among the survey's findings were the following changes from 2004 to 2005:

- Lifetime use of cigarettes declined 2 percent among 8th graders; declined 1.7 percent among 10th graders; and declined 2.8 percent among 12th-graders;

- Past year use of alcohol was down 2.7 percent among 8th graders; down 1.5 percent among 10th graders; and down 2.1 percent among 12th graders;

- Lifetime use of methamphetamine fell 1.2 percent among 10th graders and fell 1.7 percent among 12th-graders;

- And past year use of steroids declined 1.1 percent among 12th-graders.

Source: Excerpted from "2005 Monitoring the Future Survey Shows Continued Decline in Drug Use by Students," NIH News, National Institutes of Health, U.S. Department of Health and Human Services, December 2005.

- **Inhalants:** Among 10th-graders, a significant increase was seen in the percentage disapproving of using inhalants regularly.

- **LSD:** The perceived availability of LSD decreased significantly among 8th-graders. A significant increase was noted in the percentage of 12th-graders who disapprove of using LSD once or twice.

- **PCP:** The perceived availability of PCP decreased significantly among 8th-graders.

- **Cocaine And Crack:** The perceived availability of cocaine and crack decreased significantly among 8th-graders.

- **Narcotics Other Than Heroin, Amphetamines, Crystal Methamphetamine (Ice), Tranquilizers, Alcohol, And Steroids:** The perceived availability decreased significantly among 8th-graders.

The following NEGATIVE attitudinal changes are from 2003 to 2004:

- **Heroin:** A significant decrease was noted in the percentage of 12th-graders who perceived risk in using heroin regularly.

- **LSD:** A significant decrease occurred in the percentage of 8th-graders who disapprove of taking LSD regularly.

- **Inhalants:** The gradual decline among 8th-graders since 2001 in the perceived risk of using inhalants continued from 2003 to 2004.

- **Cocaine:** An increase in the perception of availability of all forms of cocaine was seen among 12th-graders.

Chapter 7

Preventing Drug Abuse

Risk Factors And Protective Factors

Principle 1: Prevention programs should enhance protective factors and reverse or reduce risk factors.

- The risk of becoming a drug abuser involves the relationship among the number and type of risk factors (for example, deviant attitudes and behaviors) and protective factors (for example, parental support).

- The potential impact of specific risk and protective factors changes with age. For example, risk factors within the family have greater impact on a younger child, while association with drug-abusing peers may be a more significant risk factor for an adolescent.

- Early intervention with risk factors (for example, aggressive behavior and poor self-control) often has a greater impact than later intervention by changing a child's life path (trajectory) away from problems and toward positive behaviors.

About This Chapter: Information in this chapter is from "Prevention Principles," National Institute on Drug Abuse, a component of the United States Department of Health and Human Services, February 2005.

- While risk and protective factors can affect people of all groups, these factors can have a different effect depending on a person's age, gender, ethnicity, culture, and environment.

Principle 2: Prevention programs should address all forms of drug abuse, alone or in combination, including the underage use of legal drugs (for example, tobacco or alcohol); the use of illegal drugs (for example, marijuana or heroin); and the inappropriate use of legally obtained substances (for example, inhalants), prescription medications, or over-the-counter drugs.

Principle 3: Prevention programs should address the type of drug abuse problem in the local community, target modifiable risk factors, and strengthen identified protective factors.

Principle 4: Prevention programs should be tailored to address risks specific to population or audience characteristics, such as age, gender, and ethnicity, to improve program effectiveness.

Prevention Planning

Family Programs

Principle 5: Family-based prevention programs should enhance family bonding and relationships and include parenting skills; practice in developing, discussing, and enforcing family policies on substance abuse; and training in drug education and information.

Family bonding is the bedrock of the relationship between parents and children. Bonding can be strengthened through skills training on parent supportiveness of children, parent-child communication, and parental involvement.

- Parental monitoring and supervision are critical for drug abuse prevention. These skills can be enhanced with training on rule setting; techniques for monitoring activities; praise for appropriate behavior; and moderate, consistent discipline that enforces defined family rules.

- Drug education and information for parents or caregivers reinforces what children are learning about the harmful effects of drugs and opens opportunities for family discussions about the abuse of legal and illegal substances.

- Brief, family-focused interventions for the general population can positively change specific parenting behavior that can reduce later risks of drug abuse.

School Programs

Principle 6: Prevention programs can be designed to intervene as early as preschool to address risk factors for drug abuse, such as aggressive behavior, poor social skills, and academic difficulties.

Principle 7: Prevention programs for elementary school children should target improving academic and social-emotional learning to address risk factors for drug abuse, such as early aggression, academic failure, and school dropout. Education should focus on the following skills:

- Self-control
- Emotional awareness
- Communication
- Social problem solving
- Academic support, especially in reading

Principle 8: Prevention programs for middle or junior high and high school students should increase academic and social competence with the following skills:

- Study habits and academic support
- Communication
- Peer relationships
- Self-efficacy and assertiveness
- Drug resistance skills
- Reinforcement of anti-drug attitudes
- Strengthening of personal commitments against drug abuse

Community Programs

Principle 9: Prevention programs aimed at general populations at key transition points, such as the transition to middle school, can produce beneficial effects even among high-risk families and children. Such interventions do not single out risk populations and, therefore, reduce labeling and promote bonding to school and community.

♣ It's A Fact!!
2003 Survey Found Teens Hear Prevention Messages

The Substance Abuse and Mental Health Services Administration (SAMHSA) released data showing that youth who reported seeing or hearing media messages on preventing drug and alcohol use are significantly less likely to report substance use.

While 10.3 percent of youths who reported seeing or hearing media prevention messages in the past year reported binge alcohol use in the past month, 12.5 percent of youth who were not exposed to media prevention messages engaged in binge drinking. Similarly, 10.8 percent of youth who saw or heard media prevention messages reported past month illicit drug use compared to 13.7 percent who received no messages. In 2003, 83.6 percent of youth (20.8 million) reported seeing or hearing an alcohol or drug prevention message.

SAMHSA extracted the data from the National Survey on Drug Use and Health, 2003, which asked youth ages 12–17 if they had seen or heard any alcohol or drug prevention messages from posters, pamphlets, radio, TV or other sources. The survey also asked about alcohol and drug use.

"Teenagers exposed to prevention messages through the media are less likely to use alcohol and illicit drugs," SAMHSA Administrator Charles Curie said. "Clearly, the media is one of the many avenues we must use to communicate with young people that drinking and drug use are dangerous and wrong."

The data also show that youth who reported talking to at least one parent about the dangers of tobacco, alcohol, or drug use in the past year were significantly less likely to report past month binge alcohol use, 10 percent, compared to 11.6 percent who did not talk to a parent. For illicit drug use, 10 percent of

Principle 10: Community prevention programs that combine two or more effective programs, such as family-based and school-based programs, can be more effective than a single program alone.

Principle 11: Community prevention programs reaching populations in multiple settings—for example, schools, clubs, faith-based organizations, and

---

teens who talked to a parent used drugs in the past month compared to 13 percent who did not talk to a parent.

John Walters, Director of National Drug Control Policy, said: "It is crucial that our youth receive clear and consistent messages about the dangers of marijuana and other drugs. Important health information delivered through print, radio, television, and online advertising by the National Youth Anti-Drug Media Campaign complements parents' efforts to keep their children healthy and drug-free. Research indicates the Media Campaign is moving in the right direction and that is good news for American teens and parents."

In 2003, 14.6 million youth ages 12–17 (58.9 percent) reported that they had talked to at least one parent during the past year about the dangers of using tobacco, alcohol, or drugs. Youth's ages 12–15 were more likely to have talked to a parent than those ages 16 or 17.

The National Survey on Drug Use and Health is an annual survey of close to 70,000 people. The survey collects information from residents of households, residents of non-institutionalized group quarters and civilians living on military bases. The survey provides estimates for 21 different measures related to substance use or mental illness.

The 2003 survey included responses from 22,665 youth ages 12 to 17.

The report is available on the web at www.oas.samhsa.gov.

Source: "SAMHSA Advisory," Substance Abuse and Mental Health Administration (SAMHSA), U.S. Department of Health and Human Services, July 2005.

the media—are most effective when they present consistent, community-wide messages in each setting.

Prevention Program Delivery

Principle 12: When communities adapt programs to match their needs, community norms, or differing cultural requirements, they should retain core elements of the original research-based intervention, which include the following:

- Structure (how the program is organized and constructed)

- Content (the information, skills, and strategies of the program)

- Delivery (how the program is adapted, implemented, and evaluated)

Principle 13: Prevention programs should be long-term with repeated interventions (i.e., booster programs) to reinforce the original prevention goals. Research shows that the benefits from middle school prevention programs diminish without follow-up programs in high school.

Principle 14: Prevention programs should include teacher training on good classroom management practices, such as rewarding appropriate student behavior. Such techniques help to foster students' positive behavior, achievement, academic motivation, and school bonding.

Principle 15: Prevention programs are most effective when they employ interactive techniques, such as peer discussion groups and parent role-playing, that allow for active involvement in learning about drug abuse and reinforcing skills.

Principle 16: Research-based prevention programs can be cost-effective. Similar to earlier research, recent research shows that for each dollar invested in prevention, a savings of up to $10 in treatment for alcohol or other substance abuse can be seen.

Chapter 8

Handling Peer Pressure

Understanding Peer Pressure

Your classmates keep asking you to have them over because you have a pool, everyone at school is wearing silly hats so you do too, and your best friend begs you to go running with her because you both need more exercise, so you go, too. These are all examples of peer pressure. Don't get it yet?

- Pressure is the feeling that you are being pushed toward making a certain choice—good or bad.

- A peer is someone in your own age group.

- Peer pressure is—you guessed it—the feeling that someone your own age is pushing you toward making a certain choice, good or bad.

Why Peer Pressure Can Work

Have you ever given in to pressure? Like when a friend begs to borrow something you don't want to give up or to do something your parents say is off limits? Chances are you probably have given into pressure at sometime in your life.

About This Chapter: Information in this chapter is excerpted from "Peer Pressure," The Cool Spot (http://www.thecoolspot.gov), National Institute on Alcohol Abuse and Alcoholism, a component of the United States Department of Health and Human Services, November 2004.

How did it feel to give into pressure? If you did something you wish you hadn't, then most likely you didn't feel too good about it. You might have felt some of these things:

- Sad

- Anxious

- Guilty

- Like a wimp or pushover

- Disappointed in yourself

♣ It's A Fact!!
People want to be accepted and liked by people their own age.

Everyone gives in to pressure at one time or another, but why do people sometimes do things that they really don't want to do? Here are a few reasons:

- They are afraid of being rejected by others.

- They want to be liked and don't want to lose a friend.

- They want to appear grown up.

- They don't want to be made fun of.

- They don't want to hurt someone's feelings.

- They aren't sure of what they really want.

- They don't know how to get out of the situation.

When you face pressure you can stand your ground.

How Peers Pressure

Almost everyone faces peer pressure once in a while. Friends have a big influence on our lives, but sometimes they push us to do things that we may not want to do. Unless you want to give in every time you face this, you're going to need to learn how to handle it.

The first step to standing up to peer pressure is to understand it.

Sometimes a friend can say something directly to you that puts a lot of pressure on you and makes it hard to say no. This is spoken pressure.

♣ It's A Fact!!
Examples Of Spoken Pressure

Rejection: Threatening to end a friendship or a relationship. This pressure can be hard to resist because nobody wants to lose friends. Here are some examples of pressure by rejection:

- "Who needs you as a friend any way?"

- "If you don't drink, we won't hang out any more."

- "Why don't you leave if you don't want to drink with us?"

Put Downs: Insulting or calling a person names to make them feel bad. Here are some examples of put downs:

- "You're never any fun."

- "You're such a baby."

- "You're so uncool."

Reasoning: Telling a person reasons why they should try something or why it would be OK if they did. (Nobody said these were good reasons.) Here are some examples of pressure by reasoning:

- "It won't hurt you."

- "Your parents will never find out."

- "You'll have more fun."

Examples Of Unspoken Pressure

This is something you feel without anyone saying anything to you. You feel unspoken pressure if you want to do the same things you see other doing. These are some unspoken pressure tricks:

- **The Huddle:** A group of kids standing together in which everyone is talking, and maybe looking at something you can't see, laughing and joking.

- **The Look:** Kids who think they're cool give you a certain look that means, "we're cool and you're not."

- **The Example:** A group of popular kids decide to get the same backpack and you want one too.

You might think you are supposed to act or dress a certain way because it seems like everyone else is doing it, or because it's the cool thing to do. When you feel this way, even though nobody has said anything to you about it, this is unspoken pressure.

If you haven't already, you are going to face both spoken and unspoken pressure in the future. It's just part of life. The most important thing is to make the right choices when a peer pressure situation comes up.

Peer Pressure Can Be Good, Too

Peer pressure isn't all bad. You and your friends can pressure each other into some things that will improve your health and social life and make you feel good about your decisions.

Think of a time when a friend pushed you to do something good for yourself or to avoid something that would've been bad.

Here are some good things friends can pressure each other to do:

- Be honest

- Avoid alcohol

- Avoid drugs

- Not smoke

- Be nice

- Respect others

- Work hard

- Exercise (together)

> ✔ **Quick Tip**
>
> *Tips On Resisting Pressure*
>
> Say no and let them know you mean it by doing the following:
> - Stand up straight.
> - Make eye contact.
> - Say how you feel.
> - Don't make excuses.
> - Stick up for yourself.

You and your friends can also use good peer pressure to help each other resist bad peer pressure.

If you see a friend taking some heat, try some of these lines:

- "We don't want to drink."

- "We don't need to drink to have fun."

- "Let's go and do something else."

- "Leave her alone. She said she didn't want any."

The Right To Resist

If someone is pressuring you to do anything that's not right or good for you, you have the right to resist. You have the right to say no, the right not to give a reason why, and the right to just walk away from a situation.

Resisting pressure can be hard for some people for the following reasons:

- They are afraid of being rejected by others.

- They want to be liked and don't want to lose a friend.

- They don't want to be made fun of.

- They don't want to hurt someone's feelings.

- They aren't sure of what they really want.

- They don't know how to get out of the situation.

Sometimes resisting isn't easy, but you can do it with practice and a little know-how. Keep trying, even if you don't get it right at first.

Resisting Spoken Pressure

Spoken pressure—when someone pressures you with words—can be difficult to resist. Most people don't want to risk making others feel bad, but it's important to stand up for yourself. Check out these strategies for dealing with spoken pressure.

Do

- Say no assertively.

- Stay alcohol free.

- Suggest something else to do.

- Stand up for others.

- Walk away from the situation.

- Find something else to do with other friends.

Don't

- Attend a party unprepared to resist alcohol

- Be afraid to say no

- Mumble

- Say no too aggressively

- Act like a know-it-all when saying no

Resisting Unspoken Pressure

Sometimes you can feel pressure just from watching how others act or dress, without them saying a word to you. This unspoken pressure is especially hard to resist, because instead of standing up to a friend, you're standing up to how you feel inside.

> **✔ Quick Tip**
>
> Being assertive means the following:
>
> - Standing up straight
>
> - Looking directly at the person or group who is pressuring you
>
> - Speaking in a firm voice
>
> - Saying it quickly and being polite
>
> - Choosing words well (instead of a wimpy "I can't," say, "I don't want to."
>
> **Added Bonus:** Return the challenge. Maybe say, "I thought you were my friend," or "I don't want to drink and if you're my friend you won't ask me to."

Unspoken pressure may come from role models like your parents, your older siblings, teachers, coaches, or celebrities you see in movies and on TV. Unspoken pressure may also come from peers—your friends or other people your age.

Here are some tips for resisting unspoken pressure:

- Take a reality check—most teens don't drink.

- Remember it's risky—drugs and alcohol can be dangerous.

- Find something else to do with other friends.

Chapter 9

Recognizing Drug Paraphernalia

What are drug paraphernalia?

The term drug paraphernalia refers to any equipment that is used to produce, conceal, and consume illicit drugs. It includes but is not limited to items such as bongs, roach clips, miniature spoons, and various types of pipes.

Under federal law the term drug paraphernalia means "any equipment, product or material of any kind which is primarily intended or designed for use in manufacturing, compounding, converting, concealing, producing, processing, preparing, injecting, ingesting, inhaling, or otherwise introducing into the human body a controlled substance."

What do drug paraphernalia look like?

Identifying drug paraphernalia can be challenging because products often are marketed as though they were designed for legitimate purposes. Marijuana pipes and bongs, for example, frequently carry a misleading disclaimer indicating that they are intended to be used only with tobacco products. Recognizing drug paraphernalia often involves considering other factors such as the manner in which items are displayed for sale, descriptive materials or instructions accompanying the items, and the type of business selling the items.

About This Chapter: Information in this chapter is from "Drug Paraphernalia Fast Facts," National Drug Intelligence Center, a component of the United States Department of Justice, Product No. 2003-L0559-025, September 2003.

The appearance of drug paraphernalia varies depending upon the manufacturer and intended purpose. Increasingly, bongs, pipes, and other paraphernalia are manufactured in bright, trendy colors and bear designs such as skulls, devils, dragons, and wizards. Manufacturers attempt to glamorize drug use and make their products attractive to teenagers and young adults.

Where are drug paraphernalia sold?

Drug paraphernalia can be obtained through various means. Many large manufacturers market their products over the Internet and through mail-order businesses. In addition, drug paraphernalia frequently are sold at tobacco shops, trendy gift and novelty shops, gas stations, and convenience stores.

What are examples of drug paraphernalia?

- Pipes (metal, wooden, acrylic, glass, stone, plastic, or ceramic)

- Water pipes

- Roach clips

- Miniature spoons

- Chillums (cone-shaped marijuana/hash pipes)

- Bongs

- Cigarette papers

- Cocaine freebase kits

♣ It's A Fact!!
Drug Paraphernalia Sales

With the rise of the drug culture in the United States in the 1960s and 1970s, the country began to see the appearance of "head shops," which were stores that sold a wide range of drug paraphernalia. While some of the paraphernalia was crude and homemade, much was being commercially manufactured to cater to a fast-growing market. Enterprising individuals even sold items openly in the street, until anti-paraphernalia laws in the 1980s eventually ended such blatant sales. Today, law enforcement faces another challenge. With the advent of the Internet, criminals have greatly expanded their illicit sales to a worldwide market for drug paraphernalia. For example, in a recent law enforcement effort, Operation Pipedreams, the 18 companies targeted accounted for more than a quarter of a billion dollars in retail drug paraphernalia sales annually. Typically, such illicit businesses operate retail stores as well as websites posing as retailers of legitimate tobacco accessories when in reality the products are intended for the illegal drug trade.

Source: Excerpted from "Drug Paraphernalia: Tools of the Illegal Drug Trade," United States Drug Enforcement Administration, United States Department of Justice, February 2003.

♣ It's A Fact!!
Rave Clothing And Paraphernalia

Many young ravers wear distinctive clothing and carry paraphernalia commonly associated with club drug use and the rave culture. Ravers dress for comfort. They usually wear lightweight, loose-fitting clothes and dress in layers, allowing them to remove clothing as they become overheated from dancing for hours. Many wear loose shorts or very wide-legged or baggy pants. Ravers wear T-shirts, bikini tops, tank tops, tube tops, and open-back halter tops to help keep cool. After hours of dancing and often after using MDMA—which elevates body temperature—many ravers have removed most of their clothing. Some ravers, especially females, wear costumes to rave events, dressing as princesses, cartoon characters, or other fantasy figures that match the theme of the rave (for example, futuristic, space, mystic).

Ravers often wear bright accessories like bracelets, necklaces, and earrings made of either plastic beads or pill-shaped sugar candies. MDMA users sometimes use these accessories to disguise their drugs, stringing MDMA tablets mixed with the candies. Many ravers chew on baby pacifiers or lollipops to offset the effects of involuntary teeth grinding caused by MDMA. Pacifiers are worn around the user's neck, often on plastic beaded necklaces.

Many people bring various items to rave events to enhance the effects of MDMA. Ravers use bright chemical lights and flashing lights to heighten the hallucinogenic properties of MDMA and the visual distortions brought on by its use. Chemical glow sticks, bracelets, and necklaces are commonly worn at raves and waved in the eyes of MDMA users for visual stimulus. Ravers often insert flashing red lights in their belly buttons (held in place with a mild adhesive) and pin blinking lights in the shape of hearts, stars, and animals to their clothing to provide additional visual stimulation to MDMA users. Ravers that use MDMA often wear painter's masks with menthol vapor rub applied to the inside of the mask. MDMA users believe that by inhaling the menthol fumes, they are enhancing the effects of the drug. They may be adding to their risk of hyperthermia, however, because the fumes cause eyes and nasal passages to dry out.

Source: Excerpted from "Information Bulletin: Raves," National Drug Intelligence Center, a component of the United States Department of Justice, Document ID No. 2001-L0424-004, April 2001.

✎ What's It Mean?

Bong: A water pipe used for smoking marijuana. The smoke goes through water, which cools the smoke before going into the smoker's lungs.

Roach Clip: A clip, which is used to hold the butt of a marijuana cigarette.

Source: Editor.

Are drug paraphernalia illegal?

Yes, drug paraphernalia are illegal. The drug paraphernalia statute, U. S. Code Title 21 Section 863, makes it "unlawful for any person to sell or offer for sale drug paraphernalia; to use the mails or any other facility of interstate commerce to transport drug paraphernalia; or to import or export drug paraphernalia."

Part Two

Abused Drugs And Chemicals

Chapter 10

Marijuana

Marijuana is a mixture of the dried and shredded leaves, stems, seeds, and flowers of the hemp plant. The mixture can be green, brown, or gray. Hemp's scientific name is *Cannabis sativa*.

A bunch of leaves seems harmless, right? But think again. Marijuana has a chemical in it called tetrahydrocannabinol. Better known as THC. A lot of other chemicals are found in marijuana too—about 400 of them, some of which can cause lung cancer. But THC is the main active ingredient.

Common Street Names

There are more than 200 slang terms for marijuana from city to city and from neighborhood to neighborhood. Some common names are: pot, grass, herb, weed, Mary Jane, reefer, skunk, boom, gangster, kif, chronic, and ganja.

How It Is Used

Marijuana is used in many ways. Some users brew it as tea or mix it with food. Others smoke blunts—cigars hollowed out and filled with the drug. And sometimes marijuana is smoked through a water pipe called a bong. The most common method is smoking loose marijuana rolled into a cigarette called a joint or nail.

About This Chapter: Information in this chapter is from "Marijuana," NIDA for Teens, National Institute on Drug Abuse, a component of the United States Department of Health and Human Services, June 2005.

Teen Use Of Marijuana

Ever heard that lame line "everybody's doing it?" Tell that person to check the facts. As part of a 2002 NIDA-funded study, researchers asked teens if they had used marijuana or hashish (another form of marijuana) in the past month. Of all the 8th graders surveyed, only 8.3% said yes; only 17.8% of 10th graders had used the drug in the past month; and just 21.5% of 12th graders.

Common Effects

Imagine this: You're in a ball game, playing out in left field. An easy fly ball comes your way, and you're psyched. When that ball lands in your glove your team will win, and you'll be a hero. But, you're a little off. The ball grazes your glove and hits dirt. So much for your dreams of glory.

♣ It's A Fact!! Why do young people use marijuana?

There are many reasons why some children and young teens start smoking marijuana. Many young people smoke marijuana because they see their brothers, sisters, friends, or even older family members using it. Some use marijuana because of peer pressure.

Others may think it's cool to use marijuana because they hear songs about it and see it on TV and in movies. Some teens may feel they need marijuana and other drugs to help them escape from problems at home, at school, or with friends.

No matter how many shirts and caps you see printed with the marijuana leaf, or how many groups sing about it, remember this: You don't have to use marijuana just because you think everybody else is doing it. Most teenagers do not use marijuana!

Source: Excerpted from "Marijuana: Facts for Teens," National Institute on Drug Abuse, a component of the United States Department of Health and Human Services, NIH Publication No. 04-4037, September 2004.

Smoking marijuana can cause such loss of coordination. And that's just one of the many negative side effects. Under the influence of marijuana, you could forget your best friend's phone number, watch your grade point average drop like a stone, or get into a car accident. Even worse, high doses of marijuana use can cause anxiety and panic attacks.

Before we look at the damage marijuana can do, let's back up for a second and discuss a tricky truth. For some people, smoking marijuana makes them feel good. Within minutes of inhaling, a user begins to feel "high," or filled with pleasant sensations. A chemical in marijuana, THC, triggers brain cells to release the chemical dopamine. Dopamine creates good feelings—for a short time.

Addiction

Here's the thing: Once dopamine starts flowing, a user feels the urge to smoke marijuana again, and then again, and then again. Repeated use could lead to addiction, and addiction is a brain disease.

THC Attaches To Specific Receptors In The Brain

THC is up to no good in the brain. THC finds brain cells, or neurons, with specific kinds of receptors called cannabinoid receptors. Then, it binds to these receptors.

When it attaches to a neuron, THC interferes with normal communication between neurons. Think of it as a disruption in the phone service, caused perhaps by too many users all at once. Let's say Neuron #1 needs to tell Neuron #2 to create a new memory. If THC is in the mix, this communication is likely to fail.

Certain parts of the brain have high concentrations of cannabinoid receptors. These areas are: the hippocampus, the cerebellum, the basal ganglia, and the cerebral cortex.

THC Creates Learning And Memory Problems

The hippocampus is a part of the brain with a funny name and a big job. It's in charge of certain types of learning and memory.

Disrupting the normal functioning of the hippocampus can lead to trouble studying and learning and problems recalling recent events. The difficulty can be a lot more serious than "Did I take out the trash this morning?"

Interference with the hippocampus may also lead to lasting memory loss. Studies in rats show that taking in a lot of THC over a long period of time can damage neurons in the hippocampus. Chances are, if it happens to rats, it's happening to people who smoke marijuana.

Smoking Marijuana Can Make Driving Dangerous

The cerebellum is the section of our brain that does most of the work on balance and coordination. When THC finds its way into the cerebellum, it makes scoring a goal in soccer or hitting a home run pretty tough.

THC also does a number on the basal ganglia, another part of the brain that's involved in movement control.

These THC effects can spell disaster on the highway. Research shows that drivers on marijuana have slow reaction times, impaired judgment, and problems responding to signals and sounds on the road. In one study of 150 reckless drivers, 33 tested positive for marijuana.

Smoking Marijuana May Lead To Lung Cancer

The list of negative effects goes on and on. Smoking marijuana may increase the risk of heart attack. Smoking marijuana may cause lung cancer because it has some of the same cancer-causing substances as tobacco. Plus, marijuana smokers tend to inhale more deeply and hold their breath longer than cigarette smokers do. So more smoke enters the lungs. Puff for puff, smoking marijuana may increase the risk of cancer even more than smoking cigarettes does.

Medical Marijuana

THC, the main active ingredient in marijuana, produces effects that potentially can be useful for treating a variety of medical conditions. It is the main ingredient in a pill that is currently used to treat nausea in cancer chemotherapy patients and to stimulate appetite in patients with wasting due to AIDS. Scientists are continuing to investigate other potential medical uses for cannabinoids.

However, smoking marijuana is difficult to justify medically because the amount of THC in marijuana is not always consistent. It would be difficult—if not impossible—to come up with a safe and effective use of the drug because you could never be sure how much THC you were getting. Moreover, the negative effects of marijuana smoke on the lungs will offset the helpfulness of smoked marijuana for some patients.

Finally, little is known about the many chemicals besides THC that are in marijuana, or their possible negative impact on patients with medical conditions.

Chapter 11

Inhalants

What Are Inhalants?

Inhalants are breathable chemical vapors that produce psychoactive (mind-altering) effects. A variety of products common in the home and in the workplace contain substances that can be inhaled. Many people do not think of these products, such as spray paints, glues, and cleaning fluids, as drugs because they were never meant to be used to achieve an intoxicating effect. Yet, young children and adolescents can easily obtain them and are among those most likely to abuse these extremely toxic substances. Household products should be stored carefully to prevent accidental inhalation by very young children.

Inhalants fall into three categories—solvents, gases, and nitrates.

Solvents

- **Industrial or household solvents or solvent-containing products**, including paint thinners or removers, degreasers, dry-cleaning fluids, gasoline, and glue

- **Art or office supply solvents**, including correction fluids, felt-tip-marker fluid, and electronic contact cleaners

About This Chapter: Information in this chapter is excerpted from "NIDA InfoFacts: Inhalants," National Institute on Drug Abuse, a component of the United States Department of Health and Human Services, March 2005.

♣ It's A Fact!!
Inhalant Abuse: Danger Under The Kitchen Sink

Drug abuse among the Nation's young people declined substantially in the past three years, with 600,000 fewer teens abusing drugs, according to the most recent National Institute on Drug Abuse (NIDA)–University of Michigan Monitoring the Future (MTF) survey. Abuse of inhalants, however, is an exception. The percentage of eighth-graders who have at least once sought intoxication by inhaling spray paints, nail polish remover, lighter fluid, glue, marking pens, aerosols, cleaning fluid, or other volatile substances has increased 2 years in a row and now stands at 17.3 percent. This trend is alarming and unacceptable.

Why would anyone empty a container of lighter fluid into a cup and inhale the fumes, or repeatedly sniff marking pens? Inhalant abusers breathe in a substance's vapors for effects resembling alcohol inebriation, including mild stimulation, loss of inhibition, and distorted perceptions. Inhalants generally affect the same areas of the brain as alcohol and other addictive drugs, so it is not surprising that abusers experience intoxication in addition to nausea, vomiting, slurred speech, and loss of coordination. Older children and young adolescents may seek out inhalants as an easily obtainable substitute for alcohol. Intoxication occurs quickly and usually lasts only a few minutes, making abuse of inhalants easier to conceal than abuse of alcohol or marijuana.

We cannot take lightly even one-time experimentation with these toxic chemicals. For some unlucky children, just a single session of repeated inhalations has

Gases

- **Gases used in household or commercial products,** including butane lighters and propane tanks, whipped cream aerosols or dispensers (whippets), and refrigerant gases

- **Household aerosol propellants** and associated solvents in items such as spray paints, hair or deodorant sprays, fabric protector sprays, and aerosol computer cleaning products

- **Medical anesthetic gases,** such as ether, chloroform, halothane, and nitrous oxide ("laughing gas") caused permanent organ damage or death. Organs at risk from inhalant abuse include the lungs, brain, liver, heart, and kidneys. From 2001 to 2002, the Nation's emergency departments reported a near tripling of the number of people requiring medical treatment after inhalant abuse (from 522 to 1,496). Some abusers experience restlessness, nausea, sweating, anxiety, and other symptoms of withdrawal when they stop taking the drug. Like any other drug when abused, inhalants can also lead to accidents and injuries.

NIDA is concerned that the latest MTF survey shows that the percentage of eighth-graders who believe it is dangerous to try inhalants once or twice has declined for three years and is now only 38.7 percent. These survey results parallel, and may help to explain, the current rise in abuse. Evidence shows that the public's perception of the risk involved in drug taking can affect rates of drug abuse. For example, an earlier peak in inhalant abuse occurred in 1995, when only 42 percent of 10th-graders believed that trying these substances was dangerous and 21.6 percent of eighth-graders had abused inhalants at least once. That trend reversed after a national media campaign, sponsored by the Partnership for a Drug-Free America, highlighted the health consequences associated with inhalant abuse. The abuse of inhalants dropped in tandem with a rise in the perception of risk.

Source: Excerpted from "Inhalant Abuse: Danger Under the Kitchen Sink" by NIDA Director Nora D. Volkow, M.D., Director's Column, *NIDA Notes*, Vol. 20, No. 3, October 2005, National Institute on Drug Abuse, a component of the United States Department of Health and Human Services.

Nitrites

- **Organic nitrites** are volatiles that include cyclohexyl, butyl, and amyl nitrites, and are commonly known as "poppers." Amyl nitrite is still used for medical purposes. Volatile nitrites are often sold in small brown bottles and labeled as "video head cleaner," "room odorizer," "leather cleaner," or "liquid aroma."

Health Hazards

Although they differ in makeup, nearly all abused inhalants produce short-term effects similar to anesthetics, which act to slow down the body's functions.

When inhaled in sufficient concentrations, inhalants can cause intoxication, usually lasting only a few minutes. Sometimes users extend this effect for several hours by breathing in inhalants repeatedly. Initially, users may feel slightly stimulated. Repeated inhalations make them feel less inhibited and less in control. If use continues, users can lose consciousness.

Sniffing highly concentrated amounts of the chemicals in solvents or aerosol sprays can directly induce heart failure and death within minutes of a session of repeated inhalations. This syndrome, known as "sudden sniffing death," can result from a single session of inhalant use by an otherwise healthy young person. Sudden sniffing death is particularly associated with the abuse of butane, propane, and chemicals in aerosols.

High concentrations of inhalants also can cause death from suffocation by displacing oxygen in the lungs and then in the central nervous system so that breathing ceases. Deliberately inhaling from a paper or plastic bag or in a closed area greatly increases the chances of suffocation. Even when using aerosols or volatile products for their legitimate purposes (such as painting or cleaning), it is wise to do so in a well-ventilated room or outdoors.

Chronic abuse of solvents can cause severe, long-term damage to the brain, the liver, and the kidneys.

Harmful irreversible effects that may be caused by abuse of specific solvents include the following:

- **Hearing loss:** toluene (spray paints, glues, dewaxers) and trichloroethylene (dry cleaning chemicals, correction fluids)
- **Peripheral neuropathies, or limb spasms:** hexane (glues, gasoline) and nitrous oxide (whipped cream dispensers, gas cylinders)
- **Central nervous system or brain damage:** toluene (spray paints, glues, dewaxers)
- **Bone marrow damage:** benzene (gasoline)

Serious but potentially reversible effects include:

- **Liver and kidney damage:** toluene-containing substances and chlorinated hydrocarbons (correction fluids, dry cleaning fluids)

- **Blood oxygen depletion:** aliphatic nitrites (known on the street as poppers, bold, and rush) and methylene chloride (varnish removers, paint thinners)

Initial use of inhalants often starts early. Some young people may use inhalants as an easily accessible substitute for alcohol. Research suggests that chronic or long-term inhalant abusers are among the most difficult drug abuse patients to treat. Many suffer from cognitive impairment and other neurological dysfunction and may experience multiple psychological and social problems.

Chapter 12

Raves And Club Drugs: An Overview

Introduction

High energy, all-night dance parties and clubs known as "raves," which feature dance music with a fast, pounding beat and choreographed laser programs, have become increasingly popular over the last decade, particularly among teenagers and young adults. Beginning as an underground movement in Europe, raves have evolved into a highly organized, commercialized, worldwide party culture. Rave parties and clubs are now found throughout the United States and in countries around the world. Raves are held either in permanent dance clubs or at temporary venues set up for a single weekend event in abandoned warehouses, open fields, or empty buildings.

Attendance can range from 30 "ravers" in a small club to tens of thousands in a sports stadium or open field. While techno music and light shows are essential to raves, drugs such as MDMA (3,4-methylenedioxymethamphetamine), ketamine, GHB (gamma-hydroxybutyrate), Rohypnol, and LSD (lysergic acid diethylamide), have become an integral component of the rave culture.

About This Chapter: Information in this chapter is excerpted from "Information Bulletin: Raves," National Drug Intelligence Center, a component of the U.S. Department of Justice, Product ID: 2001-L0424-004, April 2001.

History

Raves evolved from 1980s dance parties, aided by the emergence of European techno music and American house music. European clubs that sponsored raves in the 1980s tried to limit the exposure of attendees to the public and to law enforcement. Raves were secretive, after-hours, private dance parties and were often held in gay clubs where attendance was restricted to invitees or friends of invitees. The site of the party was often kept confidential, and invitees usually were not told the location of the host club until the night of the party. Because of the restricted access and the secrecy surrounding the locations, the growing rave culture was often described as an "underground" movement.

By the mid-1980s, rave parties overseas had developed such a following among youths and young adults that by 1987, London raves had outgrown most dance clubs. It then became common to hold all-night raves—which drew thousands of people—in large, open fields on the outskirts of the city. As the movement continued to grow in the late 1980s, the first rave parties emerged in U.S. cities such as San Francisco and Los Angeles.

Rave parties and clubs were present in most metropolitan areas of the United States by the early 1990s. Teenagers overtook the traditional young adult ravers and a new rave culture emerged; events became highly promoted, heavily commercialized, and less secretive. Many new U.S. rave promoters were career criminals who recognized the profitability of organizing events tailored to teens. Capitalizing on the growing popularity of raves, specialized industries were developed to market clothes, toys, drugs, and music. Private clubs and secret locations were replaced by stadium venues with off-duty police security.

By the late 1990s, raves in the United States had become so commercialized that events were little more than an exploitation of American youth. Today's raves are characterized by high entrance fees, extensive drug use, exorbitantly priced bottled water, very dark and often dangerously overcrowded dance floors, and "chill rooms," where teenage ravers go to cool down and often engage in open sexual activity. Moreover, many club owners and promoters appear to promote the use of drugs—especially MDMA. They provide bottled water and sports drinks to manage hyperthermia and dehydration; pacifiers to prevent involuntary teeth clenching; and menthol nasal inhalers, chemical lights, and neon glow sticks to enhance the effects of MDMA. In addition, rave promoters often print flyers featuring prominent and repeated use of the letters "E" and "X" (E and X are MDMA monikers) or the word "rollin'" (refers to an MDMA high), surreptitiously promoting MDMA use along with the rave.

The increasing notoriety of raves has caused the rave culture to spread from major metropolitan areas to more rural or conservative locations. Rave parties are emerging in areas of Colorado, Iowa, Louisiana, Michigan, Minnesota, and Wisconsin that are not always prepared to manage unexpected crowds of teenagers.

Rave Music

Rave music evolved from 1980s techno, house, and New York garage music. The mix of these different styles of dance music helped mold the modern version of electronic rave music. Today, rave music falls into several categories: ambient, techno, trance, progressive trance, cyber trance, house, jungle, drum 'n' bass, techstep, garage, and big beat.

Although a casual listener may not be able to distinguish between techno and trance, ravers know the music well, and several DJs and bands—unfamiliar to most people—are internationally famous within the rave community. Today's rave DJs are skilled stage performers and are considered artists much like musicians. They mix electronic sounds, beats, and rhythms, often synchronizing the music to a laser program. Popular DJs sell their music and perform live at the largest rave parties and clubs around the world. Rave organizers announce the appearance of famous DJs on their flyers and on the Internet to promote upcoming raves.

Rave Promotion

Despite the commercialization of raves through the 1990s, many promoters have preserved the tradition of rave location secrecy, more as a novelty than as a necessity. In this tradition, raves are rarely promoted in open media but are advertised on flyers found only at record stores and clothing shops, at other rave parties and clubs, and on rave Internet sites. The flyers or Internet advertisements typically provide only the name of the city where the rave will be held and a phone number for additional information.

The location of the rave often is given to the caller over the telephone, but many promoters further maintain secrecy by providing only a location, called a "map point," where ravers go the night of the rave. At the map point, ravers are told the actual location of the rave. The map point is usually a record or clothing store within a 20-minute drive of the rave.

Raves And Club Drugs

Drugs like MDMA, ketamine, GHB, Rohypnol, and LSD—known collectively as "club drugs"—are an integral part of the rave culture. Many ravers use club drugs and advocate their use, wrongly believing that they are not harmful if they are used "responsibly" and their effects are managed properly. Many of the commercially designed rave clothes display pro-drug messages, and rave posters and flyers often promote drug use.

Members of private drug education and drug testing organizations, called "harm

♣ It's A Fact!!

Club drugs affect your brain. The term "club drugs" refers to a wide variety of drugs often used at all-night dance parties ("raves"), nightclubs, and concerts. Club drugs can damage the neurons in your brain, impairing your senses, memory, judgment, and coordination.

Club drugs affect your body. Different club drugs have different effects on your body. Some common effects include loss of muscle and motor control, blurred vision, and seizures. Club drugs, like ecstasy, are stimulants that increase your heart rate and blood pressure and can lead to heart or kidney failure. Other club drugs, like GHB, are depressants that can cause drowsiness, unconsciousness, or breathing problems.

Club drugs affect your self-control. Club drugs like GHB and Rohypnol are used in "date rape" and other assaults because they are sedatives that can make you unconscious and immobilize you. Rohypnol can cause a kind of amnesia—users may not remember what they said or did while under the effects of the drug.

Club drugs are not always what they seem. Because club drugs are illegal and often produced in makeshift laboratories, it is impossible to know exactly what chemicals were used to produce them. How strong or dangerous any illegal drug is varies each time.

Club drugs can kill you. Higher doses of club drugs can cause severe breathing problems, coma, or even death.

Source: Excerpted from "Tips for Teens: The Truth About Club Drugs," SAMHSA's (Substance Abuse and Mental Health Services Administration) National Clearinghouse for Alcohol and Drug Information, 2004.

✔ **Quick Tip**

Know the law. It is illegal to buy or sell club drugs. It is also a federal crime to use any controlled substance to aid in a sexual assault.

Get the facts. Despite what you may have heard, club drugs can be addictive.

Stay informed. The club drug scene is constantly changing. New drugs and new variations of drugs appear all of the time.

Know the risks. Mixing club drugs together or with alcohol is extremely dangerous. The effects of one drug can magnify the effects and risks of another. In fact, mixing substances can be lethal.

Look around you. The vast majority of teens are not using club drugs. While ecstasy is considered to be the most frequently used club drug, less than 2 percent of 8th–12th graders use it on a regular basis. In fact, 94 percent of teens have never even tried ecstasy.

Source: Excerpted from "Tips for Teens: The Truth About Club Drugs," SAMHSA's (Substance Abuse and Mental Health Services Administration) National Clearinghouse for Alcohol and Drug Information, 2004.

reduction organizations," have appeared at raves over the past 10 years. They attend rave events to test samples of illegal drugs so they can inform ravers of purity levels. Members of these organizations believe that they help reduce the number of overdoses by educating users on the physical effects of specific drugs. Conversely, many law enforcement agencies believe that the practices of harm reduction organizations encourage drug use, and they support their position with national statistics that show an increase in club drug overdoses as harm reduction organizations have become more active.

MDMA is unquestionably the most popular of the club drugs, and evidence of MDMA use by teenagers can be seen at most rave parties. Ketamine and GHB also are used at raves, as is Rohypnol, although to a lesser extent. A recent resurgence in the availability and use of some hallucinogens—LSD, PCP (phencyclidine), psilocybin, and peyote or mescaline—has also been noted at raves and dance clubs and may necessitate their inclusion in the club drug category. Inhalants like nitrous oxide are sometimes found at rave events; nitrous oxide is sold in gas-filled balloons called "whippets" for $5–$10.

> ### ♣ It's A Fact!!
>
> **If somebody slipped a club drug into your drink, wouldn't you realize it immediately?**
>
> Probably not. Most club drugs are odorless and tasteless. Some are made into a powder form that makes it easier to slip into a drink and dissolve without a person's knowledge.
>
> **Are there any long-term effects of taking ecstasy?**
>
> Yes. Studies on both humans and animals have proven that regular use of ecstasy produces long-lasting, perhaps permanent damage to the brain's ability to think and store memories.
>
> **If you took a club drug at a rave, wouldn't you just dance off all of its effects?**
>
> Not necessarily. Some of ecstasy's effects, like confusion, depression, anxiety, paranoia, and sleep problems, have been reported to occur even weeks after the drug is taken.
>
> Source: Excerpted from "Tips for Teens: The Truth About Club Drugs," SAMHSA's (Substance Abuse and Mental Health Services Administration) National Clearinghouse for Alcohol and Drug Information, 2004.

Rampant use of club drugs at raves may be leading to the use of other and highly addictive drugs by youths. There have been widespread reports of increasing availability and use of Asian methamphetamine tablets (frequently referred to as "yaba") at California raves and nightclubs. Heroin is being encountered more frequently at raves and clubs in large metropolitan areas, especially in the eastern United States. A wider variety of visually appealing and easy-to-administer forms of MDMA, LSD, heroin, and combination tablets are also found at raves and on college campuses.

Anti-Rave Initiatives

In the late 1990s, many communities began attempts to reduce the number of raves in their areas and to curb the use of club drugs. Several cities passed new ordinances designed to regulate rave activity, while others began enforcing existing laws that helped authorities monitor raves more closely.

Cities such as Chicago, Denver, Gainesville, Hartford, Milwaukee, and New York took deliberate steps to combat raves. These cities reduced rave activity through enforcement of juvenile curfews, fire codes, health and safety ordinances, liquor laws, and licensing requirements for large public gatherings. Many communities also began requiring rave promoters to retain, at the promoters' expense, onsite ambulance and emergency medical services and uniformed police security for large rave events. Because of these measures, many rave promoters and organizers moved their operations to other areas.

Perhaps the most successful anti-rave initiative was "Operation Rave Review," which was initiated in January 2000 in New Orleans. Following the overdose death of a 17-year-old girl at a rave party in 1998, the Drug Enforcement Administration (DEA) assessed the extent of rave activity in the New Orleans area. The assessment indicated an apparent correlation between rave activity and club drug overdoses resulting in emergency room visits. For example, in a 2-year period, 52 raves were held at the New Orleans State Palace Theater, during which time approximately 400 teenagers overdosed and were transported to local emergency rooms.

Following this assessment, the DEA, New Orleans Police Department, and U.S. Attorney's Office developed a methodology for the potential prosecution of rave promoters who allowed open, unabated drug use at the events. They investigated rave promoters and gathered evidence that the promoters knowingly and intentionally allowed the distribution and use of numerous controlled substances during rave events. As a result of this investigation, several rave promoters were arrested and the largest rave operation in New Orleans was closed.

Since the completion of Operation Rave Review, the number of overdoses and emergency room visits caused by club drug use has dropped 90 percent, and MDMA overdoses have been eliminated, according to the DEA and New Orleans hospital officials. The law enforcement agencies that participated in Operation Rave Review developed a five-step process that might be employed effectively in other areas experiencing high levels of rave activity, club drug overdoses, and related emergency room visits. The process employed consisted of the following steps:

1. **Identify rave promoters.** Potential subjects for investigation included all parties responsible for managing the production and promotion of the raves, including the owners of the property where the event was held.

2. **Compile emergency medical service (EMS) records.** Records of medical transports from the rave venue to local emergency rooms were collected. Retrieval of medical records sometimes required grand jury or administrative subpoenas or court orders.

3. **Conduct undercover operations inside the venue during rave events.** Undercover investigators purchased paraphernalia (chemical light sticks, pacifiers, and drug test kits) at the venue and filmed ravers using drugs and using the paraphernalia to enhance or manage the effects of the drugs. Undercover investigators filmed drug purchases by undercover officers who purchased drugs from as many different people as possible and as quickly as possible to clearly demonstrate the availability of drugs at the venue. Undercover investigators filmed the actions or inaction of security personnel hired by the rave promoter, and they also filmed patrons being treated or transported to local emergency rooms.

4. **Place an undercover officer.** Undercover agents or officers posed as job applicants for security positions and obtained interviews with the rave promoter. The undercover officers asked for the promoter's general expectations of security personnel and specific expectations of security personnel observing drug use or distribution.

5. **Execute search warrants.** Search warrants were executed at the rave venue, at offsite offices, and at the home of the rave promoter. Officers and agents seized all documents and items relating to the ownership, advertisement, promotion, and operation of the rave venue, including but not limited to purchase orders for rave paraphernalia, water, and other stock. Officers and agents also seized employment records identifying security personnel and any memoranda detailing their responsibilities, correspondence or contracts with EMS services, and financial records that detailed costs and profits associated with raves.

Conclusion

Raves have developed over the past decade from a small subculture to the highly commercialized and widespread exploitation of young people by large-scale rave promoters. The growing awareness of the nature of rave activity and the effects of club drug use have moved many communities to action. In order to curtail rave activity, communities and law enforcement agencies are enforcing existing fire codes, health and safety ordinances, and liquor laws, and are establishing juvenile curfews and licensing requirements for large public gatherings. They are requiring rave promoters and club owners to pay for building or liquor licenses, medical services, and security for their events, all in an effort to force rave promoters to move or cease their operations.

Chapter 13

Ecstasy, GHB, Rohypnol, And Ketamine

Ecstasy

What is ecstasy?

Ecstasy is an illegal drug that has effects similar to hallucinogens and stimulants. Ecstasy's scientific name is "MDMA" or methylene-dioxymethamphetamine. That word is almost as long as the all-night dance club "raves" or "trances" where ecstasy is often used. That's why ecstasy is called a "club drug."

MDMA is synthetic. It does not come from a plant like marijuana does. MDMA is a chemical made in secret labs hidden around the country. Other chemicals or substances are often added to or substituted for MDMA in ecstasy tablets, such as caffeine, dextromethorphan (cough syrup), amphetamines, and even cocaine. Makers of ecstasy can add anything they want to the drug, so the purity of ecstasy is always in question.

About This Chapter: This chapter begins with "Ecstasy," from NIDA for Teens, National Institute on Drug Abuse, a component of the United States Department of Health and Human Services, June 2005. "GHB and Analogs Fast Facts," Product No. 2003-L0559-009, May 2003; "Rohypnol Fast Facts," Product No. 2003-L0559-020, August 2003, and "Ketamine Fast Facts," Product No. 2003-L0559-011, June 2003, are from the National Drug Intelligence Center, a component of the U.S. Department of Justice.

How is it used?

Ecstasy is usually taken by mouth in a pill, tablet, or capsule. These pills can be different colors, and sometimes the pills have cartoon-like images on them. Some MDMA users take more than one pill at a time, which is called "bumping."

How many teens use it?

According to a 2002 NIDA-funded study, some teens are getting smart and turning their backs on ecstasy. For 10th graders in this NIDA-funded study, use of MDMA dropped from 6.2% in 2001 to 4.9% in 2002. There was also a drop in use by 8th graders (from 3.5% to 2.9%) and 12th graders (from 9.2% to 7.4%) compared to 2001.

How many students in these grades have ever tried ecstasy?

> ♣ **It's A Fact!!**
> **Street Terms**
> **For Ecstasy**
>
> • E
> • XTC
> • X
> • Adam
> • Hug
> • Beans
> • Clarity
> • Lover's speed
> • Love drug
>
> Source: NIDA for Teens, National Institute on Drug Abuse, a component of the United States Department of Health and Human Services, June 2005.

A 2002 NIDA study reported that 4.3% of 8th graders, 6.6% of 10th graders, and 10.5% of 12th graders had tried MDMA at least once in their life.

Is MDMA addictive?

Like other stimulant drugs, MDMA appears to have the ability to cause addiction. That is, people continue to take the drug despite experiencing unpleasant side effects, and other social, behavioral, and health consequences.

No one knows how many times a person can use a drug before becoming addicted to it or who is most vulnerable to addiction. A person's genetic makeup, their living environment, and other factors probably play a role in their susceptibility to addiction.

What are the common effects?

In general, NIDA-supported research shows that use of any club drugs can cause serious health problems and, in rare instances, even death. Many drug users take combinations of drugs, including alcohol, which may further increase their danger.

For most users, a "hit" of ecstasy lasts for 3 to 6 hours. Once the pill is swallowed, it only takes about 15 minutes for ecstasy to get into the bloodstream and reach the brain. About 45 minutes later, a user experiences MDMA's peak level (high). It's downhill from there, unless the user "bumps" and takes more MDMA. But even if the user only takes one pill, the after-effects of MDMA can last for several days to a week (or longer in regular MDMA users). These include feelings of sadness, anxiety, depression, and memory difficulties.

What are the initial effects?

Users might feel very alert or "hyper" at first. They can keep on dancing for hours at a time while at a rave. Users also experience distortions in time, and other changes in perception, such as an enhanced sense of touch. Some, however, become anxious and agitated. Sweating or chills may occur, and the MDMA user may feel faint or dizzy.

Users can also become dehydrated through vigorous activity in a hot environment. MDMA can interfere with the body's ability to regulate its temperature, which can cause dangerous overheating (hyperthermia.) This, in turn, can lead to serious heart, kidney, and liver problems, and rarely, death. MDMA can be extremely dangerous in high doses, or when multiple small doses are taken within a short time period to maintain the ecstasy high. Blood levels of the drug can reach very high levels, increasing the risk of hyperthermia and other negative health consequences of MDMA.

What are other effects on the body?

Ecstasy can also cause muscle tension, clenching of teeth, nausea, blurred vision, fainting, and chills or sweating. MDMA increases your heart rate and your blood pressure.

What are the effects on the mind?

Ecstasy can cause confusion, depression, sleep problems, intense fear and worrying (anxiety). Some of these side effects can last for days or weeks (in regular drug users) after taking MDMA.

What are the dangers?

MDMA can be dangerous in high doses, and is unpredictable regarding who will be vulnerable to its harmful effects. It can cause a marked increase in body temperature (hyperthermia), which has also been associated with dehydration. Hyperthermia can lead to cardiovascular problems, seizures, liver failure, and muscle breakdown that can cause kidney failure. These have been reported in some fatal cases at raves.

MDMA has been shown to be neurotoxic in studies using animals. We do not know yet whether it is neurotoxic in humans. However, memory loss has been found in regular users of MDMA, and this may reflect damage to the neurons that release serotonin, which also affects the ability to sleep and helps to regulate mood.

What are the long-term effects?

Although we do not know whether there is long-term damage to the brain in human MDMA users, or whether effects of MDMA are reversible when someone stops using the drug, one study, in non-human primates, showed that exposure to high doses of MDMA for 4 days produced brain damage that was evident 6 to 7 years later. In this study, the researchers found that some of the damaged nerve fibers grow back, but not necessarily in the same parts of the brain. It's like cutting off a limb of a fruit tree. The tree is still alive and can sprout a new limb somewhere else, but it may not bear as much fruit as the old one.

What are the risks to the brain?

Brain imaging research in humans indicates that MDMA may affect neurons that use the chemical serotonin to communicate with other neurons. The serotonin system plays a direct role in regulating mood, aggression, sexual activity, sleep, and sensitivity to pain.

GHB And Analogs

What are GHB and its analogs?

GHB (gamma-hydroxybutyrate) is a powerful central nervous system depressant that the human body produces in small amounts. A synthetic (man-made) version of GHB was developed in the 1920s as an anesthetic. Individuals abuse synthetic GHB because of its euphoric and sedative effects. Because of its anesthetic properties, GHB also has been used by sexual predators to incapacitate their victims.

GHB analogs, which include GBL, BD, GHV, and GVL, are drugs that possess chemical structures that closely resemble GHB. These analogs produce effects similar to those associated with GHB and are often used in its place.

What do they look like?

GHB and its analogs typically are sold either as a white powder or as a clear liquid. The drugs often have a salty taste.

How are they abused?

GHB and its analogs usually are taken orally. Because of the drugs' salty taste, they often are mixed with a flavored beverage. Sexual predators who administer GHB or an analog to their victims typically slip the drug into a drink, often at a bar or party.

Who uses GHB and its analogs?

Although information about the extent of GHB and analog use in the United States is limited, the data that are available indicate that young people primarily use these drugs. According to the Drug Abuse Warning Network, individuals aged 18 to 25 account for 58 percent of all GHB mentions in drug-related emergency department visits.

GHB use among high school students is a particular concern. Nearly 2 percent of high school seniors in the United States used the drug at least once in the past year, according to the University of Michigan's Monitoring the Future Survey.

What are the risks?

Use of GHB and its analogs can cause nausea, vomiting, delusions, depression, dizziness, hallucinations, seizures, respiratory distress, loss of consciousness, slowed heart rate, lowered blood pressure, amnesia, coma, and death. Mixing GHB or its analogs with alcohol is particularly dangerous because alcohol enhances the drug's depressant effects.

Sustained use of GHB or its analogs can lead to addiction, and chronic users experience withdrawal symptoms when they stop using the drugs. These symptoms include anxiety, insomnia, tremors, tachycardia (abnormally fast heart rate), delirium, and agitation. Users may experience these symptoms within 1 to 6 hours of their last dose, and the symptoms may persist for months.

In addition to the risks associated with the drugs themselves, individuals who use GHB or its analogs may put themselves at risk of sexual assault. While many sexual predators lace unsuspecting victims' drinks with the drugs, others offer GHB or an analog to victims who consume the drug without understanding the effects it will produce.

What are they called?

The most common names for GHB are Georgia home boy, G, goop, grievous bodily harm, and liquid ecstasy.

Are GHB and its analogs illegal?

Yes, GHB and its analogs are illegal. GHB is a Schedule I substance under the Controlled Substances Act. Schedule I drugs, which include heroin and MDMA, have a high potential for abuse and serve no legitimate medical purpose. GHB analogs are treated as Schedule I drugs if they are intended for human consumption.

Rohypnol

What is Rohypnol?

Rohypnol, a trade name for the drug flunitrazepam, is a central nervous system depressant. The drug is legally manufactured and

♣ **It's A Fact!!**

Street Terms For GHB And Its Analogs

- Cherry meth
- Fantasy
- G-riffic
- Jib
- Liquid E
- Liquid X
- Organic quaalude
- Salty water
- Scoop
- Sleep
- Sleep-500
- Soap
- Vita-G

Source: National Drug Intelligence Center, a component of the U.S. Department of Justice, Product No. 2003-L0559-009, May 2003.

available outside the United States but is neither manufactured nor approved for sale within the United States. Since the 1990s individuals in the United States have used Rohypnol illegally, often as a means of mitigating the depression that results from using stimulants such as cocaine and methamphetamine. Rohypnol also has been used in the commission of sexual assaults.

What does Rohypnol look like?

Rohypnol is manufactured as a caplet. In 1997 the manufacturer responded to concerns about the drug's role in sexual assaults by reformulating the white, 2-milligram tablets. (The original tablets dissolved clear in liquid, making it nearly impossible for a victim to detect their presence in a beverage.) The new smaller dosage (0.5 mg and 1.0 mg) caplets are dull green with a blue core that, when dissolved in light-colored drinks, will dye the liquid blue. However, the dye may be disguised in blue or dark-colored liquids, and generic versions of the drug may not contain the blue dye.

How is Rohypnol abused?

Individuals who abuse Rohypnol may swallow the caplets whole, crush and then snort the powdered caplets, or dissolve the caplets in liquid and then inject the solution. Sexual predators who administer Rohypnol to their victims typically slip the drug into a drink, often at a bar or party. The blue color that results from mixing Rohypnol with a beverage often is masked by serving blue tropical drinks or by serving the drink in dark or opaque containers.

The effects of the drug typically are felt within 15 to 20 minutes of administration and may persist for more than 12 hours.

Who abuses Rohypnol?

Teenagers and young adults, primarily individuals aged 13 to 30, are the principal users of Rohypnol, and most users are male. The drug is popular on high school and college campuses and at raves and nightclubs.

Rohypnol use among high school students is a particular problem. Nearly 2 percent of high school seniors in the United States used Rohypnol at least once in the past year, according to the University of Michigan's Monitoring the Future Survey.

♣ It's A Fact!!
Street Terms For Rohypnol

- Circles
- La rocha
- Pingus
- Roach–2
- Roapies
- Rope
- Ropies
- Ruffies

- Forget-me pill
- Lunch money drug
- R-2
- Roaches
- Robutal
- Rophies
- Roples
- Wolfies

- Forget pill
- Mexican valium
- Reynolds
- Roachies
- Rochas dos
- Rophy
- Row-shay

Source: National Drug Intelligence Center, a component of the U.S. Department of Justice, Product No. 2003-L0559-020, August 2003.

What are the risks?

Individuals who abuse Rohypnol often experience drowsiness, headaches, memory impairment, dizziness, nightmares, confusion, and tremors. Although the drug is classified as a depressant, Rohypnol can induce aggression or excitability.

In addition to the risks associated with the drug itself, individuals who use Rohypnol may put themselves at risk of sexual assault. While many sexual predators lace unsuspecting victims' drinks with the drug, others offer Rohypnol to victims who consume the drug without understanding the effects it will produce.

Rohypnol users who inject the drug expose themselves to additional risks, including contracting HIV (human immunodeficiency virus), hepatitis B and C, and other blood-borne viruses.

What is it called?

The most common names for Rohypnol are forget-me drug, roche, roofies, and ruffles.

Is Rohypnol illegal in the United States?

Yes, Rohypnol is illegal in the United States. Rohypnol is a Schedule IV substance under the Controlled Substances Act. Schedule IV drugs are considered to have a lower potential for abuse but still can lead to limited physical or psychological dependence. In addition, in 1997 the U. S. Sentencing Commission increased the penalties associated with the possession, trafficking, and distribution of Rohypnol to those of a Schedule I substance. (Schedule I substances include heroin, marijuana, and MDMA.)

Ketamine

What is ketamine?

Ketamine is an anesthetic that is abused for its hallucinogenic properties. Its predominant legitimate use is as a veterinary anesthetic; however, it has been approved for use with both animals and humans. Abuse of the drug gained popularity when users discovered that it produced effects similar to those associated with PCP. Because of its anesthetic properties, ketamine also reportedly has been used by sexual predators to incapacitate their intended victims.

What does ketamine look like?

Ketamine generally is sold as either a colorless, odorless liquid or as a white or off-white powder.

How is ketamine abused?

In either its powder or liquid forms, ketamine is mixed with beverages or added to smokable materials such as marijuana or tobacco. As a powder the drug is snorted or pressed into tablets—often in combination with other drugs such as 3,4-methylenedioxymethamphetamine (MDMA, also known as ecstasy). As a liquid, ketamine is injected; it often is injected intramuscularly.

Who uses ketamine?

Teenagers and young adults represent the majority of ketamine users. According to the Drug Abuse Warning Network, individuals aged 12 to 25 accounted for 74 percent of the ketamine emergency department mentions in the United States in 2000.

Ketamine use among high school students is a particular concern. Nearly 3 percent of high school seniors in the United States used the drug at least once in the past year, according to the University of Michigan's Monitoring the Future Survey.

What are the risks?

Ketamine causes users to have distorted perceptions of sight and sound and to feel disconnected and out of control. Use of the drug can impair an individual's senses, judgment, and coordination for up to 24 hours after the drug is taken even though the drug's hallucinogenic effects usually last for only 45 to 90 minutes.

Use of ketamine has been associated with serious problems—both mental and physical. Ketamine can cause depression, delirium, amnesia, impaired motor function, high blood pressure, and potentially fatal respiratory problems.

In addition to the risks associated with ketamine itself, individuals who use the drug may put themselves at risk of sexual assault. Sexual predators reportedly have used ketamine to incapacitate their intended victims—either by lacing unsuspecting victims' drinks with the drug or by offering ketamine to victims who consume the drug without understanding the effects it will produce.

What is ketamine called?

The most common names for ketamine are K, special K, cat valium, and vitamin K.

Is ketamine illegal?

Yes, it is illegal to abuse ketamine. Ketamine is a controlled substance. Specifically, it is a Schedule III substance under the Controlled Substances Act. Schedule III drugs, which include codeine and anabolic steroids, have less potential for abuse than Schedule I (heroin) or Schedule II (cocaine) drugs. However, abuse of Schedule III substances may lead to physical or psychological dependence on the drug.

♣ **It's A Fact!!**
Street Terms For Ketamine

- Green K   • Honey oil
- Jet   • Ket
- Kit kat   • Purple
- Super acid • Super C
- Special la coke

Source: National Drug Intelligence Center, a component of the U.S. Department of Justice, Product No. 2003-L0559-011, June 2003.

Chapter 14

Stimulants: An Overview

The Brain's Response To Stimulants

Have you eaten any chocolate or drunk any soda lately? If you have, there's a good chance you gave your body a dose of a stimulant—caffeine, which is also in coffee.

Eating or drinking a large amount of caffeine can make you feel jittery, nervous, or energetic. That is because caffeine—like any stimulant—changes the way your brain works.

But caffeine is just a mild example of a stimulant. Many other stimulant drugs are much stronger—and some are illegal and very dangerous. Others require a doctor's prescription.

Miscommunication In The Brain

Cocaine and amphetamines change the way the brain works by changing the way nerve cells communicate. Nerve cells, called neurons, send messages to each other by releasing special chemicals called neurotransmitters. Neurotransmitters are able to work by attaching to key sites on neurons called receptors.

About This Chapter: Information in this chapter is from "Mind Over Matter: Stimulants," from NIDA for Teens, National Institute on Drug Abuse, a component of the United States Department of Health and Human Services, June 2005.

One of the neurotransmitters affected by cocaine is called dopamine. Dopamine is released by neurons in the limbic system—the part of the brain that controls feelings of pleasure.

Normally, once dopamine has attached to a nerve cell's receptor and caused a change in the cell, it's pumped back to the neuron that released it. But cocaine blocks the pump, called the dopamine transporter. Dopamine then builds up in the gap (synapse) between neurons.

The result: dopamine keeps affecting a nerve cell after it should have stopped. That's why someone who uses cocaine feels an extra sense of pleasure for a short time.

♣ **It's A Fact!!**
Examples Of Strong Stimulants

- **Cocaine:** Made from the leaf of the coca plant, this drug often comes in the form of a white powder that some people inhale through their nose.

- **Crack:** A form of cocaine that can be smoked.

- **Amphetamines:** Often called "speed," these pills are sometimes prescribed by doctors for medical problems.

- **Methamphetamine:** A powerful form of amphetamine that comes in clear crystals (called "ice") or powder (called "crank") that is smoked or injected.

Cocaine Can Damage The Way The Brain Works

Although cocaine may make someone feel pleasure for a while, later it can damage the ability to feel pleasure. Research suggests that long-term cocaine use may reduce the amount of dopamine or the number of dopamine receptors in the brain.

When this happens, nerve cells must have cocaine to communicate properly. Without the drug, the brain can't send enough dopamine into the receptors to create a feeling of pleasure.

If a long-term user of cocaine or crack stops taking the drug, the person feels an extremely strong craving for it, because without it he or she can't feel nearly as much pleasure.

Cocaine Tightens Blood Vessels

Cocaine causes the body's blood vessels to become narrow, constricting the flow of blood. This is a problem. It forces the heart to work harder to pump blood through the body. (If you've ever tried squeezing into a tight pair of pants, then you know how hard it is for the heart to pump blood through narrowed blood vessels.)

When the heart works harder, it beats faster. It may work so hard that it temporarily loses its natural rhythm. This is called fibrillation, and it can be very dangerous because it stops the flow of blood through the body.

Many of cocaine's effects on the heart are actually caused by cocaine's impact on the brain—the body's control center.

Scientists Discover Answers

Fortunately, scientists have figured out how to copy the gene that controls the dopamine transporter. This process is called "cloning".

By studying copies of the transporter, scientists may learn more about how cocaine affects it—and how to prevent those effects. These studies may even lead to the discovery of a treatment for cocaine addiction.

Scientists are already working to create a medication for use as a treatment. This chemical would attach to the dopamine transporter just like cocaine does, but it wouldn't block dopamine's normal movement back into neurons. By attaching to the transporter, the substitute would block the effects of cocaine.

Chapter 15

Crack, Cocaine, Methamphetamine, Khat, And Yaba

Crack And Cocaine

Cocaine is a powerfully addictive stimulant drug. The powdered, hydrochloride salt form of cocaine can be snorted or dissolved in water and injected. Crack is cocaine that has not been neutralized by an acid to make the hydrochloride salt. This form of cocaine comes in a rock crystal that can be heated and its vapors smoked. The term "crack" refers to the crackling sound heard when it is heated.

Snorting is the process of inhaling cocaine powder through the nose, where it is absorbed into the bloodstream through the nasal tissues. Injecting is the use of a needle to release the drug directly into the bloodstream; any needle use increases a user's risk of contracting HIV and other bloodborne infections. Smoking involves inhaling cocaine vapor or smoke into the lungs, where absorption into the bloodstream is as rapid as by injection.

About This Chapter: This chapter begins with "Crack And Cocaine," excerpted from NIDA InfoFacts, March 2005 and "Methamphetamine," excerpted from NIDA InfoFacts, May 2005, National Institute on Drug Abuse, a component of the United States Department of Health and Human Services. "Khat Fast Facts," Product No. 2003-L0559-014, July 2003 and "Yaba Fast Facts," Product No. 2003-L0559-015, June 2003, are from the National Drug Intelligence Center, a component of the U.S. Department of Justice.

What are the health hazards?

Cocaine is a strong central nervous system stimulant that interferes with the reabsorption process of dopamine, a chemical messenger associated with pleasure and movement. The buildup of dopamine causes continuous stimulation of "receiving" neurons, which is associated with the euphoria commonly reported by cocaine abusers.

Physical effects of cocaine use include constricted blood vessels, dilated pupils, and increased temperature, heart rate, and blood pressure. The duration of cocaine's immediate euphoric effects, which include hyperstimulation, reduced fatigue, and mental clarity, depends on the route of administration. The faster the absorption, the more intense the high. On the other hand, the faster the absorption, the shorter the duration of action. The high from snorting may last 15 to 30 minutes, while that from smoking may last 5 to 10 minutes. Increased use can reduce the period of time a user feels high and increases the risk of addiction.

> ## ♣ It's A Fact!!
> A cocaine user can experience acute cardiovascular or cerebrovascular emergencies, such as a heart attack or stroke, which could result in sudden death. Cocaine-related deaths are often a result of cardiac arrest or seizure followed by respiratory arrest.
>
> Source: "Crack And Cocaine," from NIDA InfoFacts, March 2005, National Institute on Drug Abuse, a component of the United States Department of Health and Human Services.

Some users of cocaine report feelings of restlessness, irritability, and anxiety. A tolerance to the "high" may develop, and many addicts report that they seek but fail to achieve as much pleasure as they did from their first exposure. Some users will increase their doses to intensify and prolong the euphoric effects. While tolerance to the high can occur, users can also become more sensitive to cocaine's anesthetic and convulsant effects without increasing the dose taken. This increased sensitivity may explain some deaths occurring after apparently low doses of cocaine.

Use of cocaine in a binge, during which the drug is taken repeatedly and at increasingly high doses, may lead to a state of increasing irritability, restlessness, and paranoia. This can result in a period of full-blown paranoid psychosis, in which the user loses touch with reality and experiences auditory hallucinations.

Other complications associated with cocaine use include disturbances in hearth rhythm and heart attacks, chest pain and respiratory failure, strokes, seizures and headaches, and gastrointestinal complications such as abdominal pain and nausea. Because cocaine has a tendency to decrease appetite, many chronic users can become malnourished.

Different means of taking cocaine can produce different adverse effects. Regularly snorting cocaine, for example, can lead to loss of sense of smell, nosebleeds, problems with swallowing, hoarseness, and a chronically runny nose. Ingesting cocaine can cause severe bowel gangrene due to reduced blood flow. People who inject cocaine can experience severe allergic reactions and, as with any injecting drug user, are at increased risk for contracting HIV and other blood-borne diseases.

What is cocaethylene?

When people mix cocaine and alcohol consumption, they are compounding the danger each drug poses and unknowingly forming a complex chemical experiment within their bodies. NIDA (National Institute on Drug Abuse)-funded researchers have found that the human liver combines cocaine and alcohol and manufactures a third substance, cocaethylene, that intensifies cocaine's euphoric effects, while potentially increasing the risk of sudden death.

What treatment is used?

The widespread abuse of cocaine has stimulated extensive efforts to develop treatment programs for this type of drug abuse.

One of NIDA's top research priorities is to find a medication to block or greatly reduce the effects of cocaine, to be used as one part of a comprehensive treatment program. NIDA-funded researchers are also looking at medications that help alleviate the severe craving that people in treatment for cocaine addiction often experience. Several medications are currently being investigated for their safety and efficacy in treating cocaine addiction.

In addition to treatment medications, behavioral interventions—particularly cognitive behavioral therapy—can be effective in decreasing drug use by patients in treatment for cocaine abuse. Providing the optimal combination of treatment and services for each individual is critical to successful outcomes.

Methamphetamine

Methamphetamine is an addictive stimulant drug that strongly activates certain systems in the brain. Methamphetamine is chemically related to amphetamine, but the central nervous system effects of methamphetamine are greater. Both drugs have some limited therapeutic uses, primarily in the treatment of obesity.

Methamphetamine is made in illegal laboratories and has a high potential for abuse and addiction. Street methamphetamine is referred to by many names, such as "speed," "meth," and "chalk." Methamphetamine hydrochloride, clear chunky crystals resembling ice, which can be inhaled by smoking, is referred to as "ice," "crystal," "glass," and "tina."

What are the health hazards?

Methamphetamine releases high levels of the neurotransmitter dopamine, which stimulates brain cells, enhancing mood and body movement. It also appears to have a neurotoxic effect, damaging brain cells that contain dopamine as well as serotonin, another neurotransmitter. Over time, methamphetamine appears to cause reduced levels of dopamine, which can result in symptoms like those of Parkinson's disease, a severe movement disorder.

Methamphetamine is taken orally or intranasally (snorting the powder), by intravenous injection, and by smoking. Immediately after smoking or intravenous injection, the methamphetamine user experiences an intense sensation, called a "rush" or "flash," that lasts only a few minutes and is described as extremely pleasurable. Oral or intranasal use produces euphoria—a high, but not a rush. Users may become addicted quickly, and use it with increasing frequency and in increasing doses.

Animal research going back more than 20 years shows that high doses of methamphetamine damage neuron cell endings. Dopamine- and serotonin-containing neurons do not die after methamphetamine use, but their nerve endings ("terminals") are cut back, and regrowth appears to be limited.

The central nervous system (CNS) actions that result from taking even small amounts of methamphetamine include increased wakefulness, increased

♣ It's A Fact!!
2004 Survey Found More Methamphetamine Users Meet Criteria For Dependence And Abuse

The Substance Abuse and Mental Health Services Administration (SAMHSA) released data showing that the prevalence of methamphetamine use in 2004 was similar to the number of users in the prior two years. But, the new 2004 National Survey on Drug Use and Health also showed that the number of past month methamphetamine users who met criteria for illicit drug dependence or abuse in the past 12 months increased sharply.

In 2004, 1.4 million persons ages 12 or older (0.6 percent of the population) used methamphetamine in the past year and 600,000 (0.2 percent) used in the past month. These numbers are similar to numbers in 2002 and 2003.

However, the number of past month methamphetamine users who met criteria for illicit drug dependence or abuse in the past 12 months increased from 164,000 (27.5 percent of past month methamphetamine users in 2002 to 346,000 (59.3 percent) in 2004. Of these 130,000 (22.3 percent) had stimulants, primarily methamphetamine, as their primary substance of abuse in 2004.

"Methamphetamine is undeniably a uniquely destructive drug," SAMHSA Administrator Charles Curie said. "While rates of use have remained relatively stable over the past few years, these new findings show that an increasing proportion of methamphetamine users are developing problems of drug abuse and dependence and are in need of treatment."

The survey questions ask about both illicit methamphetamine, as well as prescription methamphetamine used nonmedically. Dependence or abuse is defined using criteria specified in the Diagnostic and Statistical Manual of Mental Disorders (DSM-IV) used by psychiatrists for their diagnoses. Information on symptoms of dependence and abuse is collected for alcohol and a number of specific illicit drug categories, including stimulants, but not exclusively methamphetamine. Methamphetamine is the most frequently reported stimulant used.

The survey found that in 2004 there were an estimated 318,000 new initiates to methamphetamine use, defined as having used it for the first time in the 12 months prior to the survey. This is approximately the same number of new users in 2002 and 2003.

Source: Excerpted from "SAMHSA Advisory," Substance Abuse and Mental Health Services Administration (SAMHSA), United States Department of Health and Human Services, September 2005.

physical activity, decreased appetite, increased respiration, hyperthermia, and euphoria. Other CNS effects include irritability, insomnia, confusion, tremors, convulsions, anxiety, paranoia, and aggressiveness. Hyperthermia and convulsions can result in death.

Methamphetamine causes increased heart rate and blood pressure and can cause irreversible damage to blood vessels in the brain, producing strokes. Other effects of methamphetamine include respiratory problems, irregular heartbeat, and extreme anorexia. Its use can result in cardiovascular collapse and death.

Khat Fast Facts

What is khat?

Khat (*Catha edulis*) is a flowering shrub native to northeast Africa and the Arabian Peninsula. Individuals chew khat leaves because of the stimulant effects, which are similar to but less intense than those caused by abusing cocaine or methamphetamine.

What does khat look like?

When fresh, khat leaves are glossy and crimson-brown in color, resembling withered basil. Khat leaves typically begin to deteriorate 48 hours after being cut from the shrub on which they grow. Deteriorating khat leaves are leathery and turn yellow-green in color.

How is khat used?

Khat typically is ingested by chewing the leaves—as is done with loose tobacco. Dried khat leaves can be brewed in tea or cooked and added to food. After ingesting khat, the user experiences an immediate increase in blood pressure and heart rate. The effects of the drug generally begin to subside between 90 minutes and 3 hours after ingestion; however, they can last up to 24 hours.

Who uses khat?

The use of khat is accepted within the Somali, Ethiopian, and Yemeni cultures, and in the United States khat use is most prevalent among

♣ It's A Fact!!
Street Terms For Khat

- Abyssinian tea
- African salad
- Bushman's tea
- Chat
- Gat
- Kat
- Miraa
- Oat
- Qat
- Somali tea
- Tohai
- Tschat

Source: "Khat Fast Facts," Product No. 2003-L0559-014, July 2003, National Drug Intelligence Center, a component of the U.S. Department of Justice.

immigrants from those countries. Abuse levels are highest in cities with sizable populations of immigrants from Somalia, Ethiopia, and Yemen, including Boston, Columbus, Dallas, Detroit, Kansas City, Los Angeles, Minneapolis, Nashville, New York, and Washington, D.C. In addition, there is evidence to suggest that some non-immigrants in these areas have begun abusing the drug.

What are the risks?

Individuals who abuse khat typically experience a state of mild depression following periods of prolonged use. Taken in excess, khat causes extreme thirst, hyperactivity, insomnia, and loss of appetite (which can lead to anorexia).

Frequent khat use often leads to decreased productivity because the drug tends to reduce the user's motivation. Repeated use can cause manic behavior with grandiose delusions, paranoia, and hallucinations. (There have been reports of khat-induced psychosis.) The drug also can cause damage to the nervous, respiratory, circulatory, and digestive systems.

Is khat illegal?

Yes, khat is illegal. Fresh khat leaves contain cathinone—a Schedule I drug under the Controlled Substances Act. Schedule I drugs, which include heroin and LSD, have a high potential for abuse and serve no legitimate medical purpose. When khat leaves are no longer fresh (typically after 48 hours), their chemical composition breaks down. At that point the leaves contain cathine, a Schedule IV substance. Schedule IV drugs are considered to have a lower potential for abuse but still can lead to limited physical or psychological dependence.

Yaba Fast Facts

What is yaba?

Yaba is a combination of methamphetamine (a powerful and addictive stimulant) and caffeine. Yaba, which means crazy medicine in Thai, is produced in Southeast and East Asia. The drug is popular in Asian communities in the United States and increasingly is available at raves and techno parties.

What does yaba look like?

Yaba is sold as tablets. These tablets are generally no larger than a pencil eraser. They are brightly colored, usually reddish-orange or green. Yaba tablets typically bear one of a variety of logos; R and WY are common logos.

How is yaba used?

Yaba tablets typically are consumed orally. The tablets sometimes are flavored like candy (grape, orange, or vanilla). Another common method is called chasing the dragon. Users place the yaba tablet on aluminum foil and heat it from below. As the tablet melts, vapors rise and are inhaled. The drug also may be administered by crushing the tablets into powder, which is then snorted or mixed with a solvent and injected.

Who uses yaba?

It is difficult to determine the scope of yaba use in the United States because most data sources do not distinguish yaba from other forms of methamphetamine. Yaba has emerged as a drug of abuse in Asian communities in the United States, specifically in Northern California and in Los Angeles.

Yaba also is becoming increasingly popular at raves, techno parties, and other venues where the drug MDMA (3,4-methylenedioxy-methamphetamine, typically called ecstasy) is used. Drug distributors deliberately market yaba to young people, many of whom have already tried MDMA. The bright colors and candy flavors of yaba tablets are examples of distributors' attempts to appeal to young people.

What are the risks?

Individuals who use yaba face the same risks as users of other forms of methamphetamine: rapid heart rate, increased blood pressure, and damage to the small blood vessels in the brain that can lead to stroke. Chronic use of the drug can result in inflammation of the heart lining. Overdoses can cause hyperthermia (elevated body temperature), convulsions, and death. Individuals who use yaba also may have episodes of violent behavior, paranoia, anxiety, confusion, and insomnia.

Although most users administer yaba orally, those who inject the drug expose themselves to additional risks, including contracting HIV (human immunodeficiency virus), hepatitis B and C, and other blood-borne viruses.

What is it called?

The most common names for yaba are crazy medicine and Nazi speed.

Is yaba illegal?

Yes, yaba is illegal because it contains methamphetamine, a Schedule II substance under the Controlled Substances Act. Schedule II drugs, which include cocaine and PCP, have a high potential for abuse. Abuse of these drugs may lead to severe psychological or physical dependence.

Chapter 16

Hallucinogens: An Overview

The Brain's Response To Hallucinogens

Hallucinogens cause people to experience—you guessed it—hallucinations, imagined experiences that seem real. The word "hallucinate" comes from Latin words meaning, "to wander in the mind."

No wonder some people refer to hallucinating as tripping.

The "trips" caused by hallucinogens can last for hours. Parts of these trips can feel really good, and other parts can feel really terrible.

Hallucinogens powerfully affect the brain, distorting the way our five senses work and changing our impressions of time and space. People who use these drugs a lot may have a hard time concentrating, communicating, or telling the difference between reality and illusion.

The Source Of Hallucinogens

Some hallucinogens can be found in plants. Mescaline comes from a cactus called peyote. And certain mushrooms, also known as magic mushrooms, are hallucinogens.

But many hallucinogens are chemicals that don't occur in nature.

About This Chapter: Information in this chapter is from "Mind Over Matter: Hallucinogens," NIDA for Teens, National Institute on Drug Abuse, a component of the United States Department of Health and Human Services, June 2005.

How Hallucinogens Affect Your Senses

Your brain controls all of your perceptions—the way you see, hear, smell, taste, and feel. How does your brain communicate with the rest of your body? Chemical messengers transmit information from nerve cell to nerve cell in the body and the brain. Messages are constantly being sent back and forth with amazing speed.

♣ **It's A Fact!!**

The following are some examples of chemical hallucinogens:

• LSD, also called acid

• MDA, an amphetamine

• MDMA, an amphetamine, called ecstasy

• PCP (phencyclidine), often called angel dust

Your nerve cells are called neurons, and their chemical messengers are called neurotransmitters. When neurotransmitters attach to special places on nerve cells (called receptors), they cause changes in the nerve cells.

Chemicals like hallucinogens can disrupt this communication system, and the results are changes in the way you sense the world around you.

A Recent Discovery

MDMA and MDA cause neurons to release a neurotransmitter called serotonin. Serotonin is important to many types of nerve cells, including cells that receive sensory information and cells that control sleeping and emotions. The released serotonin can over activate serotonin receptors. In animals, MDMA and MDA have been shown to damage and destroy nerve fibers of neurons that contain serotonin. This can be a big problem, because serotonin neurons have a role in so many things, such as mood, sleep, and control of heart rate.

Scientists have recently found that the damaged serotonin neurons can regrow their fibers, but the fibers don't grow back normally. The fibers may regrow into brain areas where they don't normally grow, but not into other brain areas where they should be located. The new growth patterns may cause changes in mood, learning, or memory.

Actions Of PCP In The Brain

PCP prevents the actions normally caused when a neurotransmitter, called glutamate, attaches to its receptor in the brain. It also disrupts the actions of other neurotransmitters.

This drug's effects are very unpredictable. For example, it may make some people hallucinate and become aggressive, while others may become drowsy and passive. It is also addictive.

LSD: The Most Commonly Used Hallucinogen

LSD causes its effects mainly by activating one type of receptor for serotonin. Because serotonin has a role in many important functions, LSD use can have many effects. These may include sleeplessness, trembling, and raised heart rate and blood pressure. LSD users may feel several emotions at once (including extreme terror), and their senses may seem to get crossed—giving the feeling of hearing colors and seeing sounds.

Even a tiny speck of LSD can trigger these effects. And LSD has an unusual "echo." Many users have flashbacks—sudden repetitions of their LSD experiences—days or months after they stop using the drug.

Chapter 17

LSD, PCP, Foxy, And Psilocybin

LSD

LSD (lysergic acid diethylamide) is one of the major drugs making up the hallucinogen class. LSD was discovered in 1938 and is one of the most potent mood-changing chemicals. It is manufactured from lysergic acid, which is found in ergot, a fungus that grows on rye and other grains.

LSD, commonly referred to as "acid," is sold on the street in tablets, capsules, and, occasionally, liquid form. It is odorless, colorless, and has a slightly bitter taste and is usually taken by mouth. Often LSD is added to absorbent paper, such as blotter paper, and divided into small, decorated squares, with each square representing one dose.

The Drug Enforcement Administration reports that the strength of LSD samples obtained currently from illicit sources ranges from 20 to 80 micrograms of LSD per dose. This is considerably less than the levels reported during the 1960s and early 1970s, when the dosage ranged from 100 to 200 micrograms, or higher, per unit.

About This Chapter: This chapter begins with "LSD", February 2005, and "PCP," March 2005, excerpted from NIDA InfoFacts, National Institute on Drug Abuse, a component of the United States Department of Health and Human Services. "Foxy Fast Facts," Product No. 2003-L0559-024, September 2003, and "Psilocybin Fast Facts," Product No. 2003-L0559-018, August 2003, are from the National Drug Intelligence Center, a component of the U.S. Department of Justice.

What are the health hazards?

The effects of LSD are unpredictable. They depend on the amount taken; the user's personality, mood, and expectations; and the surroundings in which the drug is used. Usually, the user feels the first effects of the drug 30 to 90 minutes after taking it. The physical effects include dilated pupils, higher body temperature, increased heart rate and blood pressure, sweating, loss of appetite, sleeplessness, dry mouth, and tremors.

Sensations and feelings change much more dramatically than the physical signs. The user may feel several different emotions at once or swing rapidly from one emotion to another. If taken in a large enough dose, the drug produces delusions and visual hallucinations. The user's sense of time and self changes. Sensations may seem to "cross over," giving the user the feeling of hearing colors and seeing sounds. These changes can be frightening and can cause panic.

Users refer to their experience with LSD as a "trip" and to acute adverse reactions as a "bad trip." These experiences are long; typically they begin to clear after about 12 hours.

Many LSD users experience flashbacks, recurrence of certain aspects of a person's experience, without the user having taken the drug again. A flashback occurs suddenly, often without warning, and may occur within a few days or more than a year after LSD use. Flashbacks usually occur in people who use hallucinogens chronically or have an underlying personality problem; however, otherwise healthy people who use LSD occasionally may also have flashbacks. Bad trips and flashbacks are only part of the risks of LSD use. LSD users may manifest relatively long-lasting psychoses, such as schizophrenia or severe depression. It is difficult to determine the extent and mechanism of the LSD involvement in these illnesses.

> ✤ **It's A Fact!!**
> Some LSD users experience severe, terrifying thoughts and feelings, fear of losing control, fear of insanity and death, and despair while using LSD. Some fatal accidents have occurred during states of LSD intoxication.
>
> Source: "LSD," NIDA InfoFacts, National Institute on Drug Abuse, a component of the United States Department of Health and Human Services, February 2005.

Most users of LSD voluntarily decrease or stop its use over time. LSD is not considered an addictive drug since it does not produce compulsive drug-seeking behavior, as do cocaine, amphetamine, heroin, alcohol, and nicotine. However, like many of the addictive drugs, LSD produces tolerance, so some users who take the drug repeatedly must take progressively higher doses to achieve the state of intoxication that they had previously achieved. This is an extremely dangerous practice, given the unpredictability of the drug.

PCP (Phencyclidine)

PCP (phencyclidine) was developed in the 1950s as an intravenous anesthetic. Its use in humans was discontinued in 1965, because patients often became agitated, delusional, and irrational while recovering from its anesthetic effects. PCP is illegally manufactured in laboratories and is sold on the street by such names as angel dust, ozone, wack, and rocket fuel. Killer joints and crystal supergrass are names that refer to PCP combined with marijuana. The variety of street names for PCP reflects its bizarre and volatile effects.

PCP is a white crystalline powder that is readily soluble in water or alcohol. It has a distinctive bitter chemical taste. PCP can be mixed easily with dyes and turns up on the illicit drug market in a variety of tablets, capsules, and colored powders. It is normally used in one of three ways: snorted, smoked, or ingested. For smoking, PCP is often applied to a leafy material such as mint, parsley, oregano, or marijuana.

What are the health hazards?

PCP is addictive—its repeated use can lead to craving and compulsive PCP-seeking behavior. First introduced as a street drug in the 1960s, PCP quickly gained a reputation as a drug that could cause bad reactions and was not worth the risk. After using PCP once, many people will not knowingly use it again. Others attribute their continued use to feelings of strength, power, invulnerability, and a numbing effect on the mind.

At low to moderate doses, physiological effects of PCP include a slight increase in breathing rate and a pronounced rise in blood pressure and pulse rate. Breathing becomes shallow, and flushing and profuse sweating occurs. Generalized numbness of the extremities and loss of muscular coordination also may occur.

At high doses of PCP, blood pressure, pulse rate, and respiration drop. This may be accompanied by nausea, vomiting, blurred vision, flicking up and down of the eyes, drooling, loss of balance, and dizziness. High doses of PCP can also cause seizures, coma, and death (though death more often results from accidental injury or suicide during PCP intoxication). High doses can cause symptoms that mimic schizophrenia, such as delusions, hallucinations, paranoia, disordered thinking, a sensation of distance from one's environment, and catatonia. Speech is often sparse and garbled.

People who use PCP for long periods report memory loss, difficulties with speech and thinking, depression, and weight loss. These symptoms can persist up to a year after stopping PCP use. Mood disorders also have been reported. PCP has sedative effects, and interactions with other central nervous system depressants, such as alcohol and benzodiazepines, can lead to coma.

♣ It's A Fact!!

Many PCP users are brought to emergency rooms because of PCP overdose or because of the drug's unpleasant psychological effects. In a hospital or detention setting, these people often become violent or suicidal and are very dangerous to themselves and others.

Source: "PCP," NIDA InfoFacts, National Institute on Drug Abuse, a component of the United States Department of Health and Human Services, March 2005.

Foxy Fast Facts

What is foxy?

Foxy and foxy methoxy are common names for a synthetic drug with the chemical name 5-methoxy-N, N-diisopropyltryptamine (5-MeO-DIPT). Abused for the hallucinogenic effects it produces, foxy belongs to a class of chemical compounds known as tryptamines. (Other hallucinogenic tryptamines include psilocybin and psilocin.)

What does foxy look like?

Foxy is typically available as a powder, capsule, or tablet. (Generally the powder is placed into capsules or pressed into tablets before it is sold to users.) Some capsules and tablets contain foxy powder mixed with blue, green, red, purple, tan, orange, gray, or pink powders. The tablets sometimes are embossed with logos such as a spider or an alien head.

How is foxy used?

Foxy is typically consumed orally in 6- to 20-milligram dosages, although dosage amounts vary widely. The drug also may be administered via smoking or snorting. Typically, users begin to feel the drug's effects 20 to 30 minutes after administration. The hallucinogenic effects peak after approximately 60 to 90 minutes and generally last for 3 to 6 hours.

Who abuses foxy?

Teenagers and young adults typically abuse foxy. The drug often is used at raves, nightclubs, and other venues where the use of club drugs, particularly MDMA (ecstasy), is well established. In order to capitalize on the popularity of MDMA and other club drugs, dealers sell foxy and other noncontrolled synthetic substances in these environments. However, the Drug Enforcement Administration (DEA) made foxy a controlled substance through emergency scheduling in April 2003.

What are the risks?

Foxy produces a variety of negative physical and psychological effects in users. The physical effects include dilated pupils, visual and auditory disturbances and distortions, nausea, vomiting, and diarrhea. The psychological effects associated with the use of foxy include hallucinations, talkativeness, and emotional distress. Foxy also diminishes user inhibitions, often resulting in high-risk sexual activity.

In addition, foxy is a dose-dependent drug. This means that increasing the dose results in a corresponding increase in the intensity of the drug's effects. Doubling a 6-milligram dose, for instance, may produce effects similar to those associated with LSD.

Is foxy illegal?

Yes, foxy is illegal. In April 2003 DEA designated foxy a Schedule I substance under the Controlled Substances Act. Schedule I drugs, which include heroin and MDMA, have a high potential for abuse and serve no legitimate medical purpose in the United States.

Psilocybin Fast Facts

What is psilocybin?

Psilocybin is a hallucinogenic substance obtained from certain types of mushrooms that are indigenous to tropical and subtropical regions of South America, Mexico, and the United States. These mushrooms typically contain 0.2 to 0.4 percent psilocybin and a trace amount of psilocin, another hallucinogenic substance. Both psilocybin and psilocin can be produced synthetically, but law enforcement reporting currently does not indicate that this is occurring.

What does psilocybin look like?

Mushrooms containing psilocybin are available fresh or dried and have long, slender stems topped by caps with dark gills on the underside. Fresh mushrooms have white or whitish-gray stems; the caps are dark brown around the edges and light brown or white in the center. Dried mushrooms are generally rusty brown with isolated areas of off-white.

How is psilocybin abused?

Psilocybin mushrooms are ingested orally. They may be brewed as a tea or added to other foods to mask their bitter flavor. Some users coat the mushrooms with chocolate—this both masks the flavor and disguises the mushrooms as candy. Once the mushrooms are ingested, the body breaks down the psilocybin to produce psilocin.

Who abuses psilocybin?

Psilocybin mushrooms are popular at raves, clubs and, increasingly, on college campuses and generally are abused by teenagers and young adults. It is difficult to gauge the extent of psilocybin use in the United States because most data sources that quantify drug use exclude psilocybin. The Monitoring the Future Survey, conducted by the University of Michigan, does reveal that 9.2 percent of high school seniors in the United States used hallucinogens other than LSD—a category that includes psilocybin—at least once in their lifetime. Two percent of high school seniors used hallucinogens other than LSD in the past month.

What are the risks?

Use of psilocybin is associated with negative physical and psychological consequences. The physical effects, which appear within 20 minutes of ingestion and last approximately 6 hours, include nausea, vomiting, muscle weakness, drowsiness, and lack of coordination. While there is no evidence that users may become physically dependent on psilocybin, tolerance for the drug does develop when it is ingested continuously over a short period of time.

The psychological consequences of psilocybin use include hallucinations and an inability to discern fantasy from reality. Panic reactions and psychosis also may occur, particularly if a user ingests a large dose.

In addition to the risks associated with ingestion of psilocybin, individuals who seek to abuse psilocybin mushrooms also risk poisoning if one of the many varieties of poisonous mushrooms is incorrectly identified as a psilocybin mushroom.

What is psilocybin called?

The most common names for psilocybin are magic mushroom, mushroom, and shrooms.

Is psilocybin illegal?

Yes, psilocybin is illegal. Psilocybin is a Schedule I substance under the Controlled Substances Act. Schedule I drugs, which include heroin and LSD, have a high potential for abuse and serve no legitimate medical purpose in the United States.

Chapter 18

Opiates: An Overview

The Brain's Response To Opiates

If you've ever seen "The Wizard of Oz," then you've seen the poppy plant—the source of a type of drug called opiates. When Dorothy lies down in a field of poppies, she falls into a deep sleep.

No wonder the Latin name of this plant—*Papaver somniferum*—means "the poppy that makes you sleepy."

Opiates are made from opium, a white liquid in the poppy plant. They're also referred to as narcotics. Maybe you've heard of drugs called heroin, morphine, or codeine. These are examples of opiates.

Opiates can produce a quick, intense feeling of pleasure followed by a sense of well being and a calm drowsiness. But they can also become an addiction.

Nerve Cells Experience Addiction And Withdrawal

What happens to make a person and his or her brain become addicted to an opiate? Long-term opiate use changes the way nerve cells in the brain

About This Chapter: Information in this chapter is from "Mind Over Matter: Opiates," NIDA for Teens, National Institute on Drug Abuse, a component of the United States Department of Health and Human Services, June 2005.

work. These cells grow so used to having the opiate around that they actually need it to work normally.

❖ It's A Fact!!
If someone uses opiates again and again, his or her brain is likely to become dependent on them.

If opiates are taken away from dependent nerve cells, many cells become overactive. Eventually, these cells will work normally again, but in the meantime, they cause a wide range of symptoms in the brain and body. These are known as withdrawal symptoms.

Have you ever had the flu? You probably experienced symptoms such as aching, fever, sweating, shaking, or chills. These are similar to withdrawal symptoms, but withdrawal symptoms are much worse.

Drawing Away

Here's one way to illustrate how hard it is for brain cells to function without a drug they depend on: Grab a sheet of paper and try drawing any picture in a magazine without using the hand you usually use.

How Nerve Cells Respond To Opiate

Within the limbic system, brainstem and spinal cord, there are places on certain nerve cells that recognize opiates. When stimulated by opiates, these sites—called opiate receptors—trigger responses in the brain and body.

Scientists have identified three types of opiate receptors: delta, mu, and kappa (named after letters in the Greek alphabet). Each of these receptors is involved in different brain functions. For example, mu is responsible for the pain-relieving effects of the drug morphine.

Opiates Act On Many Places In The Brain And Nervous System

The limbic system controls emotions. Opiates change the limbic system to produce increased feelings of pleasure, relaxation, and contentment.

The brainstem controls things your body does automatically, like breathing or coughing. Opiates can act on the brainstem to stop coughing or slow breathing.

The spinal cord transmits pain signals from the body. By acting here, opiates block pain messages and allow people to bear even serious injuries.

Cloning Receptors

After years of experiments, scientists have discovered how to copy ("clone") the genes that control the production of opiate receptors. Now it will be easier for researchers to make opiate receptors and study how opiates affect nerve cells.

This discovery may lead to other exciting developments, such as better treatments for opiate addiction.

Opiates Stop Pain

Did you know that some opiates can have important medical uses? They're powerful painkillers, and doctors sometimes prescribe them to control severe diarrhea. If you look on a cough medicine label, you might find that codeine is one of the ingredients.

When used properly for medical purposes, opiates don't produce an intense feeling of pleasure, and patients have very little chance of becoming addicted.

Surprising Facts

Your brain produces its own versions of opiates, called endogenous opioids. These chemicals act just like opiates, binding to opiate receptors.

Endogenous opioids are your body's way of controlling pain. If you've ever felt pleasantly relaxed after exercising a lot, that feeling was probably caused by the release of this natural chemical in your brain.

Chapter 19

Heroin And Methadone

Heroin

Heroin is an addictive drug, and its use is a serious problem in America. Recent studies suggest a shift from injecting heroin to snorting or smoking because of increased purity and the misconception that these forms are safer. Heroin is processed from morphine, a naturally occurring substance extracted from the seedpod of the Asian poppy plant. Heroin usually appears as a white or brown powder.

What are the health hazards?

Heroin abuse is associated with serious health conditions, including fatal overdose, spontaneous abortion, collapsed veins, and, particularly in users who inject the drug, infectious diseases, including HIV/AIDS and hepatitis.

The short-term effects of heroin abuse appear soon after a single dose and disappear in a few hours. After an injection of heroin, the user reports feeling a surge of euphoria ("rush") accompanied by a warm flushing of the skin, a dry mouth, and heavy extremities. Following this initial euphoria, the

About This Chapter: This chapter begins with "Heroin," excerpted from NIDA InfoFacts, March 2005, National Institute on Drug Abuse, a component of the United States Department of Health and Human Services. "Methadone Fast Facts," Product No. 2003-L0559-021, September 2003 is from the National Drug Intelligence Center, a component of the U.S. Department of Justice.

user goes "on the nod," an alternately wakeful and drowsy state. Mental functioning becomes clouded due to the depression of the central nervous system. Longterm effects of heroin appear after repeated use for some period of time. Chronic users may develop collapsed veins, infection of the heart lining and valves, abscesses, cellulitis, and liver disease. Pulmonary complications, including various types of pneumonia, may result from the poor health condition of the abuser, as well as from heroin's depressing effects on respiration.

Heroin abuse during pregnancy and its many associated environmental factors (e.g., lack of prenatal care) have been associated with adverse consequences including low birth weight, an important risk factor for later developmental delay.

> ♣ **It's A Fact!!**
> **Street Names For Heroin**
> - Smack
> - H
> - Skag
> - Junk
>
> Other names may refer to types of heroin produced in a specific geographical area, such as "Mexican black tar."
>
> Source: "Heroin," NIDA InfoFacts, March 2005, National Institute on Drug Abuse, a component of the United States Department of Health and Human Services.

In addition to the effects of the drug itself, street heroin may have additives that do not readily dissolve and result in clogging the blood vessels that lead to the lungs, liver, kidneys, or brain. This can cause infection or even death of small patches of cells in vital organs.

Heroin/morphine was listed among the four most frequently mentioned drugs reported in drug-related death cases in 2002. Nationwide, heroin emergency department mentions were statistically unchanged from 2001 to 2002, but have increased 35 percent since 1995.

What are the facts regarding tolerance, addiction, and withdrawal?

With regular heroin use, tolerance develops. This means the abuser must use more heroin to achieve the same intensity of effect. As higher doses are used over time, physical dependence and addiction develop. With physical dependence, the body has adapted to the presence of the drug and withdrawal symptoms may occur if use is reduced or stopped.

Withdrawal, which in regular abusers may occur as early as a few hours after the last administration, produces drug craving, restlessness, muscle and bone pain, insomnia, diarrhea and vomiting, cold flashes with goose bumps ("cold turkey"), kicking movements ("kicking the habit"), and other symptoms. Major withdrawal symptoms peak between 48 and 72 hours after the last dose and subside after about a week. Sudden withdrawal by heavily dependent users who are in poor health is occasionally fatal, although heroin withdrawal is considered less dangerous than alcohol or barbiturate withdrawal.

How is addiction treated?

There is a broad range of treatment options for heroin addiction, including medications as well as behavioral therapies. Science has taught us that when medication treatment is integrated with other supportive services, patients are often able to stop heroin (or other opiate) use and return to more stable and productive lives.

In November 1997, the National Institutes of Health (NIH) convened a Consensus Panel on Effective Medical Treatment of Heroin Addiction. The panel of national experts concluded that opiate drug addictions are diseases of the brain and medical disorders that indeed can be treated effectively. The panel strongly recommended (1) broader access to methadone maintenance treatment programs for people who are addicted to heroin or other opiate drugs; and (2) the Federal and State regulations and other barriers impeding this access be eliminated. This panel also stressed the importance of providing substance abuse counseling, psychosocial therapies, and other supportive services to enhance retention and successful outcomes in methadone maintenance treatment programs.

Methadone, a synthetic opiate medication that blocks the effects of heroin for about 24 hours, has a proven record of success when prescribed at a high enough dosage level for people addicted to heroin. Other approved medications are naloxone, which is used to treat cases of overdose, and naltrexone, both of which block the effects of morphine, heroin, and other opiates.

For the pregnant heroin abuser, methadone maintenance combined with prenatal care and a comprehensive drug treatment program can improve many of the detrimental maternal and neonatal outcomes associated with untreated heroin abuse. There is preliminary evidence that buprenorphine also is safe and effective in treating heroin dependence during pregnancy, although infants exposed to methadone or buprenorphine during pregnancy typically require treatment for withdrawal symptoms. For women who do not want or are not able to receive pharmacotherapy for their heroin addiction, detoxification from opiates during pregnancy can be accomplished with relative safety, although the likelihood of relapse to heroin use should be considered.

Buprenorphine is a recent addition to the array of medications now available for treating addiction to heroin and other opiates. This medication is different from methadone in that it offers less risk of addiction and can be dispensed in the privacy of a doctor's office. Several other medications for use in heroin treatment programs are also under study.

There are many effective behavioral treatments available for heroin addiction. These can include residential and outpatient approaches. Several new behavioral therapies are showing particular promise for heroin addiction. Contingency management therapy uses a voucher-based system, where patients earn "points" based on negative drug tests, which they can exchange for items that encourage healthful living. Cognitive-behavioral interventions are designed to help modify the patient's thinking, expectancies, and behaviors and to increase skills in coping with various life stressors.

Methadone Fast Facts

What is methadone?

Methadone is a synthetic (man-made) narcotic. It is used legally to treat addiction to narcotics and to relieve severe pain, often in individuals who have cancer or terminal illnesses. Although methadone has been legally available in the United States since 1947, more recently it has emerged as a drug of abuse. This trend may be driven in part by the ready availability of the drug as it increasingly is used in the treatment of narcotic addiction and to relieve chronic pain.

What does methadone look like?

Methadone is available as a tablet, oral solution, or injectable liquid.

How is methadone used?

Some methadone tablets are designed to be swallowed intact, while others are intended to be dissolved first in liquid. Likewise, methadone is available either as a ready-to-drink solution or as a concentrate, which must be mixed first with water or fruit juice. Methadone also is available as a liquid that is administered via injection.

When used to treat narcotic addiction, methadone suppresses withdrawal symptoms for 24 to 36 hours. Individuals who are prescribed methadone for treatment of heroin addiction experience neither the cravings for heroin nor the euphoric rush that are typically associated with use of that drug.

Who abuses methadone?

It is difficult to gauge the extent of methadone abuse in the United States because most data sources that quantify drug abuse combine methadone with other narcotics. This lack of statistical information renders it impossible to describe a typical methadone abuser. The number of individuals who were treated for abuse of "other opiates" (a category that includes methadone) increased dramatically from 28,235 in 2000 to 36,265 in 2001. These individuals were predominantly Caucasian; they were nearly evenly split between males and females and represented various age groups.

Methadone abuse among high school students is a concern. Nearly 1 percent of high school seniors in the United States abused the drug at least once in their lifetime, according to the University of Michigan's Monitoring the Future Survey.

What are the risks?

Individuals who abuse methadone risk becoming tolerant of and physically dependent on the drug. When these individuals stop using the drug they may experience withdrawal symptoms including muscle tremors, nausea, diarrhea, vomiting, and abdominal cramps.

Overdosing on methadone poses an additional risk. In some instances, individuals who abuse other narcotics (such as heroin or OxyContin) turn to methadone because of its increasing availability. Methadone, however, does not produce the euphoric rush associated with those other drugs; thus, these users often consume dangerously large quantities of methadone in a vain attempt to attain the desired effect.

Methadone overdoses are associated with severe respiratory depression, decreases in heart rate and blood pressure, coma, and death. Methadone was involved in 10,725 emergency department visits in 2001—a 37 percent increase from the previous year.

> ♣ **It's A Fact!!**
> **Street Terms For Methadone**
>
> - Amidone
> - Chocolate chip cookies (methadone or heroin combined with MDMA)
> - Fizzies
> - Street methadone
> - Wafer
>
> Source: "Methadone Fast Facts," Product No. 2003-L0559-021, September 2003, National Drug Intelligence Center, a component of the U.S. Department of Justice.

Is abusing methadone illegal?

Yes, abusing methadone is illegal. Methadone is a Schedule II substance under the Controlled Substances Act. Schedule II drugs, which include cocaine and methamphetamine, have a high potential for abuse. Abuse of these drugs may lead to severe psychological or physical dependence.

Chapter 20

Prescription And Over-The-Counter Drugs: An Overview

Prescription medications such as pain relievers, tranquilizers, stimulants, and sedatives are very useful treatment tools, but sometimes people do not take them as directed and may become addicted. Pain relievers make surgery possible, and enable many individuals with chronic pain to lead productive lives. Most people who take prescription medications use them responsibly. However, the inappropriate or nonmedical use of prescription medications is a serious public health concern. Nonmedical use of prescription medications like opioids, central nervous system (CNS) depressants, and stimulants can lead to addiction, characterized by compulsive drug seeking and use.

Patients, healthcare professionals, and pharmacists all have roles in preventing misuse and addiction to prescription medications. For example, when a doctor prescribes a pain relief medication, CNS depressant, or stimulant, the patient should follow the directions for use carefully, learn what effects the medication could have, and determine any potential interactions with other medications. The patient should read all information provided by the pharmacist. Physicians and other healthcare providers should screen for any

About This Chapter: Information in this chapter is excerpted from "Prescription Pain and Other Medications," NIDA InfoFacts, National Institute on Drug Abuse, a component of the United States Department of Health and Human Services, February 2005.

type of substance abuse during routine history-taking, with questions about which prescriptions and over-the-counter medicines the patient is taking and why. Providers should note any rapid increases in the amount of a medication needed or frequent requests for refills before the quantity prescribed should have been used, as these may be indicators of abuse.

Opioids

Opioids are commonly prescribed because of their effective analgesic, or pain relieving, properties. Studies have shown that properly managed medical use of opioid analgesic compounds is safe and rarely causes addiction. Taken exactly as prescribed, opioids can be used to manage pain effectively.

♣ **It's A Fact!!**
Commonly Abused Prescription Medications

While many prescription medications can be abused or misused, these three classes are most commonly abused:

- **Opioids**—often prescribed to treat pain
- **CNS Depressants**—used to treat anxiety and sleep disorders
- **Stimulants**—prescribed to treat narcolepsy and attention deficit/hyperactivity disorder

Among the compounds that fall within this class—sometimes referred to as narcotics—are morphine, codeine, and related medications. Morphine is often used before or after surgery to alleviate severe pain. Codeine is used for milder pain. Other examples of opioids that can be prescribed to alleviate pain include oxycodone (OxyContin—an oral, controlled release form of the drug); propoxyphene (Darvon); hydrocodone (Vicodin); hydromorphone (Dilaudid); and meperidine (Demerol), which is used less often because of side effects. In addition to their effective pain relieving properties, some of these medications can be used to relieve severe diarrhea (Lomotil, for example, which is diphenoxylate) or severe coughs (codeine).

Opioids act by attaching to specific proteins called opioid receptors, which are found in the brain, spinal cord, and gastrointestinal tract. When these compounds attach to certain opioid receptors in the brain and spinal cord, they can effectively change the way a person experiences pain.

In addition, opioid medications can affect regions of the brain that mediate what we perceive as pleasure, resulting in the initial euphoria that many opioids produce. They can also produce drowsiness, cause constipation, and, depending upon the amount taken, depress breathing. Taking a large single dose could cause severe respiratory depression or death.

Opioids may interact with other medications and are only safe to use with other medications under a physician's supervision. Typically, they should not be used with substances such as alcohol, antihistamines, barbiturates, or benzodiazepines. Since these substances slow breathing, their combined effects could lead to life-threatening respiratory depression.

Long-term use also can lead to physical dependence—the body adapts to the presence of the substance and withdrawal symptoms occur if use is reduced abruptly. This can also include tolerance, which means that higher doses of a medication must be taken to obtain the same initial effects. Note that physical dependence is not the same as addiction—physical dependence can occur even with appropriate long-term use of opioid and other medications. Addiction, as noted earlier, is defined as compulsive, often uncontrollable drug use in spite of negative consequences.

Individuals taking prescribed opioid medications should not only be given these medications under appropriate medical supervision, but also should be medically supervised when stopping use in order to reduce or avoid withdrawal symptoms. Symptoms of withdrawal can include restlessness, muscle and bone pain, insomnia, diarrhea, vomiting, cold flashes with goose bumps ("cold turkey"), and involuntary leg movements.

Individuals who become addicted to prescription medications can be treated. Options for effectively treating addiction to prescription opioids are drawn from research on treating heroin addiction. Some pharmacological examples of available treatments are described as follows:

- Methadone, a synthetic opioid that blocks the effects of heroin and other opioids, eliminates withdrawal symptoms and relieves craving. It has been used for over 30 years to successfully treat people addicted to opioids.

- Buprenorphine, another synthetic opioid, is a recent addition to the arsenal of medications for treating addiction to heroin and other opiates.

- Naltrexone is a long-acting opioid blocker often used with highly motivated individuals in treatment programs promoting complete abstinence. Naltrexone also is used to prevent relapse.

- Naloxone counteracts the effects of opioids and is used to treat overdoses.

Central Nervous System (CNS) Depressants

CNS depressants slow normal brain function. In higher doses, some CNS depressants can become general anesthetics. Tranquilizers and sedatives are examples of CNS depressants.

✎ What's It Mean?

Analgesics: Analgesics are meant to relieve pain. These pain relievers don't get rid of what causes your pain, rather they block the nerve pathways that send pain signals from the body part to the brain so that you don't hurt as much. [1]

Attention-Deficit Hyperactivity Disorder: A behavioral condition that makes it hard for people to pay attention and concentrate. [1]

Anesthetic: An agent that causes insensitivity to pain and is used for surgeries and other medical procedures. [2]

Narcolepsy: A chronic sleep disorder characterized by excessive and overwhelming daytime sleepiness (even after adequate nighttime sleep). [3]

Source: [1] "GirlsHealth.gov Web Site Glossary," the National Women's Health Information Center (NWHIC), United States Department of Health and Human Services, Office on Women's Health, June 2005; available online at http://www.4girls.gov/glossary.htm. [2] "NIDA for Teens Glossary," National Institute on Drug Abuse, United States Department of Health and Human Services, November 2005; available online at http://teens.drugabuse.gov/utilities/glossary.asp#A. [3] "Glossary," Office of Science Education, National Institutes of Health, cited December 2005; available online at http://science.education.nih.gov/supplements/nih3/sleep/other/glossary.htm.

CNS depressants can be divided into two groups, based on their chemistry and pharmacology, and are described as follows:

- Barbiturates, such as mephobarbital (Mebaral) and pentobarbital sodium (Nembutal), which are used to treat anxiety, tension, and sleep disorders.

- Benzodiazepines, such as diazepam (Valium), chlordiazepoxide HCl (Librium), and alprazolam (Xanax), which can be prescribed to treat anxiety, acute stress reactions, and panic attacks. Benzodiazepines that have a more sedating effect, such as estazolam (ProSom), can be prescribed for short-term treatment of sleep disorders.

There are many CNS depressants, and most act on the brain similarly—they affect the neurotransmitter gamma-aminobutyric acid (GABA). Neurotransmitters are brain chemicals that facilitate communication between brain cells. GABA works by decreasing brain activity. Although different classes of CNS depressants work in unique ways, ultimately it is their ability to increase GABA activity that produces a drowsy or calming effect. Despite these beneficial effects for people suffering from anxiety or sleep disorders, barbiturates and benzodiazepines can be addictive and should be used only as prescribed.

CNS depressants should not be combined with any medication or substance that causes sleepiness, including prescription pain medicines, certain over-the-counter cold and allergy medications, or alcohol. If combined, they can slow breathing, or slow both the heart and respiration, which can be fatal.

Discontinuing prolonged use of high doses of CNS depressants can lead to withdrawal. Because they work by slowing the brain's activity, a potential consequence of abuse is that when one stops taking a CNS depressant, the brain's activity can rebound to the point that seizures can occur. Someone thinking about ending their use of a CNS depressant, or who has stopped and is suffering withdrawal, should speak with a physician and seek medical treatment.

In addition to medical supervision, counseling in an in-patient or outpatient setting can help people who are overcoming addiction to CNS depressants. For example, cognitive-behavioral therapy has been used successfully to help individuals in treatment for abuse of benzodiazepines. This type of therapy focuses on modifying a patient's thinking, expectations, and behaviors while simultaneously increasing their skills for coping with various life stressors.

Often the abuse of CNS depressants occurs in conjunction with the abuse of another substance or drug, such as alcohol or cocaine. In these cases of polydrug abuse, the treatment approach should address the multiple addictions.

Stimulants

Stimulants increase alertness, attention, and energy, which are accompanied by increases in blood pressure, heart rate, and respiration.

Historically, stimulants were used to treat asthma and other respiratory problems, obesity, neurological disorders, and a variety of other ailments. As their potential for abuse and addiction became apparent, the use of stimulants began to wane. Now, stimulants are prescribed for treating only a few health conditions, including narcolepsy, attention-deficit hyperactivity disorder (ADHD), and depression that has not responded to other treatments. Stimulants may also be used for short-term treatment of obesity and for patients with asthma.

Stimulants such as dextroamphetamine (Dexedrine) and methylphenidate (Ritalin) have chemical structures that are similar to key brain neurotransmitters called monoamines, which include norepinephrine and dopamine. Stimulants increase the levels of these chemicals in the brain and body. This, in turn, increases blood pressure and heart rate, constricts blood vessels, increases blood glucose, and opens up the pathways of the respiratory system. In addition, the increase in dopamine is associated with a sense of euphoria that can accompany the use of stimulants.

Research indicates that people with ADHD do not become addicted to stimulant medications, such as Ritalin, when taken in the form and dosage prescribed. However, when misused, stimulants can be addictive.

The consequences of stimulant abuse can be extremely dangerous. Taking high doses of a stimulant can result in an irregular heartbeat, dangerously high body temperatures, and/or the potential for cardiovascular failure or seizures. Taking high doses of some stimulants repeatedly over a short period of time can lead to hostility or feelings of paranoia in some individuals.

Stimulants should not be mixed with antidepressants or over-the-counter cold medicines containing decongestants. Antidepressants may enhance the effects of a stimulant, and stimulants in combination with decongestants may cause blood pressure to become dangerously high or lead to irregular heart rhythms.

Treatment of addiction to prescription stimulants, such as methylphenidate and amphetamines, is based on behavioral therapies proven effective for treating cocaine or methamphetamine addiction. At this time, there are no proven medications for the treatment of stimulant addiction. Antidepressants, however, may be used to manage the symptoms of depression that can accompany early abstinence from stimulants.

Depending on the patient's situation, the first step in treating prescription stimulant addiction may be to slowly decrease the drug's dose and attempt to treat withdrawal symptoms. This process of detoxification could then be followed with one of many behavioral therapies. Contingency management, for example, improves treatment outcomes by enabling patients to earn vouchers for drug-free urine tests; the vouchers can be exchanged for items that promote healthy living. Cognitive-behavioral therapies, which teach patients skills to recognize risky situations, avoid drug use, and cope more effectively with problems, are proving beneficial. Recovery support groups may also be effective in conjunction with a behavioral therapy.

Chapter 21

Ritalin, OxyContin, And DXM

Methylphenidate (Ritalin)

Methylphenidate is a medication prescribed for individuals (usually children) who have attention-deficit hyperactivity disorder (ADHD), which consists of a persistent pattern of abnormally high levels of activity, impulsivity, and/or inattention that is more frequently displayed and more severe than is typically observed in individuals with comparable levels of development. The pattern of behavior usually arises between the ages of 3 and 5, and is diagnosed during the elementary school years due to the child's excessive locomotor activity, poor attention, and/or impulsive behavior. Most symptoms improve during adolescence or adulthood, but the disorder can persist or be present in adults. It has been estimated that 3–7 percent of school-age children have ADHD. Methylphenidate also is occasionally prescribed for treating narcolepsy.

About This Chapter: This chapter begins with "Methylphenidate (Ritalin)," excerpted from NIDA InfoFacts, March 2005, National Institute on Drug Abuse, a component of the United States Department of Health and Human Services. "OxyContin Fast Facts," Product No. 2003-L0559-019, August 2003, and "DXM (Dextromethorphan)," excerpted from "Intelligence Bulletin: DXM (Dextromethorphan)," Product No. 2004-L0424-029, October 2004, from the National Drug Intelligence Center, a component of the U.S. Department of Justice.

What are the health effects of Ritalin abuse?

Methylphenidate is a central nervous system (CNS) stimulant. It has effects similar to, but more potent than, caffeine and less potent than amphetamines. It has a notably calming and "focusing" effect on those with ADHD, particularly children.

Recent research at Brookhaven National Laboratory may begin to explain how methylphenidate helps people with ADHD. The researchers used positron emission tomography (PET—a noninvasive brain scan) to confirm that administering normal therapeutic doses of methylphenidate to healthy, adult men increased their dopamine levels. The researchers speculate that methylphenidate amplifies the release of dopamine, a neurotransmitter, thereby improving attention and focus in individuals who have dopamine signals that are weak.

Methylphenidate is a valuable medicine, for adults as well as children with ADHD. Treatment of ADHD with stimulants such as Ritalin and psychotherapy help to improve the abnormal behaviors of ADHD, as well as the self-esteem, cognition, and social and family function of the patient. Research shows that individuals with ADHD do not become addicted to stimulant medications when taken in the form and dosage prescribed by doctors. In fact, it has been reported that stimulant therapy in childhood is associated with a reduction in the risk for subsequent drug and alcohol use disorders. Also, studies have found that individuals with ADHD treated with stimulants such as methylphenidate are significantly less likely than those who do not receive treatment to abuse drugs and alcohol when they are older.

Because of its stimulant properties, however, in recent years there have been reports of abuse of methylphenidate by people for whom it is not prescribed. It is abused for its stimulant effects: appetite suppression, wakefulness, increased focus/attentiveness, and euphoria. Addiction to methylphenidate seems to occur when it induces large and fast dopamine increases in the brain. In contrast, the therapeutic effect is achieved by slow and steady increases of dopamine, which are similar to the natural production by the brain. The doses prescribed by physicians start low and increase slowly until a therapeutic effect is reached. That way, the risk of addiction is very small. When abused, the tablets are either taken orally or crushed and snorted. Some abusers dissolve the tablets in water and inject the mixture; complications can arise from this because insoluble fillers in the tablets can block small blood vessels.

OxyContin Fast Facts

What is OxyContin?

OxyContin, a trade name for the narcotic oxycodone hydrochloride, is a painkiller available in the United States only by prescription. OxyContin is legitimately prescribed for relief of moderate to severe pain resulting from injuries, bursitis, neuralgia, arthritis, and cancer. Individuals abuse OxyContin for the euphoric effect it produces—an effect similar to that associated with heroin use.

What does OxyContin look like?

OxyContin is available as a 10 milligram (mg), 20 mg, 40 mg, or 80 mg tablet. The tablets vary in color and size according to dosage. The tablets are imprinted with the letters OC on one side and the number of milligrams on the opposite side.

How is OxyContin abused?

OxyContin tablets have a controlled-release feature and are designed to be swallowed whole. In order to bypass the controlled-release feature, abusers either chew or crush the tablets. Crushed tablets can be snorted or dissolved in water and injected.

Who abuses OxyContin?

Individuals of all ages abuse OxyContin. Data reported in the National Household Survey on Drug Abuse indicate that nearly 1 million U. S. residents aged 12 and older used OxyContin nonmedically at least once in their lifetime.

OxyContin abuse among high school students is a particular problem. Four percent of high school seniors in the United States abused the drug at least once in the past year, according to the University of Michigan's Monitoring the Future Survey.

What are the risks?

Individuals who abuse OxyContin risk developing tolerance for the drug, meaning they must take increasingly higher doses to achieve the same effects. Long-term abuse of the drug can lead to physical dependence and addiction. Individuals who become dependent upon or addicted to the drug may experience withdrawal symptoms if they cease using the drug.

Withdrawal symptoms associated with OxyContin dependency or addiction include restlessness, muscle and bone pain, insomnia, diarrhea, vomiting, cold flashes, and involuntary leg movements.

> ### ♣ It's A Fact!!
> ### Street Terms For OxyContin
>
> - 40 (a 40-milligram tablet)
> - 80 (an 80-milligram tablet)
> - Blue
> - Hillbilly heroin
> - Kicker
> - Oxycotton
>
> Source: "OxyContin Fast Facts," Product No. 2003-L0559-019, August 2003, National Drug Intelligence Center, a component of the U.S. Department of Justice.

Individuals who take a large dose of OxyContin are at risk of severe respiratory depression that can lead to death. Inexperienced and new users are at particular risk, because they may be unaware of what constitutes a large dose and have not developed a tolerance for the drug.

In addition, OxyContin abusers who inject the drug expose themselves to additional risks, including contracting HIV (human immunodeficiency virus), hepatitis B and C, and other blood-borne viruses.

What is OxyContin called?

The most common names for OxyContin are OCs, ox, and oxy.

Is it illegal to abuse OxyContin?

Yes, abusing OxyContin is illegal. OxyContin is a Schedule II substance under the Controlled Substances Act. Schedule II drugs, which include cocaine and methamphetamine, have a high potential for abuse. Abuse of these drugs may lead to severe psychological or physical dependence.

DXM (Dextromethorphan)

The abuse of DXM (dextromethorphan)—a common ingredient contained in over-the-counter cough and cold medicines—is an increasing concern for law enforcement officers in the United States. Adolescents are the primary abusers of the drug. Additionally, because DXM is a common ingredient in many cough and cold medicines, many adolescents do not perceive any risk in abusing the drug. Compounding the problem is that few parents know about the potential for abuse of the drug.

What is DXM?

DXM is a synthetically produced substance that is chemically related to codeine, though it is not an opiate. DXM is an ingredient in over-the-counter cough and cold remedies, and since the 1950s, has gradually replaced codeine as the most widely used cough suppressant in the United States. It is available in capsule, liquid, liquid gelatin capsule, lozenge, and tablet forms.

When ingested at recommended dosage levels, DXM generally is a safe and highly effective cough suppressant; however, when ingested in larger amounts, DXM produces negative physiological effects.

How is DXM abused?

Most DXM abusers ingest the drug orally, although some snort the pure powdered form of the drug. Abusers ingest various amounts of DXM depending on their body weight. Some abusers ingest 250 to 1,500 milligrams in a single dosage, far more than the recommended therapeutic dose of 10 to 20 milligrams every 4 hours or 30 milligrams every 6 to 8 hours.

Over-the-counter products that contain DXM often contain other ingredients such as acetaminophen, chlorpheniramine, and guaifenesin. Large dosages of acetaminophen can cause liver damage; large dosages of chlorpheniramine can cause increased heart rate, lack of coordination, seizures, and coma; and large dosages of guaifenesin can cause vomiting. Some first-time users may not abuse DXM repeatedly if they experience negative side effects—such as vomiting—commonly associated with the other ingredients contained in over-the-counter DXM medications. Nonetheless, some DXM abusers "robo shake," a practice whereby they drink a large amount of cough syrup containing DXM and then force themselves to vomit so as to absorb enough DXM through the stomach lining to achieve the desired effect while expelling the other ingredients. Some more experienced abusers use a chemical procedure to extract the DXM from the other ingredients contained in cough syrups to avoid such side effects. (This procedure cannot be used on DXM products sold in nonliquid form.)

Recommended dosages of DXM generally are safe but can cause nausea, gastrointestinal disturbances, slight drowsiness, and dizziness. Acute dosages (between 250 and 1,500 milligrams) can cause blurred vision, body itching, rash, sweating, fever, hypertension, shallow respiration, diarrhea, toxic psychosis, coma, and an increase in heart rate, blood pressure, and body temperature. Some abusers become violent after ingesting the drug. Little is known about the long-term effects of DXM abuse; however, anecdotal reporting and limited clinical research suggest that extensive and prolonged abuse may cause learning and memory impairment. While studies indicate that DXM is not addictive, some former DXM abusers report experiencing cravings for the drug.

♣ **It's A Fact!!**
Slang Terms For DXM

- DM
- Robo
- Rojo
- Velvet

Slang Terms For DXM Intoxication

- Robo tripping
- Skittling
- Dexing

Source: "Intelligence Bulletin: DXM (Dextromethorphan)," Product No. 2004-L0424-029, October 2004, National Drug Intelligence Center, a component of the U.S. Department of Justice.

Deaths caused by DXM overdoses are rare as most abusers ingest DXM products that contain other ingredients that cause vomiting, which expels the DXM from their bodies. Ingesting the drug in combination with other drugs causes most DXM-related deaths. DXM-related deaths also occur from impairment of the senses, which can lead to accidents. In 2003, a 14-year-old boy in Colorado who abused DXM died when two cars hit him as he attempted to cross a highway. State law enforcement investigators suspect that the drug affected the boy's depth perception and caused him to misjudge the distance and speed of the oncoming vehicles.

DXM abuse levels are difficult to determine. Commonly used drug toxicology screens and field tests do not accurately detect the presence of DXM. Therefore, more thorough laboratory testing must be performed. National surveys conducted to estimate rates of drug abuse do not include questions regarding DXM. However, the American Association of Poison Control Centers reports that the total number of calls to centers nationwide involving DXM abuse or misuse have increased since 2000. Calls involving abuse or misuse of DXM by teenagers increased approximately 100 percent from 2000 (1,623) through 2003 (3,271). Calls involving abuse by other age groups increased 21 percent from 2000 through 2002, before decreasing slightly in 2003.

Table 21.1. Calls Involving Abuse or Misuse of DXM to Poison Control Centers

Year	Teenagers	All Other Age Groups
2000	1,623	900
2001	2,276	1,107
2002	2,881	1,139
2003	3,271	1,111

Source of Statistics: American Association of Poison Control Centers

Chapter 22

Anabolic Steroids

Ever wondered how those bulky weight lifters got so big? While some may have gotten their muscles through a strict regimen of weight-lifting and diet, others may have gotten that way through the illegal use of steroids.

Steroids are synthetic substances similar to the male sex hormone testosterone. They do have legitimate medical uses. Sometimes doctors prescribe anabolic steroids to help people with certain kinds of anemia and men who don't produce enough testosterone on their own. Doctors also prescribe a different kind of steroid, called corticosteroids, to reduce swelling. Corticosteroids are not anabolic steroids and do not have the same harmful effects.

But doctors never prescribe anabolic steroids to young, healthy people to help them build muscles. Without a prescription from a doctor, steroids are illegal.

There are many different kinds of steroids. Here's a list of some of the most common anabolic steroids taken today: Anadrol, Oxandrin, Dianabol, Winstrol, Deca-Durabolin, and equipoise.

Common Street Names

Slang words for steroids are hard to find. Most people just say steroids. On the street, steroids may be called roids or juice. The scientific name for

About This Chapter: Information in this chapter is from "Anabolic Steroids," NIDA for Teens, National Institute on Drug Abuse, a component of the United States Department of Health and Human Services, July 2005.

this class of drugs is anabolic-androgenic steroids. Anabolic refers to muscle building. Androgenic refers to increased male characteristics. But even scientists shorten it to anabolic steroids.

How They Are Used

Some steroid users pop pills. Others use hypodermic needles to inject steroids directly into muscles. When users take more and more of a drug over and over again, they are called "abusers." Abusers have been known to take doses 10 to 100 times higher than the amount prescribed for medical reasons by a doctor.

Many steroid users take two or more kinds of steroids at once. Called stacking, this way of taking steroids is supposed to get users bigger faster. Some abusers pyramid their doses in 6 to 12-week cycles. At the beginning of the cycle, the steroid user starts with low doses and slowly increases to higher doses. In the second half of the cycle, they gradually decrease the amount of steroids. Neither of these methods has been proven to work.

Steroid Statistics

Most teens are smart and stay away from steroids. As part of a 2002 National Institute on Drug Abuse (NIDA)-funded study, teens were asked if they ever tried steroids—even once. Only 2.5% of 8th graders ever tried steroids; only 3.5% of 10th graders; and 4% of 12th graders.

Common Effects

Steroids can make pimples pop up and hair fall out. They can make guys grow breasts and girls grow beards. Steroids can cause livers to grow tumors and hearts to clog up. They can even send users on violent, angry rampages. In other words, steroids throw a body way out of whack.

Steroids do make users bulk up, but the health risks are high. It's true, on steroids biceps bulge; abs ripple; and quads balloon. But that's just on the outside. Steroid users may be very pleased when they flex in the mirror, but they may create problems on the inside. These problems may hurt them the rest of their lives. As a matter of fact steroid use can shorten their lives.

Steroids Cause Hormone Imbalances

For teens, hormone balance is important. Hormones are involved in the development of a girl's feminine traits and a boy's masculine traits. When someone abuses steroids, gender mix-ups happen.

Using steroids, guys can experience shrunken testicles and reduced sperm count. They can also end up with breasts, a condition called gynecomastia.

Using steroids, girls can become more masculine. Their voices deepen. They grow excessive body hair. Their breast size decreases.

Teens At Risk For Stunted Growth

Teens who abuse steroids before the typical adolescent growth spurt risk staying short and never reaching their full adult height. Why? Because the body is programmed to stop growing after puberty. When hormone levels reach a certain point, the body thinks it has already gone through puberty. So, bones get the message to stop growing way too soon.

Steroid Abuse Can Be Fatal

When steroids get into the body, they go to different organs and muscles. Steroids affect individual cells and makes them create proteins. These proteins spell trouble.

The liver, for example, can grow tumors and develop cancer. Steroid abusers may also develop a rare condition called peliosis hepatitis in which blood-filled cysts crop up on the liver. Both the tumors and cysts can rupture and cause internal bleeding.

Steroids are no friend of the heart, either. Abusing steroids can cause heart attacks and strokes, even in young athletes. Here's how: Steroid use can lead to a condition called atherosclerosis, which causes fat deposits inside arteries to disrupt blood flow. When blood flow to the heart is blocked, a heart attack can occur. If blood flow to the brain is blocked, a stroke can result.

To bulk up the artificial way—using steroids—puts teens at risk for more than liver disease and cardiovascular disease. Steroids can weaken the immune system, which is what helps the body fight against germs and disease. That means that illnesses and diseases have an easy target in a steroid abuser.

By injecting steroids by needle, teens can add HIV and hepatitis B and C to their list of health hazards. Many abusers share non-sterile "works" or drug injection equipment that can spread life-threatening viral infections.

Steroids Can Cause Extreme Mood Changes

Steroids can also mess with your head. Research shows that high doses of steroids can cause extreme fluctuations in emotions, from euphoria to rage. That's right. Rage can come from how steroids act on your brain.

Your moods and emotions are balanced by the limbic system of your brain. Steroids act on the limbic system and may cause irritability and mild depression. Eventually, steroids can cause mania, delusions, and violent aggression or "roid rage."

Steroids' Disfiguring Effects

Last, but not least, steroids have disfiguring effects—severe acne, greasy hair, and baldness (in both guys and girls).

The bottom line is: Science proves the serious risks of steroid use.

♣ It's A Fact!!

Research indicates that some users might turn to other drugs to alleviate some of the negative effects of anabolic steroids. For example, a study of 227 men admitted to a private treatment center for dependence on heroin or other opioids found that 9.3 percent had abused anabolic steroids before trying any other illicit drug. Of these 9.3 percent, 86 percent first used opioids to counteract insomnia and irritability resulting from the anabolic steroids.

Source: Excerpted from "Steroids (Anabolic-Androgenic)," NIDA InfoFacts, March 2005, National Institute on Drug Abuse, a component of the United States Department of Health and Human Services.

Chapter 23

Sports Supplements (Ergogenic Aids)

If you're a competitive athlete or a fitness buff, improving your sports performance is probably on your mind. Spending tons of time in the gym or at practice may offer results (along with a pile of sweaty laundry), but it's no shortcut, and teens with busy lives may be looking for fast, effective results.

Some people think that taking drugs known as sports supplements could improve their performance without so much hard work. But do sports supplements really work? And are they safe?

What Are Sports Supplements?

Sports supplements (also referred to as ergogenic aids) are products used to enhance athletic performance. They come in different forms, including vitamins, synthetic (manmade) drugs, and hormones, most of which are available over the counter without a prescription.

Some people think that supplements help them develop more muscle mass, increase strength, and build stamina. Other people use sports supplements to

About This Chapter: Information in this chapter is from "Sports Supplements." This information was provided by TeensHealth, one of the largest resources online for medically reviewed health information written for parents, kids, and teens. For more articles like this one, visit www.TeensHealth.org, or www.KidsHealth.org. © 2003 The Nemours Center for Children's Health Media, a division of The Nemours Foundation.

lose weight. If you're thinking about using sports supplements, you're not alone. Many teens who see sports medicine doctors when they want to improve their performance have questions about how supplements work and whether they're safe.

Most of the foods you see on the shelves of your local grocery store and the drugs your doctor prescribes for you are regulated by a government agency called the Food and Drug Administration (FDA). The FDA ensures that many foods, beverages, and drugs adhere to certain safety standards. But sports supplements aren't regulated by the FDA, and no sports supplements have been tested on kids and teens. That means that scientists and doctors don't know whether supplements are safe or effective for teens to use.

Lots of sports organizations have developed policies on sports supplements. The National Football League (NFL), the National Collegiate Athletic Association (NCAA), and the International Olympic Committee (IOC) have banned the use of steroids, creatine, ephedra, and androstenedione by their athletes, and competitors who use them face fines, ineligibility, and suspension from their sports.

Common Supplements And How They Affect The Body

Whether you hear about sports supplements from your teammates in the locker room or the sales clerk at your local vitamin store, chances are you're not getting the whole story about how supplements work and the risks you take by using them.

Anabolic steroids are hormones that help the body build muscle tissue and increase muscle mass. Steroids, also known as roids or juice, are similar to the male hormone testosterone, which is produced naturally in larger amounts in guys' bodies and smaller amounts in girls' bodies. When a person takes steroids, the body's muscle tissue is stimulated to grow, producing larger and stronger muscles.

But steroids can have some unwelcome, serious side effects—such as high blood pressure and heart disease, liver damage and cancer, urinary and bowel problems, strokes and blood clots, and sleep problems. A person who takes steroids may develop bigger muscles, but he or she is also at risk for baldness and severe acne. Guys who take juice can suffer from infertility, breast and nipple enlargement, and problems having an erection. Girls may find themselves with deeper voices, smaller breasts, menstrual problems, and an increase in facial and body hair.

Steroids can also have emotional effects on the user, such as severe mood swings, aggressive behavior, irritability, and depressive or suicidal thoughts. Teens who inject steroids with infected needles are also at risk for HIV or hepatitis.

Androstenedione, more commonly known as andro, is another popular nutritional supplement. When a person takes andro, the body may convert it to testosterone, which is necessary for muscle development. When it's taken in large doses, andro is said to increase muscle mass, although studies haven't shown that andro is particularly effective. Scientists don't know exactly how much andro the body absorbs, and the long-term effects of andro use haven't been determined. What is known is that andro can cause hormone imbalances in people who use it. Andro use may have the same effects as taking anabolic steroids and may lead to such dangerous side effects as testicular cancer, infertility, stroke, and an increased risk of heart disease.

Another sports supplement you may have heard about is human growth hormone (HGH). Doctors may prescribe growth hormone for some teens who have certain hormone or growth problems to help them develop normally. But growth hormone can also be abused by athletes who want to build muscle mass. Many athletes still use growth hormone even though several sports organizations (such as the NCAA) have banned it. Teen athletes who abuse growth hormone may have impaired development and altered hormone levels.

In a recent survey of high school senior athletes, about 44% said they had tried or currently used creatine to enhance athletic performance. Creatine is already manufactured by the body in the liver, kidneys, and pancreas, and it occurs naturally in foods such as meat and fish. If a person takes creatine supplements, the extra creatine is stored in the muscles, and some people think that it gives them an energy boost during workouts or competitions.

Available over the counter in pill, powder, or gel form, creatine is one of the most popular nutritional supplements, and teens make up a large portion of the supplement's users. Teens who take creatine usually take it to improve strength, but the long-term and short-term effects of creatine use haven't been studied in teens and kids. Research has not shown that creatine can

✔ **Quick Tip**

Tips For Dealing With Athletic Pressure And Competition

Advertisements for sports supplements often use persuasive before and after pictures that make it look easy to get a muscular, toned body. But remember—the goal of supplement advertisers is to make money by selling more supplements. Because sports supplements are not regulated by the FDA, sellers are not required to provide information about their dangerous side effects. Teens and kids may seem like an easy sell on supplements because they may feel dissatisfied or uncomfortable with their still-developing bodies, and many supplement companies try to convince teens like you that supplements are an easy solution.

Don't waste your hard-earned allowance or pay from your after-school job on expensive and dangerous supplements. Instead, try these tips for getting better game:

- Make down time a priority. Some studies show that teens need more than 8 hours of sleep a night—are you getting enough? If you come home from practice to a load of homework, try doing as much homework as possible on the weekend to free up your nights for sleep. If you have an after-school job that's interfering with your ZZZs, consider cutting back on your hours during your sports season.

- Try to R-E-L-A-X. Your school, work, and sports schedules may have you sprinting from one activity to the next, but taking a few minutes to relax can be helpful. Meditating or visualizing your success during the next game may improve your performance; sitting quietly and focusing on your breathing can give you a brief break and prepare you for your next activity.

- Chow down on good eats. Fried, fat-laden, or sugary foods will interfere with your performance in a major way. Instead, focus on eating foods such as lean meats, whole grains, vegetables, fruits, and low-fat dairy products. Celebrating with the team at the local pizza place after a big game is fine once in a while, but for most meals and snacks choose healthy foods to keep your body weight in a healthy range and your performance at its best.

increase endurance or improve aerobic performance—but it may leave teens prone to muscle cramps and tears. And there have been several reports of creatine use leading to seizures or kidney failure.

Fat burners (sometimes known as thermogenics) are a recent addition to the sports supplement market. Fat burners are often made with an herb called

- Eat often. Sometimes teens skip breakfast or have an early lunch and then try to play a late afternoon game. But they quickly wear out because they haven't had enough food to fuel their activity. Not eating enough may place teens at risk for injury or muscle fatigue. So make sure to eat lunch on practice and game days. If you feel hungry before the game, pack easy-to-carry, healthy snacks in your bag, such as fruit, bagels, or string cheese.

- Avoid harmful substances. Drinking, smoking, or doing drugs are all-around bad ideas for athletes. Smoking will diminish your lung capacity and ability to breathe, alcohol will make you sluggish and tired, and drugs will impair your hand-eye coordination and reduce your alertness. And you can kiss your team good-bye if you get caught using these substances—many schools have a no-tolerance policy for athletes.

- Train harder and smarter. If you get out of breath easily during your basketball game and you want to increase your endurance, improving your cardiovascular conditioning is key. If you think that more leg strength will help you excel on the soccer field, consider weight training to increase your muscle strength. Before changing your program, though, get advice from your doctor. You can't expect results overnight, but improving your strength and endurance with hard work will be a lot safer for your body in the long run.

- Consult a professional. If you're concerned about your weight or whether your diet is helping your performance, talk to your doctor or a registered dietitian who can evaluate your nutrition and steer you in the right direction. Coaches can help you too, by helping you focus on weak spots during practice. And if you're still convinced that supplements will help you, talk to your doctor or a sports medicine specialist. The doc will be able to offer alternatives to supplements based on your body and sport.

ephedra, also known as ephedrine or ma huang, which speeds up the nervous system and increases metabolism. Some teens use fat burners to lose weight or to increase energy—but using products containing ephedrine is a bad idea for anyone. Ephedra-based products can be one of the most dangerous supplements. In December 2003, the U.S. Food and Drug Administration banned ephedra from sale in the United States based on evidence that it can cause heart problems, stroke, and occasionally even death.

Will Supplements Make Me A Better Athlete?

Sports supplements haven't been tested on teens and kids. But studies on adults show that the claims of many supplements are weak at best. Most won't make you any stronger, and none will make you any faster or more skillful.

Many factors go into your abilities as an athlete—including your diet, how much sleep you get, genetics and heredity, and your training program—but the fact is that using sports supplements may put you at risk for serious health conditions. So instead of turning to supplements to improve your performance, concentrate on eating the best nutrition and following a serious weight-training and aerobic-conditioning program.

Chapter 24

Herbal Supplements

You've seen the ads: "Natural herbs melt pounds away—without diet or exercise!" or "Amazing new discovery boosts athletic performance!" They usually claim that a doctor has discovered a new dietary supplement, a miracle substance that will make you thinner, stronger, smarter, or better at whatever you do. Best of all, you're told, this supplement works without any real effort—all you have to do is send in your money and swallow what they send you.

Having trouble believing these ads? You're right to be skeptical. There's little evidence that dietary supplements have the effects that they claim.

What Are Dietary Supplements?

Dietary supplements are products that include vitamins, minerals, amino acids, herbs, or botanicals (plants)—or any concentration, extract, or combination of these—as part of their ingredients. You can purchase dietary supplements in pill, gel capsule, liquid, or powder forms.

About This Chapter: Information in this chapter is from "Dietary Supplements: Facts Vs. Fads." This information was provided by TeensHealth, one of the largest resources online for medically reviewed health information written for parents, kids, and teens. For more articles like this one, visit www.TeensHealth.org, or www.KidsHealth.org. © 2004 The Nemours Center for Children's Health Media, a division of The Nemours Foundation.

How safe are they? In many cases, no one really knows. The U.S. Food and Drug Administration (FDA), which normally checks out the safety of foods and medicines before they come on the market, does not check on the safety of dietary supplements before they're sold. The FDA has to wait until it receives reports of problems caused by supplements before it can investigate and ban a dietary supplement. This is what happened with the herb ephedra (also called ma huang or herbal fen-phen) in 2003 when the FDA pulled the supplement from the U.S. market after it was linked to the death of a well-known baseball player.

This means that if you take an untested supplement, you are serving as the manufacturer's unpaid guinea pig and risking your own health.

♣ **It's A Fact!!**
There is evidence that some supplements can cause serious damage to a user's health, especially when that user is a teen.

Source: © 2004 The Nemours Center for Children's Health Media, a division of The Nemours Foundation.

Can Supplements Make Me A Better Athlete?

Some athletes take dietary supplements believing that these improve their performances. However, claims for these improvements are often exaggerated or not based on scientific evidence.

And some supplements may be hazardous to teens. Anabolic steroids, manmade hormones similar to the male hormone testosterone, are unsafe and illegal. That's because the large quantities of these steroids that are found in the supplements can have devastating side effects on the body, including heart damage, kidney damage, and bone problems. Studies also show that steroids may be addictive, and that even small doses can interfere with growth in teens.

Because sports supplements like creatine are unregulated, there is no standard dose. So users have no way of knowing what levels, if any, are safe, especially for teens who are still growing. The same goes for androstenedione, the supplement that gained attention because professional baseball player Mark McGwire used it. Research suggests that this hormone supplement may lead to health problems such as acne, gynecomastia (breast enlargement in guys), and heart problems.

Some people think that taking amino acid powders is helpful for increasing their muscle mass, but these powders don't actually have any special muscle-building effects. Amino acids are the building blocks of protein. Although it's scientifically true that they're required to build muscle (along with enough exercise), the human body can easily get all the amino acids it needs from the protein in food. So, if you work out properly and eat a balanced diet with enough protein, taking amino acid supplements won't actually do anything for you—except maybe empty your wallet.

Energy bars are also often used as a dietary supplement. These high-calorie, fortified treats should be used with caution, though. They may serve a purpose for athletes who burn lots of calories in high-intensity activities, like competitive cycling. But for most people they can add unwanted calories to the diet, and they're not particularly filling as a meal replacement.

Can Supplements Help Me Lose Weight?

If you'd like to lose a few pounds, you might be tempted to try some of the many herbal weight-loss products available today. But none of these herbal remedies work—and some (like ephedra, the banned weight-loss supplement mentioned above) can have serious side effects.

Herbs like chickweed, ginseng, kelp, and bee pollen, often included in diet aids, do nothing to promote weight loss—and some can be harmful or deadly in large doses. The only safe and effective way to take off excess pounds remains healthy eating and exercise. If you are concerned about your weight, talk to a doctor or dietitian. He or she can help you get to a healthy weight.

What About Vitamin And Mineral Supplements?

The best way to get your daily dose of vitamins and minerals is from food. Although there's usually nothing wrong with a teen taking a basic multivitamin, if you're eating well, you probably don't need one. If you do choose to take a multivitamin, stick with a basic supplement and avoid brands

---

♣ It's A Fact!!

FDA Issues Regulation Prohibiting Sale Of Dietary Supplements Containing Ephedrine Alkaloids And Reiterates Its Advice That Consumers Stop Using These Products

The Food and Drug Administration (FDA) issued a final rule prohibiting the sale of dietary supplements containing ephedrine alkaloids (ephedra) because such supplements present an unreasonable risk of illness or injury.

"This FDA rule reflects what the scientific evidence shows—that ephedra poses an unreasonable risk to those who use it," Health and Human Services Tommy G. Thompson said. "The regulations prohibit the sale of dietary supplements containing ephedra, and we intend to take swift action against anyone who puts consumers at risk by continuing to sell such products."

"We advised consumers to stop using ephedra products, and we asked responsible companies to stop selling them," said FDA Commissioner Mark B. McClellan, M.D., Ph.D. "We intend to use this regulation to make sure consumers are protected by removing these risky products from the market."

Under the Dietary Supplement Health and Education Act (DSHEA) of 1994, FDA may remove a dietary supplement from the market if it presents a significant or unreasonable risk of illness or injury when used according to its labeling or under ordinary conditions of use. FDA's final regulation presents a framework for applying this unique statutory standard.

In recent years, dietary supplements containing ephedrine alkaloids have been extensively promoted for aiding weight control and boosting sports performance and energy. The totality of the available data showed little evidence of ephedra's effectiveness except for modest, short-term weight loss without any clear health benefit, while confirming that the substance raises blood

that contain higher doses than 100% of the RDA for any vitamin or mineral. Some vitamins can build up in the human system and cause problems when taken in excess amounts.

Talk to your doctor about additional vitamin and mineral supplements. If you can't eat dairy products for example, you might need a calcium supplement.

---

pressure and otherwise stresses the circulatory system. These effects are linked to significant adverse health outcomes, including heart attack and stroke.

Ephedra, also called Ma huang, is one of the plants that are a source of ephedrine alkaloids, including ephedrine and pseudoephedrine. When chemically synthesized, ephedrine and pseudoephedrine are regulated under the Federal Food, Drug, and Cosmetic Act as drugs. In contrast to the DSHEA-regulated dietary supplements that contain ephedrine alkaloids, the safety and effectiveness of drug products containing ephedrine alkaloids in drug products have to be proven by the manufacturer.

The issuance of this final rule continues a process that started in June, 1997 when FDA first issued a proposal that required a statement on dietary supplements containing ephedrine alkaloids warning that they are hazardous and should not be used for more than seven days. FDA also proposed to restrict the amount of ephedrine alkaloids in dietary supplements and to prevent combining ephedra with other ingredients that have a known stimulant effect.

FDA modified this proposed rule in 2000, and in February 2003 it announced a series of measures that included taking enforcement actions against firms making unsubstantiated claims regarding enhanced athletic performance for their ephedra-containing products. FDA also issued warning letters to firms promoting these products as alternatives to illicit street drugs. Many firms have complied with FDA's warning against making such claims. FDA has also followed up with seizures and injunctions and joint enforcement actions with the Federal Trade Commission and the Department of Justice. As a result, most ephedra-containing dietary supplements advertised for enhanced sport performance have been removed from the market.

Source: Excerpted from "FDA News," U.S. Food and Drug Administration, February 2004.

Vegetarians might want to take vitamin B12 (a vitamin that is found mainly in food that comes from animals and may be missing in a vegetarian diet). Teens whose doctors have put them on weight-loss diets of less than 1,200 calories a day, or teens with food allergies, should also discuss vitamin and mineral needs with their doctors.

Supplement Warning Signals

Check with your doctor before you take any dietary supplement, including vitamins and minerals. If your doctor starts you on a supplement, watch for warning signals that could indicate problems: stomach discomfort, pain, headache, rashes, or even vague symptoms like tiredness, dizziness, or lethargy.

Because it's not always clear what goes into some supplements, people with food allergies should be particularly wary. Some supplements contain ingredients from shellfish and other potential allergens, and you just don't know how you'll react to them.

When it comes to supplements, be a skeptical consumer. We all love to look for the quick fix. But if it looks too easy, it probably is.

Chapter 25

Caffeine And Energy Drinks

Caffeine

It's 11:00 P.M. and you've already had a full day of school and after-school activities. You're tired and you know you could use some sleep, but you still haven't finished your homework or watched the movie that's due back tomorrow. So instead of catching a few ZZZs, you reach for the remote—and the caffeine.

What Is Caffeine?

Caffeine is a drug that is naturally produced in the leaves and seeds of many plants. It's also produced artificially and added to certain foods. It's part of the same group of drugs sometimes used to treat asthma.

Caffeine is defined as a drug because it stimulates the central nervous system, causing increased heart rate and alertness. Most people who are sensitive to caffeine experience a temporary increase in energy and elevation in mood.

Caffeine is in tea leaves, coffee beans, chocolate, many soft drinks, pain relievers, and other over-the-counter pills. In its natural form, caffeine tastes very bitter. But most caffeinated drinks have gone through enough processing to camouflage the bitter taste. Most teens get the majority of their caffeine intake through soft drinks, which can also have added sugar and artificial flavors.

Got The Jitters?

If taken in moderate amounts (like a single can of soda or cup of coffee), many people feel that caffeine increases their mental alertness. Higher doses of caffeine can cause anxiety, dizziness, headaches, and the jitters and can interfere with normal sleep, though. And very high doses of caffeine—like taking a whole box of alertness pills—would be harmful to the body.

Caffeine is addictive and may cause withdrawal symptoms for those who abruptly stop consuming it. These include severe headaches, muscle aches, temporary depression, and irritability. Although scientists once worried that caffeine could stunt growth, this concern is not supported by research.

Caffeine sensitivity refers to the amount of caffeine that will produce an effect in someone. This amount varies from person to person. On average, the smaller the person, the less caffeine necessary to produce side effects. However, caffeine sensitivity is most affected by the amount of daily caffeine use. People who regularly drink beverages containing caffeine soon develop a reduced sensitivity to caffeine. This means they require higher doses of caffeine to achieve the same effects as someone who doesn't drink caffeinated drinks every day. In short, the more caffeine you take in, the more caffeine you'll need to feel the same effects.

Caffeine moves through the body within a few hours after it's consumed and is then passed through the urine. It's not stored in the body, but you may feel its effects for up to 6 hours if you're sensitive to it.

Although you may think you're getting plenty of liquids when you drink caffeinated beverages, caffeine works against the body in two ways: It has a mild dehydrating effect because it increases the need to urinate. And large amounts of caffeine may cause the body to lose calcium and potassium, causing sore muscles and delayed recovery times after exercise.

Caffeine has health risks for certain users. Small children are more sensitive to caffeine because they have not been exposed to it as much as older children or adults. Pregnant women or nursing mothers should consider decreasing their caffeine intake, although in small or moderate amounts there is no evidence that it causes a problem for the baby. Caffeine can aggravate heart problems or nervous disorders, and some teens may not be aware that they're at risk.

Moderation Is The Key

Although the effects of caffeine vary from one person to the next, doctors recommend that people should consume no more than about 100 milligrams (mg) of caffeine daily. That might sound like a lot, but one espresso contains about 100 milligrams of caffeine!

Cutting Back

If you're taking in too much caffeine, you may want to cut back. Kicking the caffeine habit is never easy, and the best way is to cut back slowly. Otherwise you could get headaches and feel achy, depressed, or lousy.

Try cutting your intake by substituting noncaffeinated drinks for caffeinated sodas and coffee. Examples include water, caffeine-free sodas, and caffeine-free teas. Keep track of how many caffeinated drinks you have each day, and substitute one drink per week with a caffeine-free alternative until you've gotten below the 100-milligram mark.

As you cut back on the amount of caffeine you consume, you may find yourself feeling tired. Your best bet is to hit the sack, not the sodas: It's just your body's way of telling you it needs more rest. Your energy levels will return to normal in a few days.

The Buzz About Energy Drinks

When pop princess Britney Spears needs a pick-me-up, she turns to a popular energy drink for a quick boost. Red Bull mixed with apple juice, she has said, "really pumps me up."

Table 25.1. Common Caffeinated Products and the Amounts of Caffeine They Contain

Drink/Food	Amt. of Drink/Food	Amt. of Caffeine
Jolt soft drink	12 ounces	71.2 mg
Mountain Dew	12 ounces	55.0 mg
Coca-Cola	12 ounces	34.0 mg
Diet Coke	12 ounces	45.0 mg
Pepsi	12 ounces	38.0 mg
7-Up	12 ounces	0 mg
Brewed coffee (drip method)	5 ounces	115 mg*
Iced tea	12 ounces	70 mg*
Dark chocolate	1 ounce	20 mg*
Milk chocolate	1 ounce	6 mg*
Cocoa beverage	5 ounces	4 mg*
Chocolate milk beverage	8 ounces	5 mg*
Cold relief medication	1 tablet	30 mg*
Vivarin	1 tablet	200 mg

* denotes average amount of caffeine

Source: U.S. Food and Drug Administration and National Soft Drink Association

And that's the idea. Highly caffeinated energy drinks—such as Red Bull, Go-Fast! and Monster—market themselves as sources of increased energy and concentration. Their websites feature high-flying motorcyclists and upside-down skateboarders as dynamic embodiments of all that concentrated energy.

But are these drinks good for you? Maher Karam-Hage, M.D., an addiction specialist at the University of Michigan Health System, raises some concerns about the beverages, particularly when they are mixed with alcohol, ingested before intensive exercise or used by children.

"In the United States, these energy drinks have not had any warnings. In Europe, it's been more cautionary," says Karam-Hage, medical director of the Chelsea-Arbor Treatment Center, a joint program of the U-M Health System and Chelsea Community Hospital. He notes that France has banned some of the drinks and other countries have placed restrictions on them. "In this country, our advertisements for these drinks and the marketing are ahead of the science."

The energy drinks typically contain sugar, caffeine (often 80 mg per can, about the same as a cup of coffee), and taurine, a sulfur-containing amino acid. Some countries have raised concerns about the amount of caffeine in the drinks and the uncertain health effects of taurine. Energy drinks are different from sports drinks, which tend not to have caffeine or taurine and are lower in carbohydrates.

While Karam-Hage stops short of saying people never should consume energy drinks, he says that mixing them with alcohol is dangerous and should be avoided.

"The best analogy I can come up with is it's the same as driving a car, putting one foot on the gas and one foot on the brakes," he says of combining the stimulants in caffeine and the intoxicating effects of alcohol.

Mixing alcohol and caffeine is nothing new—think of the people who try to sober up by drinking coffee after a night at the bar—but Karam-Hage says the belief that caffeine makes someone alert after drinking alcohol is a myth.

"You feel a little bit more alert and a little more awake, but in reality, your reflexes are not changed whatsoever. You're still intoxicated," he says. "And that's exactly the same problem that happens with energy drinks: people drink more and feel like, 'oh, I can handle a bit more alcohol then.'"

When people consume these beverages before intensive exercise, he says, they should be aware of the effects the drinks have on people's bodies. They can put a strain on the body due to the caffeine and, in some of the beverages, other diuretics. These can cause dehydration or even collapse, particularly if people drink more than one can before exercising, Karam-Hage says.

He is particularly concerned about the popularity of the drinks among young people. The beverages can cause children to be hyperactive, fidgety or even rageful, he says. And because the drinks are so small in size, people may be inclined to drink more than one at a time, he says.

"Most of us wouldn't really let our children drink two or three or even four cups of coffee, but children go to the store around the corner and find energy drinks," he says. "That can be dangerous."

♣ **It's A Fact!!**

• Most energy drinks contain caffeine, often about 80 mg per can (about the same as one cup of brewed coffee and more than the amount in two cans of Coca-Cola)

• Taurine, which the body produces on its own, is a sulfur-containing amino acid often marketed as an antioxidant, anti-anxiety treatment and a heartbeat regulator, but some scientists and health care providers say it is unclear what effect it has

• Caffeine will not reduce the effects of alcohol

Source: Reprinted with permission from the University of Michigan Health System, http://www.med.umich.edu. Copyright © 2005 Regents of the University of Michigan.

Part Three

Alcohol

Chapter 26

The Facts On Alcoholism And Alcohol Abuse

For many people, the facts about alcoholism are not clear. What is alcoholism, exactly? How does it differ from alcohol abuse? When should a person seek help for a problem related to his or her drinking? This chapter will answer these and other common questions about alcohol problems. It will explain alcoholism and alcohol abuse, the symptoms of each, when and where to seek help, and treatment choices.

A Widespread Problem

For most adults who drink, alcohol is a pleasant accompaniment to social activities. Moderate alcohol use—up to two drinks per day for men and one drink per day for women and older people—is not harmful for most adults. (A standard drink is one 12-ounce bottle or can of beer or wine cooler, one 5-ounce glass of wine, or 1.5 ounces of 80-proof distilled spirits.) Nonetheless, a large number of people get into serious trouble because of their drinking. Currently, nearly 14 million Americans—1 in every 13 people—abuse alcohol or are alcoholic. Several million more people engage in risky drinking

About This Chapter: Information in this chapter is from "Alcoholism: Getting the Facts," National Institute on Alcohol Abuse and Alcoholism (NIAAA), a component of the National Institutes of Health (NIH), NIH Publication No. 96-4153, September 2004.

that could lead to alcohol problems. These patterns include binge drinking and heavy drinking on a regular basis. In addition, 53 percent of men and women in the United States report that one or more of their close relatives have a drinking problem.

The consequences of alcohol misuse are serious—in many cases, life threatening. Heavy drinking can increase the risk for certain cancers, especially those of the liver, esophagus, throat, and larynx (voice box). Heavy drinking can also cause liver cirrhosis, immune system problems, brain damage, and harm to the fetus during pregnancy. In addition, drinking increases the risk of death from automobile crashes as well as recreational and on-the-job injuries. Furthermore, both homicides and suicides are more likely to be committed by persons who have been drinking. In purely economic terms, alcohol-related problems cost society approximately $185 billion per year. In human terms, the costs cannot be calculated.

> ## ✤ It's A Fact!!
>
> As a teen, your brain is still developing. New research on teens with alcohol disorders shows that heavy drinking in the teen years can cause long-lasting harm to thinking abilities.
>
> Source: Excerpted from "Too Much, Too Soon, Too Risky," The Cool Spot (http://www.thecoolspot.gov), National Institute on Alcohol Abuse and Alcoholism (NIAAA), a component of the National Institutes of Health (NIH), November 2004.

What Is Alcoholism?

Alcoholism, also known as "alcohol dependence," is a disease that includes four symptoms:

- **Craving:** A strong need, or compulsion, to drink

- **Loss of control:** The inability to limit one's drinking on any given occasion

- **Physical dependence:** Withdrawal symptoms, such as nausea, sweating, shakiness, and anxiety, occur when alcohol use is stopped after a period of heavy drinking

- **Tolerance:** The need to drink greater amounts of alcohol in order to "get high"

People who are not alcoholic sometimes do not understand why an alcoholic can't just "use a little willpower" to stop drinking. However, alcoholism has little to do with willpower. Alcoholics are in the grip of a powerful "craving," or uncontrollable need, for alcohol that overrides their ability to stop drinking. This need can be as strong as the need for food or water.

Although some people are able to recover from alcoholism without help, the majority of alcoholics need assistance. With treatment and support, many individuals are able to stop drinking and rebuild their lives.

♣ It's A Fact!!

Alcohol affects your brain. Drinking alcohol leads to a loss of coordination, poor judgment, slowed reflexes, distorted vision, memory lapses, and even blackouts.

Alcohol affects your body. Alcohol can damage every organ in your body. It is absorbed directly into your bloodstream and can increase your risk for a variety of life-threatening diseases, including cancer.

Alcohol affects your self-control. Alcohol depresses your central nervous system, lowers your inhibitions, and impairs your judgment. Drinking can lead to risky behaviors, such as driving when you shouldn't, or having unprotected sex.

Alcohol can kill you. Drinking large amounts of alcohol at one time or very rapidly can cause alcohol poisoning, which can lead to coma or even death. Driving and drinking also can be deadly. In 2002, 29 percent of drivers age 15 to 20 who died in traffic accidents had been drinking alcohol.

Alcohol can hurt you—even if you're not the one drinking. If you're around people who are drinking, you have an increased risk of being seriously injured, involved in car crashes, or affected by violence. At the very least, you may have to deal with people who are sick, out of control, or unable to take care of themselves.

Source: Excerpted from "Tips for Teens: The Truth About Alcohol," U.S. Department of Health and Human Services and SAMHSA's National Clearinghouse for Alcohol and Drug Information, 2004.

Many people wonder why some individuals can use alcohol without problems but others cannot. One important reason has to do with genetics. Scientists have found that having an alcoholic family member makes it more likely that if you choose to drink you too may develop alcoholism. Genes, however, are not the whole story. In fact, scientists now believe that certain factors in a person's environment influence whether a person with a genetic risk for alcoholism ever develops the disease. A person's risk for developing alcoholism can increase based on the person's environment, including where and how he or she lives; family, friends, and culture; peer pressure; and even how easy it is to get alcohol.

What Is Alcohol Abuse?

Alcohol abuse differs from alcoholism in that it does not include an extremely strong craving for alcohol, loss of control over drinking, or physical dependence. Alcohol abuse is defined as a pattern of drinking that results in one or more of the following situations within a 12-month period:

- Failure to fulfill major work, school, or home responsibilities

- Drinking in situations that are physically dangerous, such as while driving a car or operating machinery

- Having recurring alcohol-related legal problems, such as being arrested for driving under the influence of alcohol or for physically hurting someone while drunk

- Continued drinking despite having ongoing relationship problems that are caused or worsened by the drinking

Although alcohol abuse is basically different from alcoholism, alcoholics also experience many effects of alcohol abuse.

What Are The Signs Of A Problem?

How can you tell whether you may have a drinking problem? Answering the following four questions can help you find out:

- Have you ever felt you should cut down on your drinking?

- Have people annoyed you by criticizing your drinking?

✔ **Quick Tip**

How can you tell if a friend has a drinking problem?

Sometimes it's tough to tell. But there are signs you can look for. If your friend has one or more of the following warning signs, he or she may have a problem with alcohol:

• Getting drunk on a regular basis

• Lying about how much alcohol he or she is using

• Believing that alcohol is necessary to have fun

• Having frequent hangovers

• Feeling run-down, depressed, or even suicidal

• Having "blackouts"—forgetting what he or she did while drinking

What can you do to help someone who has a drinking problem? Be a real friend. You might even save a life. Encourage your friend to stop or seek professional help.

Source: Excerpted from "Tips for Teens: The Truth About Alcohol," U.S. Department of Health and Human Services and SAMHSA's National Clearinghouse for Alcohol and Drug Information, 2004.

• Have you ever felt bad or guilty about your drinking?

• Have you ever had a drink first thing in the morning (as an "eye opener") to steady your nerves or get rid of a hangover?

One "yes" answer suggests a possible alcohol problem. If you answered "yes" to more than one question, it is highly likely that a problem exists. In either case, it is important that you see your doctor or other health care provider right away to discuss your answers to these questions. He or she can help you determine whether you have a drinking problem and, if so, recommend the best course of action.

Even if you answered "no" to all of the above questions, if you encounter drinking-related problems with your job, relationships, health, or the law, you should seek professional help. The effects of alcohol abuse can be extremely serious—even fatal—both to you and to others.

The Decision To Get Help

Accepting the fact that help is needed for an alcohol problem may not be easy. But keep in mind that the sooner you get help, the better are your chances for a successful recovery.

Any concerns you may have about discussing drinking-related problems with your health care provider may stem from common misconceptions about alcoholism and alcoholic people. In our society, the myth prevails that an alcohol problem is a sign of moral weakness. As a result, you may feel that to seek help is to admit some type of shameful defect in yourself. In fact, alcoholism is a disease that is no more a sign of weakness than is asthma. Moreover, taking steps to identify a possible drinking problem has an enormous payoff—a chance for a healthier, more rewarding life.

When you visit your health care provider, he or she will ask you a number of questions about your alcohol use to determine whether you are having problems related to your drinking. Try to answer these questions as fully and honestly as you can. You also will be given a physical examination. If your health care provider concludes that you may be dependent on alcohol, he or she may recommend that you see a specialist in treating alcoholism. You should be involved in any referral decisions and have all treatment choices explained to you.

Getting Well

Alcoholism Treatment

The type of treatment you receive depends on the severity of your alcoholism and the resources that are available in your community. Treatment may include detoxification (the process of safely getting alcohol out of your system); taking doctor-prescribed medications, such as disulfiram (Antabuse®) or naltrexone (ReVia®), to help prevent a return (or relapse) to drinking once drinking has stopped; and individual and/or group counseling. There are promising types of counseling that teach alcoholics to identify situations and feelings that trigger the urge to drink and to find new ways to cope that do not include alcohol use. These treatments are often provided on an outpatient basis.

Because the support of family members is important to the recovery process, many programs also offer brief marital counseling and family therapy as part of the treatment process. Programs may also link individuals with vital community resources, such as legal assistance, job training, childcare, and parenting classes.

Alcoholics Anonymous

Virtually all alcoholism treatment programs also include Alcoholics Anonymous (AA) meetings. AA describes itself as a "worldwide fellowship of men and women who help each other to stay sober." Although AA is generally recognized as an effective mutual help program for recovering alcoholics, not everyone responds to AA's style or message, and other recovery approaches are available. Even people who are helped by AA usually find that AA works best in combination with other forms of treatment, including counseling and medical care.

Can Alcoholism Be Cured?

Although alcoholism can be treated, a cure is not yet available. In other words, even if an alcoholic has been sober for a long time and has regained health, he or she remains susceptible to relapse and must continue to avoid all alcoholic beverages. "Cutting down" on drinking doesn't work; cutting out alcohol is necessary for a successful recovery.

However, even individuals who are determined to stay sober may suffer one or several "slips," or relapses, before achieving long-term sobriety. Relapses are very common and do not mean that a person has failed or cannot recover from alcoholism. Keep in mind, too, that every day that a recovering alcoholic has stayed sober prior to a relapse is extremely valuable time, both to the individual and to his or her family. If a relapse occurs, it is very important to try to stop drinking once again and to get whatever additional support you need to abstain from drinking.

Help For Alcohol Abuse

If your health care provider determines that you are not alcohol dependent but are nonetheless involved in a pattern of alcohol abuse, he or she can help you to do the following:

- Examine the benefits of stopping an unhealthy drinking pattern.

- Set a drinking goal for yourself. Some people choose to abstain from alcohol. Others prefer to limit the amount they drink.

- Examine the situations that trigger your unhealthy drinking patterns, and develop new ways of handling those situations so that you can maintain your drinking goal.

Some individuals who have stopped drinking after experiencing alcohol-related problems choose to attend AA meetings for information and support, even though they have not been diagnosed as alcoholic.

New Directions

With NIAAA's support, scientists at medical centers and universities throughout the country are studying alcoholism. The goal of this research is to develop better ways of treating and preventing alcohol problems. Today, NIAAA funds approximately 90 percent of all alcoholism research in the United States. Some of the more exciting investigations focus on the causes, consequences, treatment, and prevention of alcoholism:

- **Genetics:** Alcoholism is a complex disease. Therefore, there are likely to be many genes involved in increasing a person's risk for alcoholism. Scientists are searching for these genes, and have found areas on chromosomes where they are probably located. Powerful new techniques may permit researchers to identify and measure the specific contribution of each gene to the complex behaviors associated with heavy drinking. This research will provide the basis for new medications to treat alcohol-related problems.

- **Treatment:** NIAAA-supported researchers have made considerable progress in evaluating commonly used therapies and in developing new types of therapies to treat alcohol-related problems. One large-scale study sponsored by NIAAA found that each of three commonly used behavioral treatments for alcohol abuse and alcoholism—motivation enhancement therapy, cognitive-behavioral therapy, and 12-step facilitation therapy—significantly reduced drinking in the year following treatment. This study also found that approximately one-third of the study participants who were followed up either were still abstinent or were drinking without serious problems 3 years after the study ended. Other therapies that have been evaluated and found effective in reducing alcohol problems include brief intervention for alcohol abusers (individuals who are not dependent on alcohol) and behavioral marital therapy for married alcohol-dependent individuals.

- **Medications development:** NIAAA has made developing medications to treat alcoholism a high priority. It is believed that a range of new medications will be developed based on the results of genetic and neuroscience research. In fact, neuroscience research has already led to studies of one medication—naltrexone (ReVia®)—as an anticraving medication. NIAAA-supported researchers found that this drug, in combination with behavioral therapy, was effective in treating alcoholism. Naltrexone, which targets the brain's reward circuits, is the first medication approved to help maintain sobriety after detoxification from alcohol since the approval of disulfiram (Antabuse®) in 1949.

- **Combined medications/behavioral therapies:** NIAAA-supported researchers have found that available medications work best with behavioral therapy. Thus, NIAAA has initiated a large-scale clinical trial to determine which of the currently available medications and which behavioral therapies work best together.

In addition to these efforts, NIAAA is sponsoring promising research in other vital areas, such as fetal alcohol syndrome, alcohol's effects on the brain and other organs, aspects of drinkers' environments that may contribute to alcohol abuse and alcoholism, strategies to reduce alcohol-related problems, and new treatment techniques. Together, these investigations will help prevent alcohol problems; identify alcohol abuse and alcoholism at earlier stages; and make available new, more effective treatment approaches for individuals and families.

Chapter 27

Teens And Alcohol

Alcohol is a drug, as surely as cocaine and marijuana are. And it's danger-ous. Kids who drink are more likely to do the following:

• Be victims of violent crime

• Have serious problems in school

• Be involved in drinking-related traffic crashes

Teens And Alcohol: The Risks

For young people, alcohol is the number one drug of choice. In fact, teens use alcohol more frequently and heavily than all other illicit drugs combined.

It is important to remember that alcohol is a powerful, mood-altering drug. Not only does alcohol affect the mind and body, in often-unpredictable ways, but also teens lack the judgment and coping skills to handle alcohol wisely. The result of this can be the following:

• Alcohol-related traffic crashes are a major cause of death among teens. Alcohol use also is linked with youthful deaths by drowning, suicide, and homicide.

About This Chapter: Information in this chapter is excerpted from "Make A Differ-ence: Talk To Your Child About Alcohol," National Institute on Alcohol Abuse and Alcoholism (NIAAA), a component of the National Institutes of Health (NIH), NIH Publication No. 00-4314, September 2004.

- Teens who use alcohol are more likely to become sexually active at earlier ages, to have sexual intercourse more often, and to have unprotected sex than teens who do not drink.

- Young people who drink are more likely than others to be victims of violent crime, including rape, aggravated assault, and robbery.

- Teens who drink are more likely to have problems with school work and school conduct.

✔ Quick Tip

Get the facts. One drink can make you fail a breath test. You can lose your driver's license, be subject to a heavy fine, or have your car permanently taken away.

Stay informed. "Binge" drinking means having five or more drinks on one occasion. Studies show that more than 35 percent of adults with an alcohol problem developed symptoms—such as binge drinking—by age 19.

Know the risks. Alcohol is a drug. Mixing it with any other drug can be extremely dangerous. Alcohol and acetaminophen—a common ingredient in over-the-counter pain and fever reducers—can damage your liver. Alcohol mixed with other drugs can cause nausea, vomiting, fainting, heart problems, and difficulty breathing. Mixing alcohol and drugs also can lead to coma and death.

Keep your edge. Alcohol is a depressant, or downer, because it reduces brain activity. If you are depressed before you start drinking, alcohol can make you feel worse.

Look around you. Most teens aren't drinking alcohol. Research shows that 71 percent of people 12–20 haven't had a drink in the past month.

Source: Excerpted from "Tips for Teens: The Truth About Alcohol," U.S. Department of Health and Human Services and SAMHSA's National Clearinghouse for Alcohol and Drug Information, 2004.

- An individual who begins drinking as a teen is four times more likely to develop alcohol dependence than someone who waits until adulthood to use alcohol.

The message is clear: Alcohol use is very risky business for young people. And the longer teens delay alcohol use, the less likely they are to develop any problems associated with it.

A Young Teen's World

Early adolescence is a time of enormous and often confusing changes, which makes it a challenging time for you. These are some examples:

- **Physical Changes.** Young teens experience rapid increases in height and weight as well as the beginnings of sexual development. As a result, many kids feel more self-conscious about their bodies than they did when they were younger and begin to question whether they are "good enough"—tall enough, slender enough, strong enough, attractive enough—compared with others. A young teen who feels he or she doesn't measure up in some way is more likely to do things to try to please friends, including experimenting with alcohol.

- **Thinking Skills.** Most young teens are still very "now" oriented and are just beginning to understand that their actions—such as drinking—have consequences. They also tend to believe that bad things won't happen to them, which helps to explain why they often take risks.

- **Social and Emotional Changes.** As children approach adolescence, friends and "fitting in" become extremely important. Young teens increasingly look to friends and the media for clues on how to behave and begin to question adults' values and rules.

Chapter 28

Statistics On Alcohol Consumption And Related Health Concerns

Measures Of Alcohol Consumption And Alcohol-Related Health Effects From Excessive Consumption

Current Drinking

- Current drinkers are those who consume alcohol-containing beverages.

- In 2002, 54.9% of U.S. adults (18 years and older) reported drinking at least one drink in the past month. The prevalence of past-month alcohol consumption was higher for men (62.4%) than for women (47.9%).

Binge Drinking

- Binge drinking is generally defined as having 5 or more drinks on one occasion, meaning in a row or within a short period of time. However, among women, binge drinking is often defined as having 4 or more drinks on one occasion. This lower cut-point is used for women because women are generally of smaller stature than men, and absorb and metabolize alcohol differently than men.

About This Chapter: Information in this chapter is excerpted from "General Alcohol Information," Centers for Disease Control and Prevention, a component of the Department of Health and Human Services, January 2005.

- About 1 in 3 adult drinkers in the United States report past-month binge drinking, and this ratio has changed very little since the mid-1980s.

- In 2001, there were approximately 1.5 billion episodes of binge drinking in the U.S. Binge drinking rates were highest among those aged 18 to 25 years; however, 70% of binge drinking episodes occurred among those aged 26 years and older.

- Binge drinkers were 14 times more likely to report alcohol-impaired driving than non-binge drinkers.

- Binge drinking is associated with a number of adverse health effects, including unintentional injuries (for example, motor vehicle crashes, falls, burns, drownings, and hypothermia); violence (homicide, suicide, child abuse, domestic violence); sudden infant death syndrome; alcohol poisoning; hypertension; myocardial infarction; gastritis; pancreatitis; sexually transmitted diseases; meningitis; and poor control of diabetes.

✎ What's It Mean?
Alcohol Dependence

A person is defined as being dependent on alcohol if he or she reports three or more of the following symptoms in the past year:

- Tolerance (needing more alcohol to become intoxicated).

- Withdrawal

- Alcohol use for longer periods than intended.

- Desire and/or unsuccessful efforts to cut down or control alcohol use.

- Considerable time spent obtaining or using alcohol, or recovering from its effects.

- Important social, work, or recreational activities given up because of use.

- Continued use of alcohol despite knowledge of problems caused by or aggravated by use.

In 2002, 3.7% of past-year drinkers were alcohol-dependent.

Heavy Drinking

- Heavy drinking is consuming alcohol in excess of 1 drink per day on average for women and greater than 2 drinks per day on average for men.

- In 2002, 5.9% of U.S. adults reported heavy drinking in the past 30 days; the prevalence of heavy drinking was greater for men (7.1%) than for women (4.5%).

- Heavy drinking is associated with a number of chronic health conditions, including chronic liver disease and cirrhosis, gastrointestinal cancers, heart disease, stroke, pancreatitis, depression, and a variety of social problems.

Underage Drinking

- As of 1988, all states prohibit the purchase of alcohol by youth under the age of 21 years. Consequently, underage drinking is defined as consuming alcohol prior to the minimum legal drinking age of 21 years.

- In 2003, 44.9% of 9th through 12th graders reported drinking alcohol on one or more of the past 30 days; prevalence of current drinking was higher for females (45.8%) than among males (43.8%).

- In 2003, 28.3% of 9th through 12th graders reported binge drinking (having five or more drinks of alcohol in a row or within a couple of hours) at least once during the past 30 days. The prevalence of binge drinking was higher for males (29%) than among females (27.5%).

- Alcohol use is a leading risk factor in the three leading causes of death among youth: unintentional injuries (including motor vehicle crashes and drownings); suicides; and homicides. Other adverse consequences of underage drinking include risky sexual behavior and poor school performance.

- Zero tolerance laws, which make it illegal for youth under age 21 years to drive with any measurable amount of alcohol in their system (that is, with a blood alcohol concentration (BAC) =0.02 g/dL), have reduced traffic fatalities among 18 to 20 year olds by 13% and saved an estimated 21,887 lives from 1975 through 2002.

Alcohol Use And Women's Health

- For women of childbearing age, the consequences of excessive alcohol consumption, particularly binge drinking, includes unintentional injuries, domestic violence, risky sexual behavior and sexually transmitted diseases, unintended pregnancy, and alcohol-exposed pregnancies.

- In 2001, 11.8% of women aged 18 to 44 years reported consuming alcohol within the past month, and 11% reported binge drinking (5 or more drinks on any one occasion).

- Women with unintended pregnancies were 60% more likely to binge drink during the three months before conception than women with intended pregnancies.

Alcohol-Impaired Driving

- In 2002, 2.2% of U.S. adults reported alcohol-impaired driving in the past 30 days.

- In 2001, there were approximately 1.4 million arrests for driving under the influence of alcohol or narcotics. This is an arrest rate of 1 of every 137 licensed drivers in the United States.

Alcohol-Related Health Effects From Excessive Alcohol Consumption

Total Deaths Due To Alcohol

- In 2000, there were approximately 85,000 deaths attributable to either excessive or risky drinking in the U.S., making alcohol the third leading actual cause of death.

- Alcohol-related deaths in the United States vary considerably by state, and are directly related to the amount of alcohol consumed and the pattern of alcohol use.

Alcohol Motor Vehicle Crash Deaths

- In 2002, 17,419 people in the United States died in alcohol-related motor vehicle crashes, accounting for 41% of all traffic-related deaths.

- From 1997 through 2002, 2,355 children died in alcohol-related motor vehicle crashes; 1,588 (68%) of these children were riding with a drinking driver.

Alcohol And Unintentional Injuries

- Alcohol-related unintentional injuries and deaths include motor vehicle crashes, drownings, falls, hypothermia, burns, suicides, and homicides.

- Approximately 31.1% of those who die from unintentional, non-traffic injuries in the United States have a blood alcohol concentration of 0.10 g/dL or greater.

- Patients treated in an emergency department (ED) for an unintentional injury are 13.5 times more likely to have consumed 5 or more alcohol-containing beverages within 6 hours of their injury compared to age and sex matched community controls.

Alcohol And Violence

- Approximately 72% of rapes reported on college campuses occur when victims are so intoxicated they are unable to consent or refuse.

- Two-thirds of victims of intimate partner violence reported that alcohol was involved in the incident.

- Nearly one-half of the cases of child abuse and neglect are associated with parental alcohol or drug abuse.

- Approximately 23% of suicide deaths are attributable to alcohol.

Alcohol And Pregnancy

- Adverse health effects that are associated with alcohol-exposed pregnancies include miscarriage, premature delivery, low birth weight, sudden infant death syndrome (SIDS), and prenatal alcohol-related conditions (for example, fetal alcohol syndrome (FAS) and alcohol-related neurodevelopmental disorders).

- Alcohol-related neurodevelopmental disorder and alcohol-related birth defects are believed to occur approximately three times as often as fetal alcohol syndrome.

- Fetal alcohol syndrome is one of the leading causes of mental retardation, and is directly attributable to drinking during pregnancy. FAS is characterized by growth retardation, facial abnormalities, and central nervous system dysfunction (learning disabilities and lower IQ), as well as behavioral problems.

- The incidence of FAS in the United States ranges from 0.2 to 1.5 per 1,000 live births.

- Any maternal alcohol use in the periconceptional period (that is, during the three months before pregnancy or during the first trimester) is associated with a six-fold increased risk of SIDS.

- Binge drinking (five or more drinks at a time) during a mother's first trimester of pregnancy is associated with an eight-fold increase in the odds that the infant will die of SIDS.

Alcohol And Sexually Transmitted Disease

- Alcohol use by young adults is associated with earlier initiation of sexual activity, unprotected sexual intercourse, multiple partners and an increased risk for sexually transmitted diseases.

- Among teens aged 14 to 18, 20% of those who reported drinking before age 14 also reported being sexually active compared to 7% of those who did not report drinking before this age.

- Among adults aged 18 to 30, binge drinkers were twice as likely as those who did not binge drink to have had two or more sex partners.

- People who abuse alcohol are more likely to engage in risky behaviors, such as having unprotected sex, having more sex partners, and using intravenous drugs. In a single act of unprotected sex with an infected partner, a teenage woman has a 1% risk of acquiring HIV, a 30 % risk of getting genital herpes, and a 50% chance of contracting gonorrhea.

Hepatitis C And Chronic Liver Disease

- Alcohol consumption can exacerbate the HCV infection and accelerate disease progression to cirrhosis. Alcohol may also exacerbate the side effects of antiviral treatment for HCV infection, impairing the body's response to the virus.

- In 2003, there were 12,207 deaths from alcohol-related chronic liver disease (CLD). Approximately 75% of those deaths occurred among men.

- Approximately 40% of the deaths from unspecified liver disease in the United States are attributable to heavy alcohol consumption.

Alcohol And Cancer

- Alcohol-related cancers include oral-pharyngeal, esophagus (squamous cell type), prostate, liver, and breast. In general, the risk of cancer increases with increasing amounts of alcohol.

- Excessive drinkers are 3 times more likely to develop liver cancer than non-drinkers.

- Excessive drinkers are 4 times more likely to develop esophageal cancer than non-drinkers.

- Oral cancers are six times more common in heavy alcohol users than in non-alcohol users.

- Compared to non-drinkers, women who consume an average of 1 alcoholic drink per day increase their risk of breast cancer by approximately 7%. Women who consume an average of 2 to 5 drinks per day increase their risk of developing breast cancer by approximately 50% compared to that of non-drinkers.

Effective Prevention Strategies For Alcohol-Related Health Problems

Minimum Legal Drinking Age Laws

- All states and the District of Columbia have enforced 21-year-old minimum drinking age laws. In 2002, an estimated 917 lives were saved in traffic crashes as a result of the age 21 minimum drinking age laws.

• Increasing the minimum drinking age from 18 to 21 has reduced both drinking and traffic crashes among youth by 10 to 15%.

Comprehensive Community Programs

• Comprehensive community-based programs have reduced past month alcohol consumption among underage youth by 7%.

Intervention Training Programs For Servers

• Server training programs have reduced alcohol sales by 11.5% and sales to pseudo-intoxicated buyers by 46%.

• Server training programs have reduced single vehicle nighttime injury crashes by 23%.

Chapter 29

Alcohol Poisoning

Knowing The Facts Can Save Lives

Until the 1990s, deaths due to alcohol poisoning were largely ignored by the media. Families who lost a child due to AOD (alcohol overdose) suffered in silence. College campuses, where a great many of the deaths occurred, sought to avoid adverse publicity. Death certificates said "cardiac arrest" or "asphyxiation." Medical examiners sometimes chose to tell a grieving family, "It was a freak accident," rather than "Your son/daughter drank him/herself to death."

In 1994, a Federal law was passed requiring colleges to publish all student deaths. Finally, these tragic AOD stories are in newspapers and on national television; stories like the one about a 16-year-old cheerleader in Illinois who died after drinking a bottle of schnapps on a friend's dare.

Remove Intoxicated Drivers (RID) began working on the problem of AOD in 1992. Teenagers are particularly vulnerable to AOD. Of the first 8 cases RID discovered, half were 16 years old or younger. At least half were first-time drinkers and had never been drunk before. Five were put to bed by

About This Chapter: Information in this chapter is excerpted from "Alcohol Poisoning," Youth & Generation X Planner, Safe & Sober Campaign, National Highway Traffic Safety Administration (NHTSA), U.S. Department of Transportation, 1998; reviewed January 2006 by David A. Cooke, M.D., Diplomate, American Board of Internal Medicine.

friends or their own parents to "sleep it off," only to be found dead in the morning. Their friends or parents didn't know that if a person drinks too much alcohol quickly before falling asleep, the alcohol would shut down breathing and heart functions and kill a person within a few hours.

Until now, the lack of public information about AOD has been a national failure. The following information literally saves lives. It could save a friend or maybe even you.

Mechanisms Of Alcohol Poisoning

Alcohol depresses nerves that control involuntary actions such as breathing, the heartbeat, and the gag reflex (prevents choking). A fatal dose of alcohol will eventually stop these functions. After the victim stops drinking, the heart keeps beating, and alcohol in the stomach continues to enter the bloodstream and circulate throughout the body. As a result of this, the following can happen:

- Victim chokes on own vomit

- Breathing slows, becomes irregular, stops

- Heart beats irregularly or stops

- Hypothermia (low body temperature) leads to cardiac arrest

- Hypoglycemia (too little blood sugar) leads to seizures

Even if the victim lives, AOD can lead to irreversible brain damage. Rapid binge drinking (which often happens on a bet or a dare) is especially dangerous because the victim can ingest a fatal dose before becoming unconscious.

> **♣ It's A Fact!!**
>
> Based on discussions with victims' families and county medical examiners, Remove Intoxicated Drivers (RID) estimates as many as 4,000 deaths occur each year from alcohol overdosing: drinking too much alcohol too fast. Families learn, in the most difficult way, that alcohol can be a lethal drug.

Critical Signs Of Alcohol Poisoning

- Mental confusion, stupor, coma, or person cannot be roused

- No response to pinching the skin

- Vomiting while sleeping

- Seizures

- Slow breathing (less than 8 breaths per minute)

- Irregular breathing (10 seconds or more between breaths)

- Hypothermia (low body temperature), bluish skin color, paleness

Many people try different methods to reverse the effects of alcohol to become sober. Most of these methods are myths, and they don't work.

Common Myths

- Drinking black coffee

- Taking a cold bath or shower

- Sleeping it off

- Walking it off

What To Do If You Suspect Someone May Have Ingested A Fatal Dose Of Alcohol

- Call 911 or the emergency medical number.

- Stay with the victim.

- Keep the victim from choking on vomit.

- Tell emergency medical technicians the symptoms and, if you know, how much alcohol the victim drank. Prompt action may save the life of a friend, or your own.

When Medical Personnel Arrive

Medical personnel should do they following:

- Protect the airway. This usually means inserting a tube into the trachea to protect it from vomit. Turning the victim on his/her side is not sufficient protection.

- Administer oxygen.

- Monitor breathing, and place victim on respirator if necessary.

- Monitor glucose and other levels in blood.

- Administer medication if convulsions are present.

Conventional Treatments Do Not Work For AOD

- Pumping the stomach

- Syrup of Ipecac to induce vomiting

- Activated charcoal

- Narcan (to reverse the effects of the central nervous system depressant)

Bystanders Have A Responsibility

- Know the danger signals.

- Do not wait for all symptoms to be present.

- Be aware that a person who has passed out may die.

- If there is any suspicion of AOD, call 911 or the emergency number for help. Don't try to guess the level of drunkenness.

What You Can Do

- Write letters to your local editor using this information the next time you notice a news story about an underage drinking incident or underage impaired driving crash.

- Encourage your school principal to present programs on alcohol awareness in health classes.

- Refuse to host underage drinking parties.

Chapter 30

Study Suggests Alcohol Merchandise Encourages Underage Drinking

Adolescents who collect and brandish promotional hats, shirts, bags and other merchandise displaying popular alcohol logos are far more likely to start drinking while still underage, according to a new study conducted by Dartmouth-Hitchcock Medical Center in Lebanon, New Hampshire.

In light of the apparent connection, the authors of the study recommended that the alcohol industry officially halt the practice of distributing and selling alcohol-related paraphernalia—much as the tobacco industry did with tobacco-related items in 1998.

"This study shows that promotional items are related to early onset drinking, and I think the responsible thing to do would be for these industries to quit distributing them," said Dr. James D. Sargent, study co-author from Dartmouth's department of pediatrics.

According to the study authors, the alcohol industry currently spends more than $1 billion a year on all aspects of marketing—a figure that includes expenditures for such youth-oriented promotional items as baseball caps, backpacks and T-shirts.

Such teen-targeted branding flies in the face of the 1984 federal National Minimum Drinking Age Act, which set the drinking age in the United States at 21 years—the highest in the world. The legislation mandated that all 50 states prohibit the selling of alcohol to minors under the age of 21. Public possession of alcohol by minors was similarly made illegal.

However, the law did not actually outlaw underage drinking—allowing those under 21 to legally consume alcohol in private settings or for either religious or medicinal purposes.

According to 2003 figures issued by the National Institute on Alcohol Abuse and Alcoholism, almost half of all adolescents have had at least one drink—and more than one-fifth have been drunk—by the time they enter the eighth grade.

Beginning in 1999, Sargent and his colleagues examined the drinking behavior of this age group by focusing on more than 2,400 middle school students in Vermont and New Hampshire.

The adolescents ranged in age from 9 to 15 years—attending grades five through eight. The research team established that none of the children had ever had a drink at the onset of the study.

During follow-up telephone interviews conducted one to two years later, Sargent and his team found that 14 percent of the students said they now owned at least one alcohol-related promotional item. Of the 32 students who mentioned the particular branding of their promotional possession, 29 had beer-related ones.

The researchers further found that 15 percent of the students said they now drank alcohol to some degree.

More than 24 percent of those who owned promotional items said they consumed alcohol, compared with the slightly more than 12 percent of non-owners who said they drank.

The researchers noted that ownership of alcohol promotional items was associated with being at the older range of the student group, having peers who drank, having tried smoking, "sensation-seeking," and doing less well in school.

✤ It's A Fact!!

A recent study showed that students who owned alcohol merchandise were significantly more likely to start drinking alcohol than those who did not.

"I think the beverage industry needs to take this seriously," said Sargent. "There's a tremendous amount of research showing that branded merchandise that the tobacco industry distributed clearly contributed to the teen smoking problem. There's just no doubt about it. Looking at the branded merchandise distributed by the alcohol industry is a relatively new topic, but it's such a similar situation that I would be surprised if multiple studies won't show that this is true in this case as well."

"For the wine and liquor industry," he added, "the point is that these kind of promotional things related to smoking were shown to lead to increased smoking among teens. And the tobacco industry gave up putting out the items."

Sargent said the alcohol industry should pick up on big tobacco's cue—noting that he expects a larger national study of teens he is currently conducting to further underline the urgency for such action.

David Jernigan, research director at the Center on Alcohol Marketing and Youth at Georgetown University in Washington, D.C., echoes the sentiment that the alcohol industry must take responsibility for its influence on underage drinking.

"The bottom line is that even the industry agrees that peer pressure is critical in a kid's decision to drink," he said." So it creates a whole set of walking billboards among the peer group at risk—among the underage peers. And that's not helpful to efforts to reduce underage drinking."

Chapter 31

Family History Of Alcoholism

If you are among the millions of people in this country who have a parent, grandparent, or other close relative with alcoholism, you may have wondered what your family's history of alcoholism means for you. Are problems with alcohol a part of your future? Is your risk for becoming an alcoholic greater than for people who do not have a family history of alcoholism? If so, what can you do to lower your risk?

Many scientific studies, including research conducted among twins and children of alcoholics, have shown that genetic factors influence alcoholism. These findings show that children of alcoholics are about four times more likely than the general population to develop alcohol problems. Children of alcoholics also have a higher risk for many other behavioral and emotional problems. But alcoholism is not determined only by the genes you inherit from your parents. In fact, more than one-half of all children of alcoholics do not become alcoholic.

Genes are not the only things children inherit from their parents. How parents act and how they treat each other and their children has an influence on children growing up in the family. These aspects of family life also affect

About This Chapter: Information in this chapter is from "A Family History of Alcoholism: Are You at Risk?" National Institute on Alcohol Abuse and Alcoholism, National Institutes of Health, NIH Publication No. 03-5340, September 2005.

the risk for alcoholism. Researchers believe a person's risk increases if he or she is in a family with the following difficulties:

- An alcoholic parent is depressed or has other psychological problems.

- Both parents abuse alcohol and other drugs.

- The parents' alcohol abuse is severe.

- Conflicts lead to aggression and violence in the family.

♣ **It's A Fact!!**
Research shows that many factors influence your risk of developing alcoholism. Some factors raise the risk while others lower it.

The good news is that many children of alcoholics, from even the most troubled families, do not develop drinking problems. Just as a family history of alcoholism does not guarantee that you will become an alcoholic, neither does growing up in a very troubled household with alcoholic parents. Just because alcoholism tends to run in families does not mean that a child of an alcoholic parent will automatically become an alcoholic too. The risk is higher but it does not have to happen.

If you are worried that your family's history of alcohol problems or your troubled family life puts you at risk for becoming alcoholic, here is some common-sense advice to help you:

Avoid underage drinking. First, underage drinking is illegal. Second, research shows that the risk for alcoholism is higher among people who begin to drink at an early age, perhaps as a result of both environmental and genetic factors.

Drink moderately as an adult. Even if they do not have a family history of alcoholism, adults who choose to drink alcohol should do so in moderation—no more than one drink a day for most women, and no more than two drinks a day for most men, according to guidelines from the U.S. Department of Agriculture and the U.S. Department of Health and Human Services. Some people should not drink at all, including women who are pregnant or who are trying to become pregnant, recovering alcoholics, people who plan to drive or engage in other activities that require attention or skill, people taking certain medications, and people with certain medical conditions.

People with a family history of alcoholism, who have a higher risk for becoming dependent on alcohol, should approach moderate drinking carefully. Maintaining moderate drinking habits may be harder for them than for people without a family history of drinking problems. Once a person moves from moderate to heavier drinking, the risks of social problems (for example, drinking and driving, violence, and trauma) and medical problems (for example, liver disease, brain damage, and cancer) increase greatly.

Talk to a health care professional. Discuss your concerns with a doctor, nurse, nurse practitioner, or other health care provider. They can recommend groups or organizations that could help you avoid alcohol problems.

Chapter 32

Children Of Alcoholics: It's Not Your Fault

Does Your Mom Or Dad Drink Too Much?

Millions of youth like yourself worry about their parents drinking too much or using drugs. It's a big problem that happens in every kind of family, whether rich or poor, single parent, or traditional or blended family and families that attend places of worship.

When your parents have been drinking, do they:

- embarrass you?

- blame you for things you didn't do?

- break promises?

- drive under the influence?

- behave in confusing and unpredictable ways?

Your parent could be misusing or be addicted to alcohol or drugs. Addiction to alcohol or drugs is a disease. People with this disease often do things that are confusing and hurtful. They need help to stop the alcohol or drug use. Sometimes that help is through an alcohol or drug abuse program; sometimes it is through Alcoholics Anonymous or other self-help groups, which

About This Chapter: Information in this chapter is from "It Feels So Bad," © 2005. Reprinted with permission by the National Association for Children of Alcoholics.

often meet in churches and synagogues. These groups have helped millions of moms and dads recover, regain their health, and begin to heal their families. Caring adults are available to help your mom or dad get the treatment and recovery support they need.

Things You Should Know

Lots of teens live in families with alcohol abuse or alcoholism—one in four. Many also live with parental drug abuse. You are not alone.

> **☞ Remember!!**
>
> You didn't cause it. You can't cure it. You can't control it. But you can take better care of yourself by communicating your feelings, making healthy choices, and celebrating yourself.

Addiction to alcohol or drugs affects all members of the family, even if only one person has the disease. This is why it is called a "family disease."

Nothing you have done has ever caused anyone else to drink too much or use drugs. It's not your fault. You need and deserve help for yourself.

People with alcohol or drug addiction in their families are at greater risk of getting this disease when they choose to drink or use drugs. You can never get this disease if you don't drink or use drugs.

It is important for you to concentrate on finding help and support for yourself.

Take Care Of Yourself

If you feel bad because your mom or dad is drinking too much or using drugs, there are steps you can take to make things better for yourself even though you cannot stop your parent from drinking or using.

Talk to a caring adult. There are many adults who will listen and help you deal with problems at home, even when it seems no one has noticed. Sometimes they are not sure if you want or need support and are waiting for you to say something first. Often a teacher, a counselor at school, a youth minister, a coach, doctor, nurse, friend's parent, grandparent, aunt or uncle is knowledgeable and anxious to help.

Families with alcohol or drug problems often try to keep it a secret. It is important to find caring adults who can help you. Talking to them really helps, and it is not being disloyal to your family if you seek help for yourself.

If you don't get the help you need from the first person you approach, it is important to reach out to another adult you can trust.

Get involved in youth programs. Join in activities offered through your church or synagogue, your school's extracurricular programs, or your community recreational departments. Here you can hang out with other young people, use your special talents and strengths and learn new skills while making friends and having fun.

Join A Support Group

Many schools have assistance programs that offer support groups for students who are living with alcohol or drug abuse in their families. These programs help with problem solving, and they give you the opportunity to meet other young people who are struggling with the same problems at home that you might face. They can help you see how others are able to have a good life in spite of what is happening at home.

Alateen Is For You

Alateen is a group for teens who are affected by someone else's alcohol or drug use. It holds meetings, like a club, where young people share tips on how to make their lives easier when a family member drinks too much or uses drugs.

The meetings are sponsored by Al-Anon. You can find the location of meetings near you by looking in the phone book under Al-Anon or Alateen, or ask a youth minister, your school counselor, your doctor or another adult you trust to help you get to a meeting near you. You can also find out about Alateen at www.alateen.org or by calling toll-free at 1-888-425-2666.

If It Is Your Friend's Mom Or Dad Who Drinks Too Much

Don't walk away, and don't pretend you don't see it.

Here are some things you can say that might help:

- It's not your fault that your parent drinks or uses drugs.

- You're not alone—lots of kids come from families where this is a problem.

- There are people who can help.

  Here are some things you can do:

- Tell your pastor or youth minister that you are worried about your friend.

- Be a good friend—include your friend in your activities and your family's fun.

- Encourage your friend to talk to a trusting adult.

Part Four

Tobacco

Chapter 33

The Brain's Response To Nicotine

For centuries, people have chewed and smoked tobacco, which comes from the plant *Nicotiana tabacum*. The reason tobacco is used by so many people is because it contains a powerful drug known as nicotine.

When tobacco is smoked, nicotine is absorbed by the lungs and quickly moved into the bloodstream, where it is circulated throughout the brain. All of this happens very rapidly. In fact, nicotine reaches the brain within 8 seconds after someone inhales tobacco smoke. Nicotine can also enter the bloodstream through the mucous membranes that line the mouth (if tobacco is chewed) or nose (if snuff is used), and even through the skin.

Nicotine affects the entire body. Nicotine acts directly on the heart to change heart rate and blood pressure. It also acts on the nerves that control respiration to change breathing patterns. In high concentrations, nicotine is deadly; in fact one drop of purified nicotine on the tongue will kill a person.

So why do people smoke? Because nicotine acts in the brain where it can stimulate feelings of pleasure.

About This Chapter: Information in this chapter is from "The Brain's Response to Nicotine," NIDA for Teens, National Institute on Drug Abuse, a component of the United States Department of Health and Human Services, June 2005.

How Does Nicotine Act In The Brain?

Your brain is made up of billions of nerve cells. They communicate by releasing chemical messengers called neurotransmitters. Each neurotransmitter is like a key that fits into a special "lock," called a receptor, located on the surface of nerve cells. When a neurotransmitter finds its receptor, it activates the receptor's nerve cell.

The nicotine molecule is shaped like a neurotransmitter called acetylcholine. Acetylcholine and its receptors are involved in many functions, including muscle movement, breathing, heart rate, learn-

> ♣ **It's A Fact!!**
> Nicotine is so lethal that it has been used as a pesticide for centuries.

ing, and memory. They also cause the release of other neurotransmitters and hormones that affect your mood, appetite, memory, and more. When nicotine gets into the brain, it attaches to acetylcholine receptors and mimics the actions of acetylcholine.

Nicotine also activates areas of the brain that are involved in producing feelings of pleasure and reward. Recently, scientists discovered that nicotine raises the levels of a neurotransmitter called dopamine in the parts of the brain that produce feelings of pleasure and reward. Dopamine, which is sometimes called the pleasure molecule, is the same neurotransmitter that is involved in addictions to other drugs such as cocaine and heroin. Researchers now believe that this change in dopamine may play a key role in all addictions. This may help explain why it is so hard for people to stop smoking.

Chapter 34

The Facts About Smoking

When your parents were young, people could buy cigarettes and smoke pretty much anywhere—even in hospitals. Ads for cigarettes were all over the place. Today we're more aware about how bad smoking is for our health. Smoking is restricted or banned in almost all public places and cigarette companies are no longer allowed to advertise on buses or trains, billboards, TV, and in many magazines.

Almost everyone knows that smoking causes cancer, emphysema, and heart disease; that it can shorten your life by 14 years or more; and that the habit can cost a smoker thousands of dollars a year. So how come people are still lighting up? The answer, in a word, is addiction.

Once You Start, It's Hard To Stop

Smoking's a hard habit to break because tobacco contains nicotine, which is highly addictive. Like heroin or other addictive drugs, the body and mind quickly become so used to the nicotine in cigarettes that a person needs to have it just to feel normal.

About This Chapter: Information in this chapter is from "Smoking." This information was provided by TeensHealth, one of the largest resources online for medically reviewed health information written for parents, kids, and teens. For more articles like this one, visit www.TeensHealth.org, or www.KidsHealth.org. © 2004 The Nemours Center for Children's Health Media, a division of The Nemours Foundation.

Almost no smoker begins as an adult. Statistics show that about nine out of ten tobacco users start before they're 18 years old. Some teens who smoke say they start because they think it helps them look older (it does—if yellow teeth and wrinkles are the look you want). Others smoke because they think it helps them relax (it doesn't—the heart actually beats faster while a person's smoking). Some light up as a way to feel rebellious or to set themselves apart (which works if you want your friends to hang out someplace else while you're puffing away). Some start because their friends smoke—or just because it gives them something to do.

Some people, especially girls, start smoking because they think it may help keep their weight down. The illnesses that smoking can cause, like lung diseases or cancer, do cause weight loss—but that's not a very good way for people to fit into their clothes.

Another reason people start smoking is because their family members do. Most adults who started smoking in their teens never expected to become addicted. That's why people say it's just so much easier to not start smoking at all.

The cigarette ads from when your parents were young convinced many of them that the habit was glamorous, powerful, or exciting—even though it's essentially a turnoff: smelly, expensive, and unhealthy. Cigarette ads from the 1940s even showed doctors recommending cigarettes as a way to relax.

Cigarette ads still show smokers as attractive and hip, sophisticated and elegant, or rebellious and cool. The good news is that these ads aren't as visible and are less effective today than they used to be: Just as doctors are more savvy about smoking today than they were a generation ago, teens are more aware of how manipulative advertising can be. The government has also passed laws limiting where and how tobacco companies are allowed to advertise to help prevent young kids from getting hooked on smoking.

How Smoking Affects Your Health

There are no physical reasons to start smoking—the body doesn't need tobacco the way it needs food, water, sleep, and exercise. In fact, many of the chemicals in cigarettes, like nicotine and cyanide, are actually poisons that can kill in high enough doses. The body's smart and it goes on the defense when it's being poisoned. For this reason, many people find it takes several tries to get started smoking: First-time smokers often feel pain or burning in the throat and lungs, and some people feel sick or even throw up the first few times they try tobacco.

The consequences of this poisoning happen gradually. Over the long term, smoking leads people to develop health problems like cancer, emphysema (breakdown of lung tissue), organ damage, and heart disease. These diseases limit a person's ability to be normally active—and can be fatal. Each time a smoker lights up, that single cigarette takes about 5 to 20 minutes off the person's life.

♣ It's A Fact!!

• Did you know that cigarettes contain formaldehyde, the same stuff used to preserve dead frogs?

• Did you know that the same cyanide found in rat poison is available in the cigarette smoke nearest you, whether you're a smoker or just hanging around people who smoke?

• And how about the nicotine in cigarettes? You probably already know that it's addictive, but did you know that it's also a potent insecticide found in bug spray?

Source: "Teens and Tobacco: What's Really In?" Centers for Disease Control and Prevention, Department of Health and Human Services, January 2005.

Smokers not only develop wrinkles and yellow teeth, they also lose bone density, which increases their risk of osteoporosis (pronounced: ahs-tee-o-puh-row-sus, a condition that causes older people to become bent over and their bones to break more easily). Smokers also tend to be less active than nonsmokers because smoking affects lung power. Smoking can also cause fertility problems in both men and women and can impact sexual health in males.

The consequences of smoking may seem very far off to many teens, but long-term health problems aren't the only hazard of smoking. Nicotine and the other toxins in cigarettes, cigars, and pipes can affect a person's body quickly, which means that teen smokers experience many of these problems:

- **Bad skin.** Because smoking restricts blood vessels, it can prevent oxygen and nutrients from getting to the skin—which is why smokers often appear pale and unhealthy. An Italian study also linked smoking to an increased risk of getting a type of skin rash called psoriasis.

- **Bad breath.** All those cigarettes leave smokers with a condition called halitosis, or persistent bad breath.

- **Bad-smelling clothes and hair.** The smell of stale smoke tends to linger—not just on people's clothing, but also on their hair, furniture, and cars. And it's often hard to get the smell of smoke out.

- **Reduced athletic performance.** People who smoke usually can't compete with nonsmoking peers because the physical effects of smoking—like rapid heartbeat, decreased circulation, and shortness of breath—impair sports performance.

- **Greater risk of injury and slower healing time.** Smoking affects the body's ability to produce collagen, so common sports injuries, such as damage to tendons and ligaments, will heal more slowly in smokers than nonsmokers.

- **Increased risk of illness.** Studies show that smokers get more colds, flu, bronchitis, and pneumonia than nonsmokers. And people with certain health conditions, like asthma, become sicker if they smoke (and often if they're just around people who smoke). Because teens who smoke as a way to manage weight often light up instead of eating, their bodies lack the nutrients they need to grow, develop, and fight off illness properly.

Smoking Is Expensive

Not only does smoking damage health, it costs an arm and a leg. Depending on where you live, smoking a pack of cigarettes a day can cost about $1,800 dollars a year. That adds up. It's money you could save or spend on something for yourself.

♣ **It's A Fact!!**

Scientists are learning how tobacco and nicotine affect teen smokers. Studies going on for 25 years show a link between heavy teen smoking and fear of going outside (agoraphobia). Teens who smoke were 6 times more likely to get agoraphobia. And, teen smokers were 15 times more likely to have panic attacks than teens who did not smoke. Scientists think the reason is that nicotine hurts blood vessels to the brain, and also blocks air from the lungs. Whatever the reason, teen smokers are more likely to have panic attacks, anxiety disorders, and depression.

Source: Excerpted from "Nicotine," NIDA for Teens, National Institute on Drug Abuse, a component of the United States Department of Health and Human Services, November 2005.

Kicking Butt And Staying Smoke Free

All forms of tobacco—cigarettes, pipes, cigars, and smokeless tobacco—are hazardous. It doesn't help to substitute products that seem like they're better for you than regular cigarettes—such as filter or low-tar cigarettes.

The only thing that really helps a person avoid the problems associated with smoking is staying smoke free. This isn't always easy, especially if everyone around you is smoking and offering you cigarettes. It may help to have your reasons for not smoking ready for times you may feel the pressure, such as "I just don't like it" or "I want to stay in shape for soccer" (or football, basketball, or other sport).

The good news for people who don't smoke or who want to quit is that studies show that the number of teens who smoke is dropping dramatically. Today, only about 22% of high school students smoke, down from 36% just 7 years ago.

If you do smoke and want to quit, there's more information and support out there than ever. Different approaches work for different people—for some, quitting cold turkey is best, whereas others find that a slower approach is the way to go. Some people find that it helps to go to a support group especially for teens; these are sometimes sponsored by local hospitals or organizations like the American Cancer Society. And the Internet offers a number of good resources. When quitting, it can be helpful to realize that the first few days are the hardest, and it's normal to have a few relapses before you manage to quit for good.

♣ It's A Fact!!

New research from the Harvard School of Public Health (HSPH) finds that cigarette makers are targeting young smokers with candy and liqueur-flavored new brands that mask the harsh and toxic properties found in tobacco smoke, and in one case, embedding a hidden flavor pellet within the filter. Despite assurances from cigarette makers that they no longer target the youth market, the researchers found that new brands are being marketed to young smokers and racial/ethnic groups using colorful and stylish packaging and exploiting adolescents' attraction to candy flavors. The study appears in the November/December [2005] issue of the journal, *Health Affairs*.

The researchers sifted through a database of more than 7 million internal tobacco industry documents spanning more than 30 years for information on alternative flavors and flavor technology used in the development of products targeting new and younger smokers. Carrie Carpenter, lead author of the study and a research analyst at HSPH stated, "Flavored cigarettes can promote youth smoking initiation and help young occasional smokers to become daily smokers by reducing or masking the natural harshness and taste of tobacco smoke and increasing the acceptability of a toxic product."

A 1993 internal document stated, "Growing interest in new flavor sensations (i.e. soft drinks, snack foods) among younger adult consumers may indicate new opportunities for enhanced-flavor tobacco products that could leverage [a brand's] current strength among younger adult smokers."

Internal research by the tobacco industry showed manufacturers that they could capitalize on youths' attraction to candy flavors. They used innovative product technology, such as a flavor pellet imbedded in one company's cigarette

Staying smoke free will give you a whole lot more of everything—more energy, better performance, better looks, more money in your pocket, and, in the long run, more life to live.

filters, to deliver fruit and liqueur flavors. Some of the flavored cigarettes the companies have developed include: Mandarin Mint, Mocha Taboo, Mintrigue, Kauai Kolada, Margarita Mixer, and others. Fruit and candy flavors were also added to smokeless tobacco products, cigars, and cigarette rolling papers.

Gregory Connolly, senior author of the study and a professor of the practice of public health at HSPH noted, "Tobacco companies are using candy-like flavors and high tech delivery devices to turn a blowtorch into a flavored popsicle, misleading millions of youngsters to try a deadly product. Adding candy flavors to a toxic product (cigarettes) isn't any different than adding sugar to contaminated meat a century ago. The only difference is that today one is regulated by the FDA and the other is not."

Dr. Cheryl Healton, president and CEO of the American Legacy Foundation, a funder of the study, commented, "The public should recognize these products for what they are—a tool to lure younger smokers to their brands, and then potentially to a lifetime of tobacco addiction."

The study, "New Cigarette Brands with Flavors That Appeal to Youth: Tobacco Marketing Strategies; *Health Affairs*, November/December 2005, Volume 24, Number 6, was funded by the American Legacy Foundation and the National Cancer Institute.

Source: This information is from "Internal Documents Show Cigarette Manufacturers Developed Candy-Flavored Brands Specifically to Target Youth Market Despite Promises." Reprinted with permission from the Harvard School of Public Health Office of Communications, © 2005.

Chapter 35

Teens And Tobacco

Cigarette smoking during childhood and adolescence produces significant health problems among young people, including cough and phlegm production, an increase in the number and severity of respiratory illnesses, decreased physical fitness, an unfavorable lipid profile and potential retardation in the rate of lung growth and the level of maximum lung function.

- Tobacco use primarily begins in early adolescence. One-third of all smokers had their first cigarette by the age of 14. Ninety percent of all smokers begin before the age of 21.

- Each day, 6,000 children under 18 years of age smoke their first cigarette. Almost 2,000 of them will become regular smokers—that's 757,000 annually.

- If current tobacco use patterns persist, an estimated 6.4 million children will die prematurely from a smoking-related disease.

- Although smoking rates among high school students increased 32 percent between 1991 and 1997, rates have declined by almost 40% since 1997. In 2003, 22% of high school students were current smokers.

About This Chapter: Information in this chapter is from "Smoking and Teens Fact Sheet." Reprinted with permission © 2005 American Lung Association. For more information about the American Lung Association or to support the work it does, call 1-800-LUNG-USA (1-800-586-4872) or log on to www.lungusa.org.

- In 2002, 10 percent of middle school students smoked.

- After seeing a dramatic increase in teen cigar smoking throughout the 80s and early 90s cigar smoking has declined 30% since 1997. In 2002, 11.6% of high school students and 6 percent of middle school students were current cigar users.

- In 2002, 6.1 percent of all high school students and 3.7% of middle school students used smokeless tobacco. Although smokeless tobacco use previously was uncommon among adolescents, older teens began using it between 1970 and 1985, at the same time that the smokeless tobacco industry was strengthening their marketing efforts.

- Other tobacco products used by high school and middle school students includes pipes (2.6% and 3.5%), bidis (2.6% and 2.4%) and kreteks (2.7% and 2.0%).

- Tobacco use is associated with alcohol and illicit drug use, and acts as a "gateway drug." Adolescents (12–17 year olds) who reported having smoked in the past 30 days were three times more likely to use alcohol, eight times more likely to smoke marijuana, and 22 times more likely to use cocaine, within those past 30 days than those 12–17 year olds who had not smoked during that time.

- Tobacco use in adolescence is also associated with a range of health-compromising behaviors, including being involved in fights, carrying weapons, engaging in high-risk sexual behavior, and using alcohol and other drugs.

✎ What's It Mean?

<u>Bidi:</u> A cigarette made by rolling tobacco by hand in a dried leaf from the tendu tree (a member of the ebony family). Most bidis are made in India and they come in different flavors.

<u>Kretek:</u> A cigarette made of a mixture of tobacco and clove.

Source: "Dictionary of Cancer Terms," National Cancer Institute, U.S. National Institutes of Health, cited December 2005; available online at http://www.cancer.gov.

- People who begin smoking at an early age are more likely to develop severe levels of nicotine addiction than those who start at a later age. Of adolescents who have smoked at least 100 cigarettes in their life-time, most of them report that they would like to quit, but are not able to do so.

- In 2000, 59 percent of high school and 60 percent of middle school students seriously tried to quit smoking.

- Peers, siblings, and friends are powerful influences. The most common situation for first trying a cigarette is with a friend who already smokes.

- Youth who have two parents who smoke are more than twice as likely as youth without smoking parents to become smokers. More than 6 million youth (23 percent) are exposed to secondhand smoke daily, and more than 10 million youth aged 12 to 18 live in a household with at least one smoker.

- A recent survey indicated that among students under 18 years old who were current smokers, 69.4% reported never being asked for proof of age when buying cigarettes in a store and 62.4% were not refused purchase because of their age.

- The 1998 Master Settlement Agreement prohibited tobacco companies from advertising their product in markets that target people younger than 18 years of age. However, this ban has not sufficiently accomplished its intended goal of curtailing tobacco exposure in children.

- Cigarette advertisements tend to emphasize youthful vigor, sexual attraction and independence themes, which appeal to teenagers and young adults struggling with these issues. A recent study found that 34% of teens begin smoking as a result of tobacco company promotional activities.

- Another study found that 52 percent of teens with non-smoking parents started smoking because of exposure to smoking in movies.

Chapter 36

Cigar And Pipe Smoking

Cigars

In recent years, cigars have had something of a "come-back", mainly due to increased promotion through cigar bars, films, and articles in magazines and newspapers. Often these articles have downplayed the serious health risks of cigar smoking, or omitted them altogether—some have even implied that it's safe! This is not true. Cigars are not a safe alternative to cigarettes.

How Do Cigars Differ From Cigarettes?

Cigars consist of filler, binder, and wrapper, which are made of air-cured and fermented tobaccos. Like the tobacco in cigarettes, cigar tobacco, when burnt, produces over 4,000 chemicals. At least 63 of these chemicals are known to cause cancer in animals, including 11 known to cause cancer in humans.

Cigars are different from cigarettes because they contain fermented tobacco. Fermentation is a controlled treatment where the leaves are packed in rooms with high temperatures and humidity for weeks at a time. As a result, cigar smoke contains higher levels of ammonia, nitrogen oxides, carbon monoxide, and cancer-causing compounds, such as nitrosamines. Tar produced by cigars is more carcinogenic than cigarette tar.

About This Chapter: Information in this chapter is excerpted from "Stopping Smoking: Cigars and Pipes," December 2003. Reproduced with permission by Quit Victoria, Australia. To view the complete text, including references, visit http://www.quit.org.au.

Cigar smoke is alkaline (i.e., less acidic than cigarette smoke), and has higher levels of nicotine, which can be more easily absorbed through the lining of the mouth. For this reason, cigar smokers tend not to inhale the smoke into their lungs, as cigarette smokers do.

Smoking Related Disease And Death Rates For Cigar Smokers

Note: "Cigar smokers" refer to people who only smoke cigars and have never smoked cigarettes.

Cigar smokers have higher death rates than non-smokers for most smoking-related diseases. However, cigar smokers generally have lower overall disease and death rates than cigarette smokers.

This is because the level of risk from cigar smoking is related to the following:

- How deeply the smoke is inhaled: Most cigar smokers do not inhale the smoke into their lungs. Instead, they absorb the nicotine through the lining of their mouth.

- How often a person smokes cigars: The majority of cigar smokers smoke occasionally, whereas most cigarette smokers smoke every day.

If a cigar smoker smokes as much tobacco and inhales as deeply as a cigarette smoker, then they have a similar level of risk for smoking-related diseases as a cigarette smoker.

Ex-Cigarette Smokers Who Smoke Cigars

Studies show that smokers who have switched from cigarettes to cigars are more likely to inhale cigar smoke into their lungs. Cigar smokers who inhale are at a much higher risk for all major smoking related diseases.

People Who Smoke Both Cigarettes And Cigars

People who smoke both cigarettes and cigars have high risks for smoking-related diseases, close to that of cigarette only smokers.

The majority of these smokers inhale cigar smoke.

Cigars And Disease

When comparing cigar smokers who have never smoked cigarettes with cigarette smokers, the following is true:

- Cigar smokers have high risks for cancers of the mouth, throat, larynx, and esophagus—similar to cigarette smokers.

- Cigar smokers have lower risks than cigarette smokers for lung cancer, heart disease, emphysema, and chronic bronchitis.

Cigar smoking also causes cancers of the pancreas, stomach, and bladder. A recent study of middle-aged men has linked cigar smoking with erection problems.

♣ It's A Fact!!

Cigar smokers also suffer from higher levels of gum disease and tooth loss than non-smokers. Cigar smoke contains more sulfur than cigarette smoke, so cigar smokers tend to suffer from halitosis (bad breath) more than cigarette smokers.

Are Cigars Addictive?

Cigar smoke contains high levels of nicotine, the addictive drug in tobacco. Nicotine from cigars can reach the brain at a sufficiently rapid rate to produce addiction. This is still true even if the smoke is not inhaled into the lungs.

However, while most cigarette smokers smoke daily, the majority of cigar smokers smoke only occasionally, suggesting that cigars may not be as similarly addictive as cigarettes. Addiction to cigars could also be related to the age at which smoking is started. Research on cigar addiction is still too limited to draw definite conclusions.

In summary, cigars may be addictive.

Cigars And Passive Smoking

Cigar smoke can be a major source of indoor air pollution. When equal amounts of tobacco from cigarettes and cigars are burnt, the smoke from the burning tip of the cigar produces more toxic and cancer causing compounds than cigarette smoke.

Pipes

Pipe tobacco is usually a blend of tobacco. It may contain a large percentage of additives, such as sweeteners. Like cigar smoke, pipe smoke is alkaline.

Pipes And Disease

Note: "Pipe smokers" refer to people who only smoke pipes and have never smoked cigarettes.

Pipe smokers have higher death rates for smoking related disease than non-smokers, but lower death rates than cigarette smokers. The reasons for this are similar to those for cigar smokers: In particular, they tend not to inhale the smoke into their lungs.

When comparing disease rates of pipe smokers who have never smoked cigarettes with cigarette smokers, the following is true:

- Pipe smokers have a higher risk for cancer of the lip than any other tobacco users.

- Pipe smokers have similar risks to cigarette smokers for cancers of the mouth, throat, larynx, and esophagus.

- Pipe smokers have lower risks than cigarette smokers for lung cancer, heart disease, emphysema, and chronic bronchitis. These risks are higher than non-smokers'.

Pipe smoking also causes cancers of the pancreas, stomach, and bladder.

Although there is limited research on pipe smoking, it appears to have similar risks to cigar smoking for contracting smoking-related diseases.

Chapter 37

Hookahs And Tobacco

The practice of smoking tobacco through elaborate water pipes called hookahs emerged centuries ago, in the palaces and harems of the Middle East. But experts say hookahs are now almost as popular in Denver as they are in Damascus, with the current fad for water pipe use growing among U.S. students.

Many young Americans may be attracted to hookahs because they believe smoke that passes through water is somehow filtered and safer, experts add.

Unfortunately, that's just not true.

"The data we have clearly shows that carbon monoxide is present in large amounts in smoke from water pipes, as is nicotine and the compounds we call 'tar,' " said Thomas Eissenberg, a researcher at the Institute for Drug and Alcohol Studies at Virginia Commonwealth University.

"In fact, carcinogen exposure in hookah smoke is equal to, or more than, that found in cigarettes," said Eissenberg, who has published research on the health dangers of the hookah fad in numerous medical journals.

The hookah, also called nargile, is comprised of four parts—the head, where burning charcoal heats a bed of tobacco; the body, through which

inhaled smoke is drawn into the third
section, a water-filled bowl at the
hookah's base, and the hose, a flex-
ible pipe through which the user
inhales the smoke after it has
bubbled through the water.

> ♣ **It's A Fact!!**
> Carbon monoxide is present
> in large amounts in smoke from
> water pipes, as is nicotine
> and tar.

"What you get, then, is smoke that has
been cooled by the water," Eissenberg said. Hookah use is, by its nature, a
very social act, with groups of users often sharing the same pipe.

"Water pipes have been around for centuries, but it looks like they are
making a real comeback," Eissenberg said. "They're making a new appearance in the U.S., but they're also coming back in the Middle East. They've
also shown up in Germany and Brazil, and in Thailand—where they were
recently outlawed."

The exact number of water pipe users in America remains unknown, he
said, but new users typically discover hookahs in local Middle Eastern restaurants or bars, where they can be rented for short-term use.

"Then later they might say, 'Hey, this would be cool for me to have,' and
go to the Internet and buy one. They aren't expensive," Eissenberg said.

While traditional Middle Eastern hookah users tended to favor harsher,
dryer tobacco, American users prefer maassel—sweetened tobacco with
tempting flavors like apple, watermelon, and licorice.

"The upsurge in use of water pipes, here and in the Middle East, is highly
correlated with the mass-production of these sweetened and flavored tobaccos," Eissenberg said.

He stressed that the U.S. hookah fad isn't restricted to fringe populations
in cities such as New York or San Francisco. "Washington state, Louisiana,
Tennessee, here in Virginia—it's popping up everywhere," he said.

While cigarette use has largely fallen out of favor, the exotic allure of
hookahs—and the misperception that hookah smoke is filtered and safer—
may be driving the trend.

"We really need to counter this idea that, just because there's water present, the smoke is safe," Eissenberg said. "We really need to get that across to people."

Legal restrictions might be in order, too, he said. "I suspect that we need to discourage the renting of water pipes, especially to underage individuals. They should be controlled in the same way that cigarettes are controlled."

The real danger, according to Eissenberg, is that hookahs may be getting many young, new users hooked on nicotine.

"Water pipes aren't convenient to use," Eissenberg pointed out. "So if somebody begins to find a water pipe and tobacco pleasurable, but they don't have a lot of time, what are they going to do? They're going to pick up cigarettes. So hookahs are, unfortunately, a potential gateway to smoking for young adults, and we certainly don't need a new gateway to tobacco use."

Dr. Norman H. Edelman, director of scientific affairs for the American Lung Association, said hookah users are taking a big chance if they think water pipes are safe.

"I've seen no data to support that. They're really rolling the dice when it comes to their health," he said.

Even if hookah smoke was somehow filtered, it probably wouldn't make any difference in terms of the actual amount of carcinogens inhaled per puff, Edelman said.

"We saw something similar with filtered cigarettes. Smoking is really all about getting nicotine into the system. So, with filtered cigarettes, people just dragged harder and longer on the cigarette to get the same amount of nicotine," he said.

Eissenberg agreed, adding that the time is now to nip the hookah craze in the bud.

"We don't want to get caught by surprise," he said. "I think we need to be vigilant when it comes to any new tobacco use method that comes into vogue."

Chapter 38

Smokeless Tobacco

You don't smoke it. You don't swallow it. All you do is slosh it around your mouth and spit out the brown juices every few seconds. OK, so it actually is pretty disgusting. But so what? After all, it's called smokeless or chewing tobacco. That means you chew and spit it, not smoke it, so it can't be as bad as inhaling tobacco smoke into your lungs, right?

Wrong. Unfortunately, smokeless doesn't mean harmless. The fact is, chewing tobacco is every bit as dangerous as smoking it.

What is smokeless tobacco?

Smokeless tobacco, also called spit tobacco, chewing tobacco, chew, chaw, dip, plug, and probably a few other things, comes in two forms: snuff and chewing tobacco.

Snuff is a fine-grain tobacco that often comes in teabag-like pouches that users "pinch" or "dip" between their lower lip and gum. Chewing tobacco comes in shredded, twisted, or "bricked" tobacco leaves that users put between their cheek and gum. Whether it's snuff or chewing tobacco, you're

About This Chapter: Information in this chapter is from "Smokeless Tobacco." This information was provided by TeensHealth, one of the largest resources online for medically reviewed health information written for parents, kids, and teens. For more articles like this one, visit www.TeensHealth.org, or www.KidsHealth.org. © 2004 The Nemours Center for Children's Health Media, a division of The Nemours Foundation.

supposed to let it sit in your mouth and suck on the tobacco juices, spitting often to get rid of the saliva that builds up. This sucking and chewing allows nicotine, which is a drug you can become addicted to, to be absorbed into the bloodstream through the tissues in your mouth. You don't even need to swallow.

Where does it come from?

Smokeless tobacco has been around for a long time. Native people of North and South America chewed tobacco, and snorting and chewing snuff was popular in Europe and Scandinavia (the word "snuff" comes from the Scandinavian word "snus").

In the United States, chewing tobacco has long been associated with baseball. Players chewed it to keep their mouths moist, spit it into their gloves to soften them up, and used it to make a "spitball," a special pitch that involved the pitcher dabbing the ball with saliva to cause it to spin off the fingers easily and break sharply. (Spitballs were banned from the sport in 1920.) By the 1950s, chewing tobacco had fallen out of favor in most of America, so by that time not too many baseball players were spitting big brown gobs all over the infield. Instead of chewing their tobacco, most people were smoking it.

But, in the 1970s, people became more aware of the dangers of smoking. Thinking it was a safe alternative to lighting up, baseball players started chewing on their tobacco again. Some players even developed the habit of mixing their chewing tobacco with bubble gum and chewing the whole thing. Gross, huh?

These days, you don't find the majority of professional ballplayers with wads of chaw in their cheeks. But lots of guys and girls, athletes or not, still find time for chewing and spitting.

Who chews?

As many as 20% of high school boys and 2% of high school girls use smokeless tobacco, according to the Centers for Disease Control and Prevention. Of the 12 to 14 million American users, one third are under age 21, and more than half of those developed the habit before they were 13. Peer pressure is just one of the reasons for starting the habit. Serious users often graduate from brands that deliver less nicotine to stronger ones. With each use, you need a little more of the drug to get the same feeling.

So what's the danger?

Just like smoking cigarettes, chewing smokeless tobacco can eventually rip apart your body and kill you. It's that simple, really. There's no such thing as a "safe" tobacco product.

Take Bill Tuttle, for example. An outfielder for the Detroit Tigers, the Kansas City Athletics (before they moved to Oakland), and the Minnesota Twins, Tuttle chewed tobacco for most of his career. In fact, a lot of Tuttle's baseball cards over the years pictured him with a cheek bulging with chewing tobacco. Thirty-eight years after the end of his baseball career, Tuttle had a more ominous bulge in his cheek—a huge tumor that was so big that it came through his cheek and extended through his skin. Doctors removed the tumor, along with much of Tuttle's face. Chewing tobacco as a young man had cost him his jawbone, his right cheekbone, a lot of his teeth and gum line, and his taste buds. Cancer caused by his chewing habit finally claimed him in 1998, but Tuttle spent the rest of his life trying to steer young people, as well as grown athletes, away from smokeless tobacco.

Other baseball players have met a similar fate. Even one of the greatest of all time, Babe Ruth, was fond of dipping and chewing tobacco. He died at age 52 of an oropharyngeal tumor, which is a cancerous tumor in the back part of the throat.

But, of course, it isn't just baseball players who learn to regret their choice to start chewing tobacco. According to the Centers for Disease Control and Prevention, each year, about 30,000 Americans learn they have mouth and throat cancers, and nearly 8,000 Americans die of these diseases. Sadly, only about half of people with diagnosed mouth or throat cancer survive more than 5 years.

What can chewing tobacco do to me?

The more immediate effects can disrupt your social life: bad breath and yellowish-brown stains on your teeth. You'll also get mouth sores (about 70% of spit tobacco users have them). But, it gets a lot more serious than that.

Oral cancer means cancer of the mouth and can happen in the lips, the tongue, the floor of the mouth, the roof of the mouth, the cheeks, or gums. It's been medically proven that long-time use of chewing tobacco can lead to cancer. But cancer from chewing tobacco doesn't just occur in the mouth. Some of the cancer-causing agents in the tobacco can get into the lining of your stomach, your esophagus, and into your bladder.

Quitting The Dipping

If you're a dipper, put some long thought into breaking the habit and quitting now. When you decide to quit, don't do it alone. Tell friends or family and enlist their support. Strategies for breaking the habit include the following:

> ♣ **It's A Fact!!**
>
> Consequences of chewing and spitting tobacco include the following:
>
> - Cracking and bleeding lips and gums
>
> - Receding gums, which can eventually make your teeth fall out
>
> - Increased heart rate, high blood pressure, and irregular heartbeats, all leading to a greater risk of heart attacks and brain damage (from a stroke)
>
> - Cancer

- Using a nicotine gum or a patch (ask your doctor about these options first)

- Planning ahead and using substitutes such as tobacco-free, mint-leaf snuff; sugarless gum; hard candy; beef jerky; sunflower seeds; shredded coconut; raisins; or dried fruit

- Getting involved in healthier activities: lifting weights, shooting baskets, going for a swim, etc.

It's tough to quit, but realize that backsliding is common, so don't give up. Your chances of success increase with each try!

Chapter 39

Secondhand Smoke

What is secondhand smoke?

Secondhand smoke, also called environmental tobacco smoke (ETS), is the combination of two forms of smoke from burning tobacco products: sidestream smoke and mainstream smoke. Sidestream smoke, which makes up about half of all secondhand smoke, comes from the burning end of a cigarette, cigar, or pipe. The smoker exhales mainstream smoke. Exposure to secondhand smoke is also called involuntary smoking or passive smoking.

What chemicals are present in secondhand smoke?

Many factors affect what chemicals are present in secondhand smoke. These factors include the type of tobacco, the chemicals added to the tobacco, how the product is smoked, and the paper in which the tobacco is wrapped. More than 4,000 chemicals have been identified in mainstream tobacco smoke; however, the actual number may be more than 100,000. Of the chemicals identified in secondhand smoke, at least 60 are carcinogens (substances that cause cancer), such as formaldehyde. Six others are substances that interfere with normal cell development, such as nicotine and carbon monoxide.

About This Chapter: Information in this chapter is excerpted from "Secondhand Smoke: Questions and Answers," National Cancer Institute, U.S. National Institutes of Health, February 2005.

Some of the compounds present in secondhand smoke become carcinogenic only after they are activated by specific enzymes (proteins that control chemical reactions) in the body. After these compounds are activated, they can then become part of a cell's DNA and may interfere with the normal growth of cells. In 1993, the U.S. Environmental Protection Agency (EPA) determined that there is sufficient evidence that secondhand smoke causes cancer in humans and classified it as a Group A carcinogen. In 2000, the U.S. Department of Health and Human Services (DHHS) formally listed secondhand smoke as a known human carcinogen in The U.S. National Toxicology Program's 10th Report on Carcinogens.

Scientists do not know what amount of exposure to secondhand smoke, if any, is safe. Because it is a complex mixture of chemicals, measuring secondhand smoke exposure is difficult and is usually determined by testing blood, saliva, or urine for the presence of nicotine, particles inhaled from indoor air, or cotinine (the primary product resulting from the breakdown of nicotine in the body). Nicotine, carbon monoxide, and other evidence of secondhand smoke exposure have been found in the body fluids of nonsmokers exposed to secondhand smoke. Nonsmokers who live with smokers in homes where smoking is allowed are at the greatest risk for suffering the negative health effects of secondhand smoke exposure.

What are the health effects of exposure to secondhand smoke?

Secondhand smoke exposure is a known risk factor for lung cancer. Approximately 3,000 lung cancer deaths occur each year among adult nonsmokers in the United States as a result of exposure to secondhand smoke. Secondhand smoke is also linked to nasal sinus cancer. Some research suggests an association between secondhand smoke and cancers of the cervix, breast, and bladder. However, more research is needed in order to confirm a link to these cancers.

Secondhand smoke is also associated with the following noncancerous conditions:

• Chronic coughing, phlegm, and wheezing

• Chest discomfort

• Lowered lung function

- Severe lower respiratory tract infections, such as bronchitis or pneumonia, in children

- More severe asthma and increased chance of developing asthma in children

- Eye and nose irritation

- Severe and chronic heart disease

- Middle ear infections in children

- Sudden infant death syndrome (SIDS)

- Low birth weight or small size at birth for babies of women exposed to secondhand smoke during pregnancy

Certain other noncancerous health conditions may also be associated with secondhand smoke. However, more research is needed in order to confirm a link between these conditions and secondhand smoke. These conditions include the following:

- Spontaneous abortion (miscarriage)

- Adverse effect on cognition and behavior in children

- Worsening of cystic fibrosis (a disease that causes excessive mucus in the lungs)

What is being done to reduce nonsmokers' exposure to secondhand smoke?

In January 2000, the DHHS launched Healthy People 2010, a comprehensive, nationwide health promotion and disease prevention agenda designed to help improve the health of all people in the United States during the first decade of the 21st century. Several objectives of this program relate to tobacco use and exposure to secondhand smoke, including the goal of reducing the proportion of nonsmokers exposed to secondhand smoke from 65 percent to 45 percent by 2010.

Studies have shown that separating smokers and nonsmokers within the same air space may reduce, but not eliminate, nonsmokers' exposure to secondhand smoke. Individuals can reduce their exposure to secondhand smoke by not allowing smoking in their home or car. Educational, clinical, and policy interventions have also been shown to reduce secondhand smoke exposure. Such policies include adoption of worksite restrictions, passage of clean indoor air laws, and enforcement of smoking restrictions in shared environments.

On the national level, several laws restricting smoking in public places have been passed. For instance, effective January 1, 2005, smoking was banned in all DHHS buildings. In other Federal office buildings, smoking is limited to designated areas. Smoking is also banned on all domestic airline flights and nearly all flights between the United States and foreign destinations. All interstate bus travel is smoke free. Smoking is also prohibited or restricted to specially designated areas on trains traveling within the United States.

Many states and local governments have passed laws prohibiting smoking in public facilities such as schools, hospitals, airports, and bus terminals.

> ☞ **Remember!!**
> **Benefits of a**
> **Smoke-Free Home**
>
> • The health risks associated with secondhand tobacco smoke will be eliminated.
>
> • The house will smell much better.
>
> • Food will taste better.
>
> • Less time will be spent cleaning curtains, walls, windows, and mirrors.
>
> • Insurance rates may be lower.
>
> • Pets will be healthier. Secondhand smoke increases the risk of lung cancer in dogs.
>
> Source: Excerpted from "Secondhand Smoke in Your Home," Centers for Disease Control and Prevention, U.S. Department of Health and Human Services, January 2005.

Some states also require private employers to create policies that protect employees who do not smoke, and several local communities have enacted nonsmokers' rights laws, most of which are stricter than state laws. Although it is still a significant public health concern, nonsmoker exposure to secondhand smoke declined by more than 70 percent from 1988–1991 to 1999–2000. In 1999, nearly 7 out of every 10 U.S. workers reported having a smoke-free policy in their workplace.

Chapter 40

Tobacco And Cancer

Smoking And Cancer In The United States: A Report Of The Surgeon General

- Cancer is the second leading cause of death and was among the first diseases causally linked to smoking.

- Lung cancer is the leading cause of cancer death, and cigarette smoking causes most cases.

- Compared to nonsmokers, men who smoke are about 23 times more likely to develop lung cancer and women who smoke are about 13 times more likely. Smoking causes about 90% of lung cancer deaths in men and almost 80% in women.

- In 2003, an estimated 171,900 new cases of lung cancer occurred and approximately 157,200 people died from lung cancer.

About This Chapter: This chapter begins with "Smoking And Cancer In The United States: A Report Of The Surgeon General," from "The Health Consequences of Smoking: A Report of the Surgeon General," Centers for Disease Control and Prevention, U.S. Department of Health and Human Services, January 2005. "Cigarette Smoking And Cancer," November 2004, "Cigar Smoking And Cancer," March 2000, and "Smokeless Tobacco And Cancer," May 2003, are from the National Cancer Institute, U.S. National Institutes of Health. Reviewed January 2006 by David A. Cooke, M.D., Diplomate, American Board of Internal Medicine.

- The 2004 Surgeon General's report adds more evidence to previous conclusions that smoking causes cancers of the oral cavity, pharynx, larynx, esophagus, lung, and bladder.

- Cancer-causing agents (carcinogens) in tobacco smoke damage important genes that control the growth of cells, causing them to grow abnormally or to reproduce too rapidly.

- Cigarette smoking is a major cause of esophageal cancer in the United States. Reductions in smoking and smokeless tobacco use could prevent many of the approximately 12,300 new cases and 12,100 deaths from esophageal cancer that occur annually.

- The combination of smoking and alcohol consumption causes most laryngeal cancer cases. In 2003, an estimated 3800 deaths occurred from laryngeal cancer.

- In 2003, an estimated 57,400 new cases of bladder cancer were diagnosed and an estimated 12,500 died from the disease.

- For smoking-attributable cancers, the risk generally increases with the number of cigarettes smoked and the number of years of smoking, and generally decreases after quitting completely.

- Smoking cigarettes that have a lower yield of tar does not substantially reduce the risk for lung cancer.

- Cigarette smoking increases the risk of developing mouth cancers. This risk also increases among people who smoke pipes and cigars.

- Reductions in the number of people who smoke cigarettes, pipes, cigars, and other tobacco products or use smokeless tobacco could prevent most of the estimated 30,200 new cases and 7,800 deaths from oral cavity and pharynx cancers annually in the United States.

New Cancers Confirmed By This Report

- The 2004 Surgeon General's report newly identifies other cancers caused by smoking, including cancers of the stomach, cervix, kidney, and pancreas and acute myeloid leukemia.

✎ What's It Mean?

Benzene: Benzene is a colorless liquid formed from both human-made activities and natural processes. Exposure to low levels of benzene can cause eye and skin irritation, drowsiness, dizziness, rapid heartbeat, headaches, nausea, tremors, confusion, and unconsciousness. Exposure to high levels of benzene can cause those symptoms plus vomiting, seizures, irregular heartbeats, coma, and death. [1]

Cervix: The lower, narrow end of the uterus that forms a canal between the uterus and vagina. [2]

Esophagus: The muscular tube through which food passes from the throat to the stomach. [2]

Larynx: The area of the throat containing the vocal cords and used for breathing, swallowing, and talking. Also called the voice box. [2]

Myeloid Leukemia: One form of cancer of the blood-forming tissue, primarily the bone marrow and lymph nodes. [3]

Pancreas: A glandular organ located in the abdomen. It makes pancreatic juices, which contain enzymes that aid in digestion, and it produces several hormones, including insulin. The stomach, intestines, and other organs surround the pancreas. [2]

Pharynx: The hollow tube inside the neck that starts behind the nose and ends at the top of the trachea (windpipe) and esophagus (the tube that goes to the stomach). The pharynx is about 5 inches long, depending on body size. Also called the throat. [2]

Source: [1] "Glossary of Volatile Organic Compounds," Centers for Disease Control and Prevention, U.S. Department of Health and Human Services, cited December 2005; available online at http://www.cdc.gov/nceh/clusters/Fallon/Glossary-VOC.pdf. [2] "Dictionary of Cancer Terms," National Cancer Institute, U.S. National Institutes of Health, cited December 2005; available online at http://www.cancer.gov/dictionary/. [3] "Glossary of Terms," U.S. Environmental Protection Agency, June 2004.

- In 2003, an estimated 22,400 new cases of stomach cancer were diagnosed, and an estimated 12,100 deaths were expected to occur.

- Former smokers have lower rates of stomach cancer than those who continue to smoke.

- For women, the risk of cervical cancer increases with the duration of smoking.

- In 2003, an estimated 31,900 new cases of kidney cancer were diagnosed, and an estimated 11,900 people died from the disease.

- In 2003, an estimated 30,700 new cases of pancreatic cancer were diagnosed, attributing to 30,000 deaths. The median time from diagnosis to death from pancreatic cancer is about 3 months.

- In 2003, approximately 10,500 cases of acute myeloid leukemia were diagnosed in adults.

- Benzene is a known cause of acute myeloid leukemia, and cigarette smoke is a major source of benzene exposure. Among U.S. smokers, 90% of benzene exposures come from cigarettes.

Cigarette Smoking And Cancer

Tobacco use, particularly cigarette smoking, is the single most preventable cause of death in the United States. Cigarette smoking alone is directly responsible for approximately 30 percent of all cancer deaths annually in the United States. Cigarette smoking also causes chronic lung disease (emphysema and chronic bronchitis), cardiovascular disease, stroke, and cataracts. Smoking during pregnancy can cause stillbirth, low birth weight, Sudden Infant Death Syndrome (SIDS), and other serious pregnancy complications. Quitting smoking greatly reduces a person's risk of developing the diseases mentioned, and can limit adverse health effects on the developing child.

What are the effects of cigarette smoking on cancer rates?

Cigarette smoking causes 87 percent of lung cancer deaths. Lung cancer is the leading cause of cancer death in both men and women. Smoking is also responsible for most cancers of the larynx, oral cavity and pharynx, esophagus, and bladder. In addition, it is a cause of kidney, pancreatic, cervical, and stomach cancers, as well as acute myeloid leukemia.

Are there any health risks for nonsmokers?

The health risks caused by cigarette smoking are not limited to smokers. Exposure to secondhand smoke, or environmental tobacco smoke (ETS), significantly increases the risk of lung cancer and heart disease in nonsmokers, as well as several respiratory illnesses in young children. (Secondhand smoke is a combination of the smoke that is released from the end of a burning cigarette and the smoke exhaled from the lungs of smokers.) The U.S. Environmental Protection Agency (EPA), the National Institute of Environmental Health Science's National Toxicology Program, and the World Health Organization's International Agency for Research on Cancer (IARC) have all classified secondhand smoke as a known human carcinogen—a category reserved for agents for which there is sufficient scientific evidence that they cause cancer. The U.S. EPA has estimated that exposure to secondhand smoke causes about 3,000 lung cancer deaths among nonsmokers and is responsible for up to 300,000 cases of lower respiratory tract infections in children up to 18 months of age in the United States each year.

How does exposure to tobacco smoke affect the cigarette smoker?

Smoking harms nearly every major organ of the body. The risk of developing smoking-related diseases, such as lung and other cancers, heart disease, stroke, and respiratory illnesses, increases with total lifetime exposure to cigarette smoke. This includes the number of cigarettes a person smokes each day, the intensity of smoking (i.e., the size and frequency of puffs), the age at which smoking began, the number of years a person has smoked, and a smoker's secondhand smoke exposure.

How would quitting smoking affect the risk of developing cancer and other diseases?

Smoking cessation has major and immediate health benefits for men and women of all ages. Quitting smoking decreases the risk of lung and other cancers, heart attack, stroke, and chronic lung disease. The earlier a person quits, the greater the health benefit. For example, research has shown that people who quit before age 50 reduce their risk of dying in the next 15 years by half compared with those who continue to smoke. Smoking low-yield cigarettes, as compared to cigarettes with higher tar and nicotine, provides no clear benefit to health.

♣ It's A Fact!!
What harmful chemicals are
found in cigarette smoke?

Cigarette smoke contains about 4,000 chemical agents, including over 60 carcinogens. In addition, many of these substances, such as carbon monoxide, tar, arsenic, and lead, are poisonous and toxic to the human body. Nicotine is a drug that is naturally present in the tobacco plant and is primarily responsible for a person's addiction to tobacco products, including cigarettes. During smoking, nicotine is absorbed quickly into the bloodstream and travels to the brain in a matter of seconds. Nicotine causes addiction to cigarettes and other tobacco products that is similar to the addiction produced by using heroin and cocaine.

Source: "Cigarette Smoking And Cancer," National
Cancer Institute, November 2004.

Cigar Smoking And Cancer

What are the health risks associated with cigar smoking?

Scientific evidence has shown that cancers of the oral cavity (lip, tongue, mouth, and throat), larynx, lung, and esophagus are associated with cigar smoking. Furthermore, evidence strongly suggests a link between cigar smoking and cancer of the pancreas. In addition, daily cigar smokers, particularly those who inhale, are at increased risk for developing heart and lung disease.

Like cigarette smoking, the risks from cigar smoking increase with increased exposure. For example, compared with someone who has never smoked, smoking only one to two cigars per day doubles the risk for oral and esophageal cancers. Smoking three to four cigars daily can increase the risk of oral cancers to more than eight times the risk for a nonsmoker, while the chance of esophageal cancer is increased to four times the risk for someone who has never smoked. Both cigar and cigarette smokers have similar levels of risk for oral, throat, and esophageal cancers.

The health risks associated with occasional cigar smoking (less than daily) are not known. About three-quarters of cigar smokers are occasional smokers.

What is the effect of inhalation on disease risk?

One of the major differences between cigar and cigarette smoking is the degree of inhalation. Almost all cigarette smokers report inhaling while the majority of cigar smokers do not because cigar smoke is generally more irritating. However, cigar smokers who have a history of cigarette smoking are more likely to inhale cigar smoke. Cigar smokers experience higher rates of lung cancer, coronary heart disease, and chronic obstructive lung disease than non-smokers, but not as high as the rates for cigarette smokers. These lower rates for cigar smokers are probably related to reduced inhalation.

How are cigars and cigarettes different?

Cigars and cigarettes differ in both size and the type of tobacco used. Cigarettes are generally more uniform in size and contain less than 1 gram of tobacco each. Cigars, on the other hand, can vary in size and shape and can measure more than 7 inches in length. Large cigars typically contain between 5 and 17 grams of tobacco. It is not unusual for some premium cigars to contain the tobacco equivalent of an entire pack of cigarettes. U.S. cigarettes are made from different blends of tobaccos, whereas most cigars are composed primarily of a single type of tobacco (air-cured or dried burley tobacco). Large cigars can take between 1 and 2 hours to smoke, whereas most cigarettes on the U.S. market take less than 10 minutes to smoke.

How are the health risks associated with cigar smoking different from those associated with smoking cigarettes?

Health risks associated with both cigars and cigarettes are strongly linked to the degree of smoke exposure. Since smoke from cigars and cigarettes are composed of many of the same toxic and carcinogenic (cancer causing) compounds, the differences in health risks appear to be related to differences in daily use and level of inhalation.

Most cigarette smokers smoke every day and inhale. In contrast, as many as three-quarters of cigar smokers smoke only occasionally, and the majority do not inhale.

All cigar and cigarette smokers, whether or not they inhale, directly expose the lips, mouth, tongue, throat, and larynx to smoke and its carcinogens.

Holding an unlit cigar between the lips also exposes these areas to carcinogens. In addition, when saliva containing smoke constituents is swallowed, the esophagus is exposed to carcinogens. These exposures probably account for the fact that oral and esophageal cancer risks are similar among cigar smokers and cigarette smokers.

Cancer of the larynx occurs at lower rates among cigar smokers who do not inhale than among cigarette smokers. Lung cancer risk among daily cigar smokers who do not inhale is double that of nonsmokers, but significantly less than the risk for cigarette smokers. However, the lung cancer risk from moderately inhaling smoke from five cigars a day is comparable to the risk from smoking up to one pack of cigarettes a day.

What are the hazards for nonsmokers exposed to cigar smoke?

Environmental tobacco smoke (ETS), also known as secondhand or passive smoke, is the smoke released from a lit cigar or cigarette. The ETS from cigars and cigarettes contains many of the same toxins and irritants (such as carbon monoxide, nicotine, hydrogen cyanide, and ammonia), as well as a number of known carcinogens (such as benzene, nitrosamines, vinyl chloride, arsenic, and hydrocarbons). Because cigars contain greater amounts of tobacco than cigarettes, they produce greater amounts of ETS.

There are, however, some differences between cigar and cigarette smoke due to the different ways cigars and cigarettes are made. Cigars go through a long aging and fermentation process. During the fermentation process, high concentrations of carcinogenic compounds are produced. These compounds are released when a cigar is smoked. Also, cigar wrappers are less porous than cigarette wrappers. The nonporous cigar wrapper makes the burning of cigar tobacco less complete than cigarette tobacco. As a result, compared with cigarette smoke, the concentrations of toxins and irritants are higher in cigar smoke. In addition, the larger size of most cigars (more tobacco) and longer smoking time produces higher exposures to nonsmokers of many toxic compounds (including carbon monoxide, hydrocarbons, ammonia, cadmium, and other substances) than a cigarette. For example, measurements of the carbon monoxide (CO) concentration at a cigar party and a cigar banquet in a restaurant showed indoor CO levels comparable to those measured on a crowded

California freeway. Such exposures could place nonsmoking workers attending such events at significantly increased risk for cancer as well as heart and lung diseases.

Are cigars addictive?

Nicotine is the agent in tobacco that is capable of causing addiction or dependence. Cigarettes have an average total nicotine content of about 8.4 milligrams, while many popular brands of cigars will contain between 100 and 200 milligrams, or as many as 444 milligrams of nicotine.

♣ It's A Fact!!
Addiction studies of cigarettes and spit tobacco show that addiction to nicotine occurs almost exclusively during adolescence and young adulthood when young people begin using these tobacco products.

Source: "Cigar Smoking And Cancer," National Cancer Institute, U.S. National Institutes of Health, March 2000.

As with cigarette smoking, when cigar smokers inhale, nicotine is absorbed rapidly. However, because of the composition of cigar smoke and the tendency of cigar smokers not to inhale, the nicotine is absorbed predominantly through the lining of the mouth rather than in the lung. It is important to note that nicotine absorbed through the lining of the mouth is capable of forming a powerful addiction, as demonstrated by the large number of people addicted to smokeless tobacco. Both inhaled and noninhaled nicotine can be addictive. The infrequent use by the average cigar smoker, low number of cigars smoked per day, and lower rates of inhalation compared with cigarette smokers have led some to suggest that cigar smokers may be less likely to be dependent than cigarette smokers.

Several studies raise the concern that use of cigars may predispose individuals to the use of cigarettes. A recent survey showed that the relapse rate of former cigarette smokers who smoked cigars was twice as great as the relapse rate of former cigarette smokers who did not smoke cigars. The study also observed that cigar smokers were more than twice as likely to take up cigarette smoking for the first time than people who never smoked cigars.

What are the benefits of quitting?

There are many health benefits to quitting cigar smoking. The likelihood of developing cancer decreases. Also, when someone quits, an improvement in health is seen almost immediately. For example, blood pressure, pulse rate, and breathing patterns start returning to normal soon after quitting. People who quit will also see an improvement in their overall quality of life. People who decide to quit have many options available to them. Some people choose to quit all at once. Other options gaining popularity in this country are nicotine replacement products, such as patches, gum, and nasal sprays. If considering quitting, ask your doctor to recommend a plan that could best suit you and your lifestyle.

Smokeless Tobacco And Cancer

What is smokeless tobacco?

There are two types of smokeless tobacco—snuff and chewing tobacco. Snuff, a finely ground or shredded tobacco, is packaged as dry, moist, or in sachets (tea bag-like pouches). Typically, the user places a pinch or dip between the cheek and gum. Chewing tobacco is available in loose leaf, plug (plug-firm and plug-moist), or twist forms, with the user putting a wad of tobacco inside the cheek. Smokeless tobacco is sometimes called "spit" or "spitting" tobacco because people spit out the tobacco juices and saliva that build up in the mouth.

What harmful chemicals are found in smokeless tobacco?

- Chewing tobacco and snuff contain 28 carcinogens (cancer-causing agents). The most harmful carcinogens in smokeless tobacco are the tobacco-specific nitrosamines (TSNAs). They are formed during the growing, curing, fermenting, and aging of tobacco. TSNAs have been detected in some smokeless tobacco products at levels many times higher than levels of other types of nitrosamines that are allowed in foods, such as bacon and beer.

- Other cancer-causing substances in smokeless tobacco include N-nitrosamino acids, volatile N-nitrosamines, benzo(a)pyrene, volatile aldehydes, formaldehyde, acetaldehyde, crotonaldehyde, hydrazine, arsenic, nickel, cadmium, benzopyrene, and polonium–210.

- All tobacco, including smokeless tobacco, contains nicotine, which is addictive. The amount of nicotine absorbed from smokeless tobacco is 3 to 4 times the amount delivered by a cigarette. Nicotine is absorbed more slowly from smokeless tobacco than from cigarettes, but more nicotine per dose is absorbed from smokeless tobacco than from cigarettes. Also, the nicotine stays in the bloodstream for a longer time.

What cancers are caused by or associated with smokeless tobacco use?

- Smokeless tobacco users increase their risk for cancer of the oral cavity. Oral cancer can include cancer of the lip, tongue, cheeks, gums, and the floor and roof of the mouth.

- People who use oral snuff for a long time have a much greater risk for cancer of the cheek and gum than people who do not use smokeless tobacco.

- The possible increased risk for other types of cancer from smokeless tobacco is being studied.

What are some of the other ways smokeless tobacco can harm users' health?

Some of the other effects of smokeless tobacco use include addiction to nicotine, oral leukoplakia (white mouth lesions that can become cancerous), gum disease, and gum recession (when the gum pulls away from the teeth). Possible increased risks for heart disease, diabetes, and reproductive problems are being studied.

Is smokeless tobacco a good substitute for cigarettes?

In 1986, the Surgeon General concluded that the use of smokeless tobacco "is not a safe substitute for smoking cigarettes. It can cause cancer and a number of noncancerous conditions and can lead to nicotine addiction and dependence." Since 1991, the National Cancer Institute has officially recommended that the public avoid and discontinue the use of all tobacco products, including smokeless tobacco. NCI also recognizes that nitrosamines, found in tobacco products, are not safe at any level. The accumulated scientific evidence does not support changing this position.

What about using smokeless tobacco to quit cigarettes?

Because all tobacco use causes disease and addiction, NCI recommends that tobacco use be avoided and discontinued. Several non-tobacco methods have been shown to be effective for quitting cigarettes. These methods include pharmacotherapies such as nicotine replacement therapy and bupropion SR, individual and group counseling, and telephone quit lines.

♣ It's A Fact!!
Who uses smokeless tobacco?

In the United States, the 2000 National Household Survey on Drug Abuse, which was conducted by the Substance Abuse and Mental Health Services Administration, reported the following statistics:

- An estimated 7.6 million Americans age 12 and older (3.4 percent) had used smokeless tobacco in the past month.

- Smokeless tobacco use was most common among young adults ages 18 to 25.

- Men were 10 times more likely than women to report using smokeless tobacco (6.5 percent of men age 12 and older compared with 0.5 percent of women).

People in many other countries and regions, including India, parts of Africa, and some Central Asian countries, have a long history of using smokeless tobacco products.

Source: "Smokeless Tobacco And Cancer," National Cancer Institute, May 2003.

Chapter 41

Smoking And Emphysema

What Is Emphysema?

Emphysema is a condition in which the walls between the alveoli, or air sacs, within the lung lose their ability to stretch and recoil. The air sacs become weakened and break. Elasticity of the lung tissue is lost, causing air to be trapped in the air sacs and impairing the exchange of oxygen and carbon dioxide. Also, the support of the airways is lost, allowing for airflow obstruction.

Symptoms of emphysema include shortness of breath, cough and a limited exercise tolerance. Emphysema and chronic bronchitis frequently co-exist together to comprise chronic obstructive pulmonary disease (COPD). COPD does not include other obstructive lung diseases such as asthma.

What Causes Emphysema?

Cigarette smoking is by far the most common cause of emphysema. Smoking is responsible for approximately 80–90% of deaths due to COPD.

In addition, it is estimated that 100,000 Americans living today were born with a deficiency of a "lung protector" protein known as alpha 1-antitrypsin

About This Chapter: Information in this chapter is from "What Is Emphysema?" Reprinted with permission © 2005 American Lung Association. For more information about the American Lung Association or to support the work it does, call 1-800-LUNG-USA (1-800-586-4872) or log on to www.lungusa.org.

(AAT). Another 25 million Americans carry a single deficient gene that could be passed on to their children.

In the absence of AAT, an inherited form of emphysema called alpha 1-antitrypsin deficiency related emphysema is almost inevitable. Symptoms of AAT deficiency emphysema usually begin between 32 and 41 years of age. Smoking significantly increases the severity of emphysema in AAT-deficient individuals.

How Serious Is Emphysema?

Over 3.1 million Americans have been diagnosed with emphysema, of which 91% were 45 years of age or older. Emphysema rarely occurs in those under 45. Men tend to have higher rates of emphysema. In 2002 the emphysema prevalence rate was 52% higher in males compared to females.

Together with chronic bronchitis and other chronic lower respiratory diseases, excluding asthma, chronic obstructive pulmonary disease (COPD) is the fourth leading cause of death in the U.S. claiming the lives of more than 120,000 Americans.

How Does Emphysema Develop?

Emphysema begins with the destruction of air sacs (alveoli) in the lungs where oxygen from the air is exchanged for carbon dioxide in the blood. The walls of the air sacs are thin and fragile. Damage to the air sacs is irreversible and results in permanent "holes" in the tissues of the lower lungs.

As air sacs are destroyed, the lungs are able to transfer less and less oxygen to the bloodstream, causing shortness of breath. The lungs also lose their elasticity, which is important to keep airways open. The patient experiences great difficulty exhaling.

Emphysema doesn't develop suddenly. It comes on very gradually. Years of exposure to the irritation of cigarette smoke usually precede the development of emphysema.

A person may initially visit the doctor because he or she has begun to feel short of breath during activity or exercise. As the disease progresses, a brief walk can be enough to bring on difficulty in breathing. Some people may have had chronic bronchitis before developing emphysema.

Treatment For Emphysema

Doctors can help persons with emphysema live more comfortably with their disease. The goal of treatment is to provide relief of symptoms and prevent progression of the disease with a minimum of side effects. The doctor's advice and treatment may include:

Quitting smoking: the single most important factor for maintaining healthy lungs.

Bronchodilator drugs (prescription drugs that relax and open air passages in the lungs): may be prescribed to treat emphysema if there is a tendency toward airway constriction or tightening. These drugs may be inhaled as aerosol sprays or taken orally.

Antibiotics: if you have a bacterial infection, such as pneumococcal pneumonia.

Steroids: these may be used for relapses or "acute exacerbations."

Exercise: including breathing exercises to strengthen the muscles used in breathing as part of a pulmonary* rehabilitation program to condition the rest of the body.

*The term "pulmonary" refers to the lungs.

Alpha 1-Proteinase Inhibitor (A1PI): only if a person has AAT deficiency-related emphysema. A1PI is not recommended for those who develop emphysema as a result of cigarette smoking or other environmental factors.

Lung transplantation: a major procedure, which can be effective.

Lung volume reduction surgery: a surgical procedure in which the most severely diseased portions of the lung are removed to allow the remaining lung and breathing muscles to work better. The short-term results are promising but those with severe forms are at higher risk of death. Recently, the Centers for Medicare and Medicaid Services (CMS) announced that they intend to cover

LVRS for people with non-high risk severe emphysema, who meet the criteria stated in the National Emphysema Treatment Trial (NETT). In addition, CMS has decided that LVRS is "reasonable and necessary" only for qualified patients that undergo therapy before and after the surgery. CMS is currently composing accreditation standards for LVRS facilities and will use these standards to determine where the surgery will be covered.

Prevention Of Emphysema

Continuing research is being done to find answers for many questions about emphysema, especially about the best ways to prevent the disease.

Researchers know that quitting smoking can prevent the occurrence and decrease the progression of emphysema. Other environmental controls can also help prevent the disease.

If an individual has emphysema, the doctor will work hard to prevent the disease from getting worse by keeping the patient healthy and clear of any infection. The patient can participate in this prevention effort by following these general health guidelines:

Emphysema is a serious disease. It damages your lungs, and it can damage your heart. See your doctor at the first sign of symptoms.

DON'T SMOKE. The majority of those who get emphysema are smokers. Continued smoking makes emphysema worse, especially for those who have AAT deficiency, the inherited form of emphysema.

Maintain overall good health habits, which include proper nutrition, adequate sleep, and regular exercise to build up your stamina and resistance to infections.

Reduce your exposure to air pollution, which may aggravate symptoms of emphysema. Refer to radio or television weather reports or your local newspaper for information about air quality. On days when the ozone (smog) level is unhealthy, restrict your activity to early morning or evening. When pollution levels are dangerous, remain indoors and stay as comfortable as possible.

Consult your doctor at the start of any cold or respiratory infection because infection can make your emphysema symptoms worse. Ask about getting vaccinated against influenza and pneumococcal pneumonia.

Chapter 42

Smoking And Asthma

Smoking causes asthma, according to new research from Finland.

Scientists studied 521 people aged 21–63 who were newly diagnosed with asthma over a period of two and a half years, comparing them with a control group of 932 people who had no asthma symptoms.

They found that those who were currently smokers were one-third more likely to develop asthma than their non-smoking counterparts. However, ex-smokers were even more at risk, with a 49% greater likelihood of having asthma.

Gender was also a factor, said the researchers, with women who smoked 143% more likely than men to develop asthma symptoms.

Previous studies have examined the links between asthma and smoking, but have been complicated by exposures to other factors such as pet allergens or second-hand smoke, or by the presence of other respiratory conditions such as chronic obstructive pulmonary disease (COPD).

This is the first study to control these other factors and draw conclusions about the effect of being a smoker on developing asthma.

"We know that smoking, both active and passive, makes asthma worse," said Professor Martyn Partridge, Asthma UK's Chief Medical Adviser. "We haven't previously had any evidence that smoking causes asthma, and previous associations have been difficult to interpret because you only have to have a few patients who have smoking induced COPD misclassified as asthma, to skew the results.

"This new research is a carefully carried out study, which has tried very hard to exclude the previous problems with misdiagnosis, and it does suggest a possibility that smoking may be among the numerous lifestyle changes that may have enhanced the risk of adults developing asthma."

♣ It's A Fact!!

Tobacco smoke is an exceptionally aggravating trigger that can worsen asthma symptoms for the nearly 20.3 million people in the United States who suffer from asthma. Quitting smoking should be a priority for people who have asthma, or have family members with asthma, according to the American Academy of Allergy, Asthma and Immunology (AAAAI).

What is asthma?

Asthma is a chronic inflammatory lung disease that blocks air flow of the tubes (airways) that leads air to the lungs. By squeezing the muscles around the airways and causing swelling, inflammation of the inside of the air tubes, and producing excess mucus, the airways become narrower; therefore, more difficult for air to move in and out of the lungs.

How does smoking affect a person's asthma?

Smoking can harm your body in many ways, but it is very harmful to the lungs. The airways in a person with asthma are very sensitive and "twitchy"; therefore, can easily be squeezed down by the smooth muscle that surrounds these tubes. Many things can trigger symptoms such as coughing, wheezing, experiencing chest tightness, and shortness of breath. When a person inhales tobacco smoke whether for personal smoking or passive smoke, these irritating substances can set off an asthma attack.

Source: Excerpted from "No Butts about It; Smoking Makes Asthma Worse." © 2004 American Academy of Allergy, Asthma and Immunology. Reprinted with permission.

Chapter 43

Smoking And Bronchitis

What is bronchitis?

Bronchitis (pronounced: brahn-kite-uss) is an inflammation of the lining of the bronchial tubes, the airways that connect the trachea (windpipe) to the lungs. This delicate, mucus-producing lining covers and protects the respiratory system, the organs and tissues involved in breathing. When a person has bronchitis, it may be harder for air to pass in and out of the lungs than it normally would, the tissues become irritated and more mucus is produced. The most common symptom of bronchitis is a cough.

When you breathe in (inhale), small, bristly hairs near the openings of your nostrils filter out dust, pollen, and other airborne particles. Bits that slip through become attached to the mucus membrane, which has tiny, hair-like structures called cilia (pronounced: sih-lee-uh) on its surface. But sometimes germs get through the cilia and other defense systems in the respiratory tract and can cause illness.

Bronchitis can be acute or chronic. An acute medical condition comes on quickly and can cause severe symptoms, but it lasts only a short time (no longer than a few weeks). Acute bronchitis is most often caused by one of a

About This Chapter: Information in this chapter is from "Bronchitis." This information was provided by TeensHealth, one of the largest resources online for medically reviewed health information written for parents, kids, and teens. For more articles like this one, visit www.TeensHealth.org, or www.KidsHealth.org. © 2004 The Nemours Center for Children's Health Media, a division of The Nemours Foundation.

number of viruses that can infect the respiratory tract and attack the bronchial tubes. Infection by certain bacteria can also cause acute bronchitis. Most people have acute bronchitis at some point in their lives.

Chronic bronchitis, on the other hand, can be mild to severe and is longer lasting—from several months to years. With chronic bronchitis, the bronchial tubes continue to be inflamed (red and swollen), irritated, and produce excessive mucus over time. The most common cause of chronic bronchitis is smoking.

People who have chronic bronchitis are more susceptible to bacterial infections of the airway and lungs, like pneumonia. (In some people with chronic bronchitis, the airway becomes permanently infected with bacteria.) Pneumonia is more common among smokers and people who are exposed to secondhand smoke.

What are the signs and symptoms?

Acute bronchitis often starts with a dry, annoying cough that is triggered by the inflammation of the lining of the bronchial tubes. Other symptoms may include the following:

- Cough that may bring up thick white, yellow, or greenish mucus

- Headache

- Generally feeling ill

- Chills

- Fever (usually mild)

- Shortness of breath

- Soreness or a feeling of tightness in the chest

> **♣ It's A Fact!!**
> Tobacco smoke is the cause of more than 80% of all cases of chronic bronchitis. People who smoke also have a much harder time recovering from acute bronchitis and other respiratory infections.

- Wheezing (a whistling or hissing sound with breathing)

Chronic bronchitis is most common in smokers, although people who have repeated episodes of acute bronchitis sometimes develop the chronic condition. Except for chills and fever, a person with chronic bronchitis has a chronic productive cough and most of the symptoms of acute bronchitis, such as shortness of breath and chest tightness, on most days of the month, for months or years.

A person with chronic bronchitis often takes longer than usual to recover from colds and other common respiratory illnesses. Wheezing, shortness of breath, and cough may become a part of daily life. Breathing can become increasingly difficult.

In people with asthma, bouts of bronchitis may come on suddenly and trigger episodes in which they have chest tightness, shortness of breath, wheezing, and difficulty exhaling (breathing out). In a severe episode of asthmatic bronchitis, the airways can become so narrowed and clogged that breathing is very difficult.

What causes bronchitis?

Viruses usually cause acute bronchitis, and it may occur together with or following a cold or other respiratory infection. Coughing can spread germs such as viruses from person to person. They can also be spread if you touch your mouth, nose, or eyes after coming into contact with respiratory fluids from an infected person.

Smoking (even for a brief time) and being around tobacco smoke, chemical fumes, and other air pollutants for long periods of time puts a person at risk for developing chronic bronchitis.

Some people who seem to have repeated bouts of bronchitis—with coughing, wheezing, and shortness of breath—may actually have asthma.

What do doctors do?

If a doctor thinks you may have bronchitis, he or she will examine you and listen to your chest with a stethoscope for signs of wheezing and congestion.

In addition to this physical examination, the doctor will ask you about any concerns and symptoms you have, your past health, your family's health, any medications you're taking, any allergies you may have, and other issues including if you smoke. This is called the medical history. Your doctor may order a chest x-ray to rule out a condition like pneumonia, and may sometimes order a breathing test (called spirometry) to rule out asthma.

Because acute bronchitis is most often caused by a virus, the doctor may not prescribe an antibiotic (antibiotics only work against bacteria, not viruses).

The doctor will recommend that you drink lots of fluids, get plenty of rest, and may suggest using an over-the-counter or prescription cough medicine to relieve your symptoms as you recover.

In some cases, the doctor may prescribe a bronchodilator (pronounced: bronko-dy-lay-ter) or other medication typically used to treat asthma. These medications are often given through inhalers or nebulizer machines and help to relax and open the bronchial tubes and clear mucus so it's easier to breathe.

If you have chronic bronchitis, the goal is to reduce your exposure to whatever is irritating your bronchial tubes. For people who smoke, that means quitting! Quitting can be hard, of course.

If you have bronchitis and don't smoke, try to avoid exposure to secondhand smoke.

Smoking And Bronchitis

Smoking causes lung damage in many ways. For example, it can cause temporary paralysis of the cilia and over time kills the ciliate airway lining cells completely. Eventually, the airway lining stops clearing smoking-related debris, irritants, and excess mucus from the lungs altogether. When this happens, a smoker's lungs become even more vulnerable to infection. Over time, harmful substances in tobacco smoke permanently damage the airways, increasing the risk for emphysema, cancer, and other serious lung diseases. Smoking also causes the mucus-producing glands to enlarge and make more mucus. Along with the toxic particles and chemicals in smoke, this causes a smoker to have a chronic cough.

What's the best way to avoid getting bronchitis? Washing your hands often helps to prevent the spread of many of the germs that cause the condition—especially during cold and flu season. If you don't smoke, don't ever start smoking—and if you do smoke, try to quit or cut down. Try to avoid being around smokers because even secondhand smoke can make you more susceptible to viral infections and increase congestion in your airway. Also, be sure to get plenty of rest and eat right so that your body can fight off any illnesses that you come in contact with.

Chapter 44

You Can Quit Smoking

First, congratulate yourself. Just reading this chapter is a great first step toward becoming tobacco free. Many people don't quit smoking because they think that it's too much trouble—or too difficult. They think they'll quit someday, and they keep on smoking.

Quitting isn't easy. After all, the nicotine in cigarettes is a powerfully addictive drug. But there are lots of good reasons to quit:

- Smoking is the number one preventable cause of death in the United States. Nearly one in five deaths in this country is related to tobacco. By quitting, you'll significantly lower the chance that you'll get cancer. It will be highly likely that you'll live a lot longer—and in better health.

- It's expensive. If you smoke a pack a day, it can cost you more than $2,000 a year. You'll be able to save the money you spend on tobacco to buy yourself a closet full of clothes, a bike, or put a down payment on a car!

- It turns your teeth yellow and it makes your breath, hair, and clothes stink.

About This Chapter: Information in this chapter is from "How Can I Quit Smoking?" This information was provided by TeensHealth, one of the largest resources online for medically reviewed health information written for parents, kids, and teens. For more articles like this one, visit www.TeensHealth.org, or www.KidsHealth.org. © 2003 The Nemours Center for Children's Health Media, a division of The Nemours Foundation.

- Smoking keeps athletes from reaching their peak performance because smokers get short of breath more easily. Being smoke-free will help improve your athletic abilities.

- Nonsmokers might not want to be around people while they're smoking, so smokers can miss out on spending time with potential friends, girlfriends, or boyfriends. And because many places don't allow smoking, smokers often have to stand outside while everyone else is inside. When you quit smoking, you'll have more freedom to go where you want—when you want.

Why is it hard to quit? Quitting can be tough—at least for many people. Smokers may have started smoking because their friends did or because it seemed cool. But they keep on smoking because they're addicted to nicotine, one of the chemicals in cigarettes and smokeless tobacco. Nicotine is both a stimulant and a depressant. That means nicotine increases the heart rate at first and makes people feel more alert (like caffeine, another stimulant). Then it causes depression and fatigue. The depression and fatigue—and the drug withdrawal from nicotine—make people crave another cigarette to perk up again. According to many experts, the nicotine in tobacco is as addictive as cocaine or heroin. But don't be discouraged; about 44 million Americans have already quit smoking for good. These strategies can help you quit, too:

Get support. Teens whose friends and family help them quit are much more likely to succeed. If you don't want to tell your parents or family that you smoke, make sure your friends know, and consider confiding in a counselor or other adult you trust. And if you're having a hard time finding people to support you (if, say, all your friends smoke and none of them is interested in quitting), you might consider joining a support group, either in person or online.

Set a quit date. You should pick a day that you'll stop smoking. Tell your friends (and your family, if they know you smoke) that you're going to quit smoking on that day. Just think of that day as a dividing line between the smoking you and the new and improved nonsmoker you'll become. Mark it on your calendar.

♣ It's A Fact!!
Five Common Myths About Quitting Smoking

Myth 1: Smoking is just a bad habit.

Fact: Tobacco use is an addiction. Nicotine is a very addictive drug. For some people, it can be as addictive as heroin or cocaine.

Myth 2: Quitting is just a matter of willpower.

Fact: Because smoking is an addiction, quitting is often very difficult. A number of treatments are available that can help.

Myth 3: If you can't quit the first time you try, you will never be able to quit.

Fact: Quitting is hard. Usually people make two or three tries, or more, before being able to quit for good.

Myth 4: The best way to quit is "cold turkey."

Fact: The most effective way to quit smoking is by using a combination of counseling and nicotine replacement therapy (such as the nicotine patch, inhaler, gum, or nasal spray) or non-nicotine medicines (such as bupropion SR). Your health care provider or smoking cessation clinic is the best place to go to for help with quitting.

Myth 5: Quitting is expensive.

Fact: Treatments cost from $3 to $10 a day. A pack-a-day smoker spends more than $2000 per year. Check with your health insurance plan to find out if smoking cessation medications and/or counseling are covered.

Source: Office of the Surgeon General, U.S. Department of Health and Human Services, March 2001. Updated January 2006 by David A. Cooke, M.D., Diplomate, American Board of Internal Medicine.

Throw away your cigarettes—all of your cigarettes. People can't stop smoking with cigarettes around to tempt them, so you should trash all your cigarettes—even that emergency pack you have stashed in the secret pocket of your backpack. Get rid of your ashtrays and lighters, too. This way, you'll make it a little bit harder to smoke.

Wash all your clothes. Get rid of the smell of cigarettes as much as you can by washing all your clothes and having your coats or sweaters dry-cleaned. If you smoked in your car, clean that out, too.

Getting Ready To Quit   ✔ Quick Tip

- Set a quit date.

- Get rid of all cigarettes and ashtrays in your home, car, and at work.

- Do not let people smoke in your home and car.

Get Medicine To Help You Quit

- Buy nicotine gum or nicotine patches at a drug store. You can ask your pharmacist for more information.

- Ask your doctor about other medicines that can help you such as nicotine nasal spray, a nicotine inhaler, or bupropion SR (pill).

Get Support

- Tell your family, friends, and people you work with that you are going to quit. Ask for their support.

- Talk to your doctor, nurse, or other health care worker. They can help you quit.

- Get together with other people who are trying to quit, or call a hotline.

Stay Quit

- Avoid being around smoking.

- Eat healthy food and get exercise.

- Keep a positive attitude.

Source: Excerpted from "Good Information for Smokers," Office of the Surgeon General, U.S. Department of Health and Human Services, March 2003.

Think about your triggers. You've probably smoked a lot of cigarettes since you started smoking, and you're aware of the situations when you tend to smoke, such as after you eat meals, when you're at your best friend's house, while drinking coffee after the movies, or as you're driving. These situations are your triggers for smoking—it feels automatic to have a cigarette when you're in them. Once you've figured out your triggers, you can make sure they don't block you from quitting smoking. Try these tips:

- Avoid these situations. For example, if you smoke when you drive, get a ride to school, walk, or take the bus for a few weeks. If you normally smoke after meals, make it a point to do something else, like read or call a friend.

- Change the place. If you and your friends usually smoke in restaurants or get takeout and eat in the car, suggest that you sit in the no-smoking section the next time you go out to eat.

- Substitute something else for cigarettes. It can be hard to get used to not holding something and having something in your mouth. If you have this problem, stock up on carrot sticks, gum, mints, toothpicks, or even sugar-free lollipops.

Expect some physical symptoms. If you smoke regularly, you're probably physically addicted to nicotine and your body may experience some symptoms of withdrawal when you quit. These symptoms may include the following:

- Headaches or stomachaches
- Crabbiness, jumpiness, or depression
- Lack of energy
- Dry mouth or sore throat
- Desire to pig out

The good news is that these symptoms of nicotine withdrawal will pass—so be patient and don't give in and sneak a smoke, or you'll just have to deal with the symptoms longer.

Keep yourself busy. Many people find it's best to quit on a Monday, when they have school or work to keep them busy. The more distracted you are, the less likely you'll be to crave cigarettes. Staying active is also a good way to make sure you keep your weight down and your energy up, even as you're experiencing the symptoms of nicotine withdrawal.

Quit gradually. Some people find that gradually decreasing the number of cigarettes that they smoke each day is an effective way to quit. (This strategy doesn't work for everyone—you may find you have to quit cold turkey.)

Use a nicotine replacement if you need to. If you find that none of these strategies is working, you might talk to your doctor about treatments. Using a nicotine replacement, such as gum, patches, inhalers, or nasal sprays, can be very helpful. Sprays and inhalers are available by prescription only, and it's important to see your doctor before buying the patch and gum over the counter. That way, your doctor can help you find the solution that will work best for you. For example, the patch requires the least effort on your part, but it doesn't offer the almost instantaneous nicotine kick that gum does.

If you slip up, don't give up! Major changes sometimes have false starts. If you're like many people, you may quit successfully for weeks or even months and then suddenly have a craving that's so strong you feel like you have to give in. Or maybe you accidentally find yourself in one of your trigger situations and give in to temptation. If you slip up, it doesn't mean you've failed, it just means you're human. Here are some ways to get back on track:

- Think about your slip as one mistake. Take notice of when and why it happened and move on.

- Did you become a heavy smoker after one cigarette? We didn't think so— it happened more gradually, over time. Keep in mind that one cigarette didn't make you a smoker to start with; so smoking one cigarette (or even two or three) after you've quit doesn't make you a smoker again.

- Remind yourself why you've quit and how well you've done—or have someone in your support group, family, or friends do this for you.

Reward yourself. Hey, quitting smoking isn't easy. Give yourself a reward! Set aside the money you usually spend on cigarettes. When you've stayed tobacco free for a week, 2 weeks, or a month, buy yourself a treat, such as a new CD, book, or some clothes. And every smoke-free year, celebrate again. You deserve it.

Chapter 45

You Can Control Your Weight As You Quit Smoking

Many people gain weight when they quit smoking. Even so, the best action you can take to improve your health is to quit smoking. Focus on stopping smoking first. Then you can continue to improve your health in other ways. These may include reaching and staying at a healthy weight for life.

Gain Weight After Quitting Smoking

Not everyone gains weight when they stop smoking. Among people who do, the average weight gain is between 6 and 8 pounds. Roughly 10 percent of people who stop smoking gain a large amount of weight—30 pounds or more.

When smokers quit, they may gain weight for a number of reasons. These include the following:

- **Feeling hungry:** Quitting smoking may make a person feel hungrier than usual. This feeling usually goes away after several weeks.

- **Having more snacks and alcoholic drinks:** Some people eat more high-fat, high-sugar snacks and drink more alcoholic beverages after they quit smoking.

About This Chapter: Information in this chapter is from "You Can Control Your Weight as You Quit Smoking," Weight-control Information Network, an information service of the National Institute of Diabetes and Digestive and Kidney Diseases (NIDDK), National Institutes of Health (NIH), NIH Publication No. 03-4159, May 2003.

- **Burning calories at normal rate again:** Smoking cigarettes makes the body burn calories faster. After quitting smoking, the body's normal rate of burning calories returns. When calories are burned more slowly again, weight gain may take place.

Avoiding Weight Gain

To help yourself gain only a small amount or no weight when you stop smoking, try to do the following:

- Accept yourself.

- Get regular moderate-intensity physical activity.

- Limit snacking and alcohol.

- Consider using medication to help you quit.

Get Regular Moderate-Intensity Physical Activity

Regular physical activity may help you avoid large weight gains when you quit smoking. It may help you look and feel good, and fit into your clothes better. You will likely find that you can breathe easier during physical activity after you quit smoking.

> ### ✔ Quick Tip
> ### Accept Yourself
>
> Do not worry about gaining a few pounds. Instead, feel proud that you are helping your health by quitting smoking. Stopping smoking may make you feel better about yourself in many ways.
>
> Stopping smoking may help you have the following:
>
> - More energy
>
> - Whiter teeth
>
> - Fresher breath and fresher smelling clothes and hair
>
> - Fewer wrinkles and healthier-looking skin
>
> - A clearer voice

Try to get 30 minutes or more of moderate-intensity physical activity on most days of the week, preferably every day. The ideas below may help you to be active every day.

Here are some ideas for being active every day:

- Take a walk after dinner.

- Sign up for a class such as dance or yoga. Ask a friend to join you.

- Get off the bus one stop early if you are in an area safe for walking.

- Park the car farther away from entrances to stores, movie theatres, or your home.

- Take the stairs instead of the elevator. Make sure the stairs are well lit.

Limit Snacking

Having more high-fat, high-sugar snacks may lead to large weight gains when you quit smoking. The following ideas may help you make healthy eating and drinking choices as you quit smoking:

- Do not go too long without eating. Being very hungry can lead to less healthy food choices.

- Eat enough at meal times to satisfy you.

- Choose healthy snacks, such as fresh fruit or canned fruit packed in juice (not syrup), air-popped popcorn, or fat-free yogurt, when you are hungry between meals.

- Do not deny yourself an occasional "treat." If you crave ice cream, enjoy a small cone.

- Choose an herbal tea, hot cocoa made with nonfat milk, or sparkling water. [Note: Teens should not drink alcoholic beverages, and they are high in calories.]

Weight Gain And Health Risks

A small—or even large—weight gain will not hurt your health as much as continuing to smoke will. The health risks of smoking are dramatic. Some of the risks are as follows:

- **Death:** Tobacco use is the leading cause of preventable death in the United States. It kills more than 400,000 people in the U.S. each year.

- **Cancer:** Smoking greatly increases the risk for lung cancer, the leading cause of cancer death in the U.S. Smoking is also linked to cancer of the esophagus, larynx, kidney, pancreas, and cervix.

- **Other Health Problems:** Smoking increases the risk for lung disease and heart disease. In pregnant women, smoking is linked to premature birth and low birth weight babies.

By quitting smoking, you are taking a big step to improve your health. Instead of worrying about weight gain, focus on quitting. Once you are tobacco-free, you can work toward having a healthy weight for life by becoming more physically active and choosing healthier foods.

Part Five

Other Drug-Related Health Concerns

Chapter 46

Drug Abuse And Mental Illness

What is the relationship between drug abuse and mental illness?

Many chronic drug abusers—the individuals we commonly regard as addicts—often simultaneously suffer from a serious mental disorder. Drug treatment and medical professionals call this condition a co-occurring disorder or a dual diagnosis.

What is chronic drug abuse?

Chronic drug abuse is the habitual abuse of licit or illicit drugs to the extent that the abuse substantially injures a person's health or substantially interferes with his or her social or economic functioning. Furthermore, any person who has lost the power of self-control over the use of drugs is considered a chronic drug abuser.

What are some serious mental disorders associated with chronic drug abuse?

Chronic drug abuse may occur in conjunction with any mental illness identified in the American Psychiatric Association (DSM-IV). Some common serious mental disorders associated with chronic drug abuse include

About This Chapter: Information in this chapter is from "Drug Abuse and Mental Illness Fast Facts," National Drug Intelligence Center, a component of the United States Department of Justice, Product No. 2004-L0559-005, April 2004.

schizophrenia, bipolar disorder, manic depression, attention deficit hyperactivity disorder (ADHD), generalized anxiety disorder, obsessive-compulsive disorder, post-traumatic stress disorder, panic disorder, and antisocial personality disorder. Some of these disorders carry with them an increased risk of drug abuse.

Table 46.1. Disorders With Increased Risk of Drug Abuse

Disorder	Risk
Antisocial personality disorder	15.5%
Manic episode	14.5%
Schizophrenia	10.1%
Panic disorder	04. 3%
Major depressive episode	04.1%
Obsessive-compulsive disorder	03.4%
Phobias	02.1%

Source: National Institute of Mental Health.

How prevalent are co-occurring disorders?

Co-occurring disorders are very common. In 2002 an estimated 4.0 million adults met the criteria for both serious mental illness and substance dependence or abuse in the past year.

Which occurs first—chronic drug abuse or serious mental illness?

It depends. In some cases, people suffering from serious mental disorders (often undiagnosed ones) take drugs to alleviate their symptoms—a practice known as self-medicating. According to the American Psychiatric Association, individuals with schizophrenia sometimes use substances such as marijuana to mitigate the disorder's negative symptoms (depression, apathy, and social withdrawal), to combat auditory hallucinations and paranoid delusions, or to lessen the adverse effects of their medication, which can include depression and restlessness.

In other cases mental disorders are caused by drug abuse. For example, MDMA (3,4-methylenedioxymethamphetamine, commonly known as ecstasy), produces long-term deficits in serotonin function in the brain, leading to mental disorders such as depression and anxiety.

Finally, chronic substance abuse and serious mental disorders may exist completely independently of one another.

Can people with co-occurring disorders be treated effectively?

Yes, chronic drug abusers who also suffer from mental illness can be treated. Researchers currently are investigating the most effective way to treat drug abusers with mental illness, and especially whether or not treating both conditions simultaneously leads to better recovery. Currently, the two conditions often are treated separately or without regard to each other. As a result, many individuals with co-occurring disorders are sent back and forth between substance abuse and mental health treatment settings.

♣ It's A Fact!!

Chronic drug abuse by adolescents during formative years is a particular concern because it can interfere with normal socialization and cognitive development and thus frequently contributes to the development of mental disorders.

Chapter 47

Substance Abuse And Suicide

Sadness, despair, and depression are prevalent problems among alcoholics and addicts. It can be difficult to differentiate the clinical syndrome of major depressive disorder from the emotional turbulence of addiction for any of the following reasons:

- Many drugs themselves are depressants, including alcohol, sedatives, and minor tranquilizers.

- Alcohol or drugs may provide a chemical cushion or buffer to ward off the emotional impact of everyday events. Without the drug, a person experiences feelings again, some painful, that the person may misidentify as abnormal.

- Many apparent symptoms of depression appear during normal withdrawal from drugs. For example, cocaine addicts typically experience a "crash" three to five days after their last use.

- The normal course of addiction may have brought about many tragedies (divorce, loss of custody of children, fatal car accidents) that cause intense but normal grief.

About This Chapter: Information in this chapter is from "Research Update—Depression, Suicide, and Addiction," March 2000. Copyright 2000 Hazelden Foundation. Reprinted by permission of Hazelden Foundation, Center City, MN.

• Loss of the relationship with the drug of choice causes grief. Alcohol or other drugs often becomes a "best friend" that is always there to provide solace and relief.

Prevalence Of Depression

Most research suggests that the rate of major depressive disorder is 2–4 times higher among alcoholics and addicts than in the general population, with rates of about 30%–40% among people seeking help for alcohol and drug problems.[1,2] The correspondence is higher between dependence and depression (as opposed to abuse) and higher for drugs other than alcohol.[3] The association between depression and alcohol/drug problems increases with age.[3]

As in the general population, the rate of depression among female alcoholics and addicts is about twice as high as in males.[4] There seems to be an especially large overlap between addiction and bipolar illness (or manic depressive disorder), with the rate of bipolar illness three times higher in treatment populations (3% vs. 1%).[2]

♣ It's A Fact!!

"An independent major mood disorder requires long-term antidepressant and/or cognitive behavioral therapies, whereas a medication-induced or an alcohol-induced mood disorder is likely to remit much more rapidly with little evidence that antidepressant medications alleviate the syndrome faster than the passage of time."[2]

Source: "Research Update—Depression, Suicide, and Addiction," March 2000. Copyright 2000 Hazelden Foundation. Reprinted by permission of Hazelden Foundation, Center City, MN.

Depression In Treatment And Recovery

Careful differential diagnosis is critical. A study that tracked depressive symptoms in alcoholic men during alcohol treatment found that, while 67% of alcoholics with a primary diagnosis of depression remained depressed four weeks later, none of the alcoholics with a secondary diagnosis of depression showed symptoms of depression.[5] In this study, primary and secondary referred to the timing of the disorders. If depression preceded alcoholism, it was likely to remain even after sobriety; if the alcoholism came first, depression was likely to subside. In actual practice it is difficult at best to differentiate between primary and secondary depression. While this study had a small sample size, the results of this study do suggest that there is no "one size fits all" approach to depression.

Typically, depression in alcoholism or addiction is treated with psychotherapy and, often, antidepressants. Studies have demonstrated that antidepressant therapy is effective in reducing depression among alcoholics.[2] The use of antidepressants is understood and supported by Alcoholics Anonymous.[6] However, it is important that medication is part of the treatment plan (and not a replacement for it), and does not supplant the work of recovery.[7]

Results of outcome studies provide no definitive answers about the effect of depression on the course of alcoholism or addiction. Some studies show worse outcomes, some show no effect, and some, remarkably, show better outcomes.[8] It may be that results differ according to the validity or homogeneity of the diagnosis of depression, and the extent to which depression is treated during the alcohol/drug treatment episode.

Suicide, Depression, And Addiction

Suicide is a tragic consequence of depression. Suicide is the eighth leading cause of death for all Americans, and is the third leading cause of death for young people aged 15–24.[9] Suicide rates are higher among men than women.

✤ It's A Fact!!

Antidepressants are an acceptable and effective treatment method for depression. Cognitive behavioral psychotherapy and some lifestyle changes are effective treatment methods for depression as well.[7,17] Some alcoholics and addicts may prefer to first try non-medication methods to treat their depression. However, it is a mistake to go to the opposite extreme, avoiding the use of antidepressants in the face of serious, unremitting depression.

Source: "Research Update—Depression, Suicide, and Addiction," March 2000. Copyright 2000 Hazelden Foundation. Reprinted by permission of Hazelden Foundation, Center City, MN.

♣ It's A Fact!!

Alcoholics and addicts with depression need longer-term assessment, treatment, and continuing care. The interaction of the two disorders is complex in that one may mask the other, and during the recovery phase, relapse of one may trigger relapse to the other. Both disorders need to be addressed, together, over an extended time period.

Depression may prevent a person from establishing a stable recovery from addiction. Any alcoholic or addict who remains depressed after becoming sober should seek help; being depressed is not a sign of weakness or of not working the Twelve Step program well enough. Suicide risk needs to be carefully monitored.

Source: "Research Update—Depression, Suicide, and Addiction," March 2000. Copyright 2000 Hazelden Foundation. Reprinted by permission of Hazelden Foundation, Center City, MN.

A history of alcohol/drug use disorders is a major risk factor for suicide.[10] In a variety of studies, unemployment, interpersonal loss, hopelessness, recent physical illness, family history of alcoholism, and childhood trauma have appeared in various combinations as additional risk factors.[11] It is generally agreed, however, that "the combination of depression and alcohol use disorders is particularly lethal, conferring a higher risk of suicide than any other clinical or demographic predictor."[12] Suicide attempts may be associated with higher addiction severity and use of more substances.[12]

Aaron T. Beck,[14] a major researcher in the field of depression, did a series of studies examining the relationship between suicide and addiction. Overall, he found alcoholics who completed suicide had a higher degree of hopelessness, lethality, and the intent not to be discovered during their plans. A study of the blood alcohol levels of people who completed suicides also shows the connection between alcoholism and suicide: A review of 19,347 deaths from 331 medical examiner reports from 1975 to 1995 found that almost one-fourth (22.7%) were determined to have been intoxicated at the time of death.[15]

Early sobriety is a high-risk time for suicide, in that individuals may be more cognitively clear and capable of carrying out suicidal thoughts than they were during the active phase of their addiction.[1]

References

1. Rosenthal, R.N., and Westrich, L. (1999). Treatment of persons with dual diagnoses of substance use disorder and other psychological problems. In B.S. McCrady and E.E. Epstein, (eds.) *Addiction: A comprehensive guidebook.* New York: Oxford University Press. 2. Raimo, E.B. and Schuckit, M.A. (1999). Alcohol dependence and mood disorders. *Addictive Behaviors.* 23, 933-946. 3. Grant, F.F. and Dawson, D.A. (1999). Alcohol and drug use, abuse and dependence: Classification, prevalence, and comorbidity. In B.S. McCrady and E.E. Epstein, (eds.) *Addiction: A comprehensive guidebook.* New York: Oxford University Press. 4. Regier, D.A., Farmer, M.E., Rae, S.S. et al. (1990). Comorbidity of mental disorders with alcohol and other drug abuse: results from the Epidemiologic Catchment Area (ECA) Study. *Journal of the American Medical Association,* 264, 2511-2518. 5. Brown, S.A., Inaba, R.K., Gillin, J.C. et al. (1995). Alcoholism and affective disorder: Clinical course of depressive symptoms. *American Journal of Psychiatry,* 152,45–52. 6. Alcoholics Anonymous, (1995) The forgotten chapter: Alcoholism and mental illness. Grapevine, March, 5–13. 7. DeRubeis, R.J., Gelfand, L.A., Tang, T.Z. et al. (1999). Medications versus cognitive behavioral therapy for severely depressed outpatients: Mega-analysis of four randomized comparisons. *American Journal of Psychiatry,* 156, 1007–1013. 8. Gastfriend, D.R. (1993). Pharmacotherapy of psychiatric syndromes with comorbid chemical dependency. *Journal of addictive Disease,* 12, 155–170. 9. Charney, D.A. Paraherakis, A.M. et al. (1998). Impact of depression on the outcome of addictions treatment. *journal of Substance Abuse Treatment,* 15:123–130. 10. Centers for Disease Control and Prevention, Suicide in the United States. www.cdc.gov/nipc/factsheets/suifacts.htm. Review date 1/28/00. 11. Grant, B.F., and Hasin, D.S. (1999). Suicidal ideation among the United States drinking population. *Journal of Studies on Alcohol,* 60, 422–429. 12. Kingree, J.B. Thompson, M.P., and Kaslow, N.J. (1999). Risk factors for suicide attempts among low-income women with a history of alcohol problems. *Addictive Behaviors,* 24:583–587. 13. Mueller, T.I. (1999). Depression and alcohol use disorders: Is the road twice as long or twice as steep? *Harvard Review of Psychiatry,* 7 (1): 51–53. 14. O'Boyle, M., and Brandon,

E. (1998). Suicide attempts, substance abuse, and personality. *Journal of Substance Abuse Treatment*, 15, 353–356. **15.** Beck, A.T., Steer, R.A., and Kovacs, M. et al. (1985). Hopelessness and eventual suicide: A 10-year prospective study of patients hospitalized with suicidal ideation. *American Journal of Psychiatry*, 142, 559–563. Beck, A.T., Steer, R.A., and Trexler, L.D. (1989). Alcohol abuse and eventual

♣ It's A Fact!!
Substance Use And The Risk Of Suicide Among Youths

The National Household Survey on Drug Abuse (NHSDA) asks youths aged 12 to 17 whether they had thought seriously about killing themselves or tried to kill themselves during the 12 months before the survey interview. For the purpose of this report, youths who thought about or tried to kill themselves during the past year were considered to be at risk for suicide. Geographic regions analyzed responses for comparative purposes.

Respondents were also queried about their use of alcohol and illicit drugs during the 12 months before the survey interview. "Any illicit drug" refers to marijuana/hashish, cocaine (including crack), inhalants, hallucinogens, heroin, or prescription-type drugs used nonmedically. Youths were also asked whether they had received treatment or counseling services during the past year for emotional or behavioral problems that were not caused by alcohol or drugs. Respondents who received treatment or counseling were asked to identify reasons for the last time they received these services.

Suicide Risk Among Youths

Suicide is an important cause of mortality among youths in the United States. The 2000 NHSDA estimated that almost 3 million youths were at risk for suicide during the past year. Of youths at risk for suicide, 37 percent actually tried to kill themselves during the past year.

Females (16 percent) were almost twice as likely as males (8 percent) to be at risk for suicide during the past year. The likelihood of suicide risk was also greater among youths aged 14 to 17 than it was among those aged 12 or 13. The likelihood of suicide risk was similar among white, black, Hispanic, and Asian youths.

suicide. *Journal of Studies on Alcohol*, 50, 202–209. **16.** Smith, G.S., Branas, C.C., and Miller, T.R. (1999). Fatal nontraffic injuries involving alcohol: A meta-analysis. *Annals of Emergency Medicine*, 659–66. **17.** Fava, G.A., Grandi, S., Zielezny, M., et al. (1996). Four-year outcome for cognitive behavioral treatment of residual symptoms in major depression. *American Journal of Psychiatry*, 153, 945–947.

Substance Use And Suicide Risk

Prior research has associated substance use with an increased risk of suicide among youths. The 2000 NHSDA found that youths who reported alcohol or illicit drug use during the past year were more likely than those who did not use these substances to be at risk for suicide during this same time period. For instance, youths who reported past year use of any illicit drug other than marijuana (29 percent) were almost three times more likely than youths who did not (10 percent) to be at risk for suicide during this time period.

Regional Differences Of Suicide Risk

Regionally, youths from the West (14 percent) were more likely to be at risk for suicide during the past year than those who lived in the Midwest (12 percent) or Northeast (11 percent). The risk of suicide was similar among youths from large metropolitan, small metropolitan, and non-metropolitan counties.

Mental Health Treatment Utilization Among Suicidal Youths

Research has demonstrated that the most effective way to prevent suicide is through the early identification and treatment of those at risk. Yet, according to the 2000 NHSDA, only 36 percent of youths at risk for suicide during the past year received mental health treatment during this same time period. Less than one-fifth of youths at risk for suicide received help from a private therapist, psychologist, psychiatrist, social worker, or counselor. More than 15 percent received treatment from school counselors, school psychologists, or having regular meetings with teachers. Among youths at risk for suicide who received mental health treatment, 38 percent reported suicidal thoughts or attempts as the reason for the last time they received these services.

Source: "Substance Use and the Risk of Suicide Among Youths," The NHSDA Report, a publication of the Office of Applied Studies, Substance Abuse and Mental Health Services Administration (SAMHSA), July 2002.

Chapter 48

Drugs And Driving

Drugged Driving

"Have one [drink] for the road" was, until recently, a commonly used phrase in American culture. It has only been within the past 20 years that as a Nation, we have begun to recognize the dangers associated with drunk driving. Through a multipronged and concerted effort involving many stakeholders, including educators, media, legislators, law enforcement, and community organizations, such as Mothers Against Drunk Driving (MADD), the Nation has seen a decline in the numbers of people killed or injured due to drunk driving. It is now time that we recognize and address the similar dangers that can occur with drugged driving.

In 12 states (Arizona, Georgia, Indiana, Illinois, Iowa, Michigan, Minnesota, Nevada, Pennsylvania, Rhode Island, Utah, and Wisconsin), it is illegal to operate a motor vehicle with any detectable level of a prohibited drug, or its metabolites, in the driver's blood. Other state laws define "drugged driving" as driving when a drug "renders the driver incapable of driving safely," or "causes the driver to be impaired."

About This Chapter: Information in this chapter is from "NIDA InfoFacts: Drugged Driving," National Institute on Drug Abuse, a component of the United States Department of Health and Human Services, August 2005.

In reality, the principal concern regarding drugged driving is that driving under the influence of any drug that acts on the brain could impair one's motor skills, reaction time, and judgment. Drugged driving is a public health concern because it puts not only the driver at risk, but passengers and others who share the road.

Statistics About Drugs And Driving

The National Highway Traffic Safety Administration (NHTSA) reports that 16,000 people are killed annually due to drunk and drugged driving. Furthermore, NHTSA estimates that drugs are used by approximately 10 to 22 percent of drivers involved in crashes, often in combination with alcohol. According to the 2003 National Survey on Drug Use and Health, an estimated 10.9 million people reported driving under the influence of an illicit drug during the year prior to being surveyed. This corresponds to 4.8 percent of the population aged 15 or older, but 14.1 percent among young adults aged 18 to 25. In addition the following is true:

- Younger adult drivers were more likely to have driven under the influence of alcohol or illicit drugs than older adult drivers, with more than one in three drivers aged 21 to 25 (33.8 percent) and nearly one in four drivers aged 26 to 34 (24.3 percent) having driven under the influence of drugs or alcohol during the previous year. These percentages go down further in drivers over age 35.

- Male drivers were nearly twice as likely as female drivers to have driven under the influence of alcohol or drugs during the previous year (22 percent compared with 11.4 percent).

In recent years, drugs other than alcohol have increasingly been recognized as hazards to road traffic safety. Research examining these drugs indicates that marijuana is the most prevalent illegal drug detected in impaired drivers, fatally injured drivers, and motor vehicle crash victims. A variety of other drugs, such as benzodiazepines, cocaine, opiates, and amphetamines, have also been reported in fatal and nonfatal motor vehicle crashes.

A number of studies have examined illicit drug use in drivers involved in motor vehicle crashes, reckless driving, or in fatal accidents. Here are some examples:

- A recent study found that 34 percent of drivers admitted to a Maryland trauma center tested positive for drugs only, while 16 percent tested positive for alcohol only; 50 percent of those under 18 tested positive for alcohol and/or drugs. While it is interesting that more people in this study tested positive for drugs only compared to alcohol only, it should be noted that this represents one geographic location, so findings cannot be generalized. In fact, many studies among similar populations have found higher prevalence rates of alcohol compared with drug use.

- In one study of 168 fatally injured truck drivers in 8 states, 33 percent tested positive for psychoactive drugs or alcohol.

- Studies conducted in a number of localities have found that approximately 4 to 14 percent of drivers who sustained injury or death in traffic accidents tested positive for delta-9-tetrahydrocannabinol (THC), the active ingredient in marijuana.

- In a large study of almost 3,400 fatally injured drivers from 3 Australian states (Victoria, New South Wales, and Western Australia) between 1990 and 1999, drugs other than alcohol were present in 26.7 percent of the cases. These included cannabis (13.5 percent), opioids (4.9 percent), stimulants (4.1 percent), benzodiazepines (4.1 percent), and other psychotropic drugs (2.7 percent). Almost 10 percent of the cases involved both alcohol and drugs.

Teens And Drugged Driving

- According to NHTSA, vehicle accidents are the leading cause of death among those aged 15 to 20. It is generally accepted that because teens are the least experienced drivers as a group, they have a higher risk of being involved in an accident compared with more experienced drivers. When this lack of experience is combined with the use of marijuana or other substances that impact cognitive and motor abilities, the results can be tragic.

- Analyses from NIDA's Monitoring the Future survey indicate that in 2001, one in six (15 percent) teens reported driving under the influence of marijuana, a number nearly equivalent to those who reported driving under the influence of alcohol (16 percent), despite higher prevalence of alcohol consumption among teens.

- The State of Maryland's Adolescent Survey indicates that 26.8 percent of the State's licensed, 12th-grade drivers reported driving under the influence of marijuana during 2001.

Drugged Driving Hazards

Drugs act on the brain and can alter perception, cognition, attention, balance, coordination, and other faculties required for safe driving. The effects of specific drugs of abuse differ depending on their mechanisms of action, the amount consumed, the history of the user, and other factors.

✎ What's It Mean?

Amphetamines: Stimulant drugs whose effects are very similar to cocaine. [1]

Benzodiazepines: A class of drugs used in medicine as minor tranquilizers, which is frequently prescribed to treat anxiety. They are central nervous system depressants. [2]

Cannabis: The botanical name for the plant from which marijuana comes. [1]

Cocaine: A highly addictive stimulant drug derived from the coca plant that produces profound feelings of pleasure. [1]

Opiates: Drugs derived from opium such as morphine and codeine. [2]

Stimulants: A class of drugs that elevates mood, increases feelings of well being, and increases energy and alertness. Stimulants include cocaine, Methamphetamine, and methylphenidate (Ritalin). [1]

Source: [1] "NIDA for Teens Glossary," NIDA for Teens, National Institute on Drug Abuse, a component of the United States Department of Health and Human Services, cited January 2006; available online at http://teens.drugabuse.gov/utilities/glossary.asp. [2] "Glossary of Terms," U.S. Department of Labor, Office of the Assistant Secretary for Policy, cited January 2006; http://www.dol.gov/asp/programs/drugs/said/GlossaryTerm.asp?ID=303.

Marijuana

THC affects areas of the brain that control the body's movements, balance, coordination, memory, and judgment abilities, as well as sensations. Because these effects are multifaceted, more research is required to understand marijuana's impact on the ability of drivers to react to complex and unpredictable situations. However, we do know the following is true:

- A meta-analysis of approximately 60 experimental studies, including laboratory, driving simulator, and on-road experiments, found that behavioral and cognitive skills related to driving performance were impaired in a dose-dependent fashion with increasing THC blood levels.

- Evidence from both real and simulated driving studies indicates that marijuana can negatively impact a driver's attentiveness, perception of time and speed, and the ability to draw on information obtained through past experiences.

- Research shows that impairment increases significantly when marijuana use is combined with alcohol.

- Studies have found that many drivers who test positive for alcohol also test positive for THC, making it clear that drinking and drugged driving are often linked behaviors.

Other Drugs

- Prescription drugs: Many medications (e.g., benzodiazepines and opiate analgesics) act on systems in the brain that could impair driving ability. In fact, many prescription drugs come with warnings against the operation of machinery—including vehicles—for a specified period of time after use. When prescription drugs are taken without medical supervision (i.e., when abused), impaired driving and other harmful reactions can also result.

☞ Remember!!
Drugged driving is a dangerous activity that puts us all at risk.

Chapter 49

Substance Use And Risky Sexual Behavior

Sexual activity and substance use are not uncommon among youth today. According to the Centers for Disease Control and Prevention, 79 percent of high school students report having experimented with alcohol at least once, and a quarter report frequent drug use. Half of all 9th–12th graders have had sexual intercourse, and 65 percent will by the time they graduate. While it has been difficult to show a direct causal relationship, there is some evidence that alcohol and drug use by young people is associated with risky sexual activity.

Risky Sexual Behaviors And Substance Use

Sexual Initiation

- Current data suggest that those who engage in any "risk behaviors" tend to take part in more than one, and that many health risk behaviors occur in combination with other risky activities.

- Prior substance use increases the probability that an adolescent will initiate sexual activity, and sexually experienced adolescents are more likely to initiate substance use including alcohol and cigarettes.

About This Chapter: Information in this chapter is from "Substance Use and Sexual Health Among Teens and Young Adults in the U.S.," © February 2002. This information was reprinted with permission from the Henry J. Kaiser Family Foundation. The Kaiser Family Foundation, based in Menlo Park, California, is a nonprofit, independent national health care philanthropy and is not associated with Kaiser Permanente or Kaiser Industries.

- Teens who use alcohol or drugs are more likely to have sex than those who do not: Adolescents who drink are seven times more likely, while those who use illicit substances are five times more likely—even after adjusting for age, race, gender, and parental educational level.

- Up to 18 percent of young people aged 13 to 19 report that they were drinking at the time of first intercourse. Among teens aged 14 to 18 who reported having used alcohol before age fourteen, 20 percent said they had sex at age fourteen or earlier, compared with seven percent of other teens.

- One-quarter of sexually active 9–12th grade students report using alcohol or drugs during their last sexual encounter, with males more likely than females to have done so (31% vs. 19%).

- For a significant proportion of adults aged 18 to 30, having sex and heavy drinking occur together in a single episode. Among men, 35 percent said they had sex when consuming five to eight drinks, compared with 17 percent of those who had one or two drinks. Among women aged 18 to 30, 39 percent had sex while consuming five to eight drinks, compared with 14 percent of women who had one or two drinks.

Unprotected Sex

- Thirty-eight percent (38%) of sexually active teenage women and 26 percent of women aged 20 to 24 rely on the condom as their contraceptive method, making it second only to the pill (used by 44% of teens and 52% of young adults).

- Research on the association between condom use and substance use is mixed. According to one analysis of a large national sample of high school students, sexually active adolescents who use alcohol and/or drugs are somewhat less likely than other students to have used a condom the last time they had sex. However, the differences were not statistically significant after controlling for other factors.

- The more substances that sexually active teens and young adults have ever tried, the less likely they are to have used a condom the last time they had sex: Among those aged 14 to 22, 78 percent of boys and 67 percent of girls who reported never using a substance said that they used a condom, compared with only 35 percent of boys and 23 percent of girls who reported ever having used five substances.

- Teen girls and young women aged 14 to 22 who have recently used multiple substances are less likely to have used a condom the last time they had sex: 26 percent of young women with four recent alcohol or drug use behaviors reported using a condom at last intercourse, compared with 44 percent of those who reported no recent alcohol or drug use.

Multiple Partners

- For teenagers as well as adults aged 18 to 30, having multiple sexual partners has been associated with both ever-use and current use of alcohol or other substances.

- Thirty-nine percent (39%) of sexually active students in 9th–12th grades who report ever using alcohol have had sex with four or more partners, compared with 29 percent of students who never drink.

- Forty-four percent (44%) of sexually active students in 9th–12th grades who report ever using drugs have had sex with four or more partners, compared with 24 percent of students who use drugs.

- Among sexually active young people aged 14 to 22 who used a substance the last time they had intercourse, 61 percent of men and 44 percent of women had had multiple partners during the three months prior to being surveyed, compared with 32 percent of men and 14 percent of women who did not use drugs or alcohol the last time they had sex.

- Sexually active women aged 14 to 22 who recently used alcohol or drugs four times are more likely than those who do not drink or take drugs to have had more than one sex partner in the last three months (48% compared with 8%). The number of different substances women aged 14 to 22 use in their lifetimes significantly increases their likelihood of having multiple sex partners. Among 18 to 22-year-old men and women, an earlier age at initiation of alcohol use is associated with the later likelihood of having multiple sex partners. For example, among those who reported having initiated alcohol use at age 10 or younger, 44 percent of men and 31 percent of women said they had had more than one sex partner in the three months prior to the survey, compared with 37 percent of men and 12 percent of women who said that they first drank alcohol at age 17 or older.

Unintended Consequences

Sexually Transmitted Diseases (STDs)

- There are approximately fifteen million new cases of sexually transmitted diseases (STDs) annually in the United States. About two-thirds of new cases occur among adolescents and young adults under 25, a group that is also more likely to engage in both risky sexual activity and alcohol and drug use.

- Young women may be biologically more susceptible to chlamydia, gonorrhea, and HIV than older women.

- In a single act of unprotected sex with an infected partner, a teenage woman has a one percent risk of acquiring HIV, a 30 percent risk of getting genital herpes, and a 50 percent chance of contracting gonorrhea.

Unintended Pregnancy

- Substance use and unintended pregnancies often occur among the same populations.

- Fifty-five percent of teenagers say that having sex while drinking or on drugs is often a reason for unplanned teen pregnancies.

- Almost one million adolescents—or 19 percent of those who have had sexual intercourse—become pregnant each year. Among women aged 15 to 19, 78 percent of pregnancies are believed to be unintended, accounting for about one-quarter of all accidental pregnancies each year.

- The pregnancy rate among women aged 20 to 24 is 183.3 per 1,000 women; it is thought that 59 percent of pregnancies in this age group are unintended.

✔ Quick Tip

- Thinking "it won't happen to me" is stupid; if you don't protect yourself, it probably will. Sex is serious. Make a plan.

- Just because you think everyone is doing it, doesn't mean they are. Some are, some aren't—and some are lying.

- There are a lot of good reasons to say "no, not yet." Protecting your feelings is one of them.

- You're in charge of your own life. Don't let anyone pressure you into having sex.

- You can always say "no"—even if you've said "yes" before.

- Carrying a condom is just being smart—it doesn't mean you're pushy or easy.

- If you think birth control "ruins the mood," consider what a pregnancy test will do to it.

- If you're drunk or high, you can't make good decisions about sex. Don't do something you might not remember or might really regret.

- Sex won't make him yours, and a baby won't make him stay.

- Not ready to be someone's father? It's simple: Use protection every time or don't have sex.

Source: © 2001 The National Campaign to Prevent Teen Pregnancy. Reprinted with permission. For additional information, visit http://www.teenpregnancy.org.

Sexual Assault And Violence

- Estimates of substance use during instances of sexual violence and rape in the general population range from 30 to 90 percent for alcohol use, and from 13 to 42 percent for the use of illicit substances.

- Alcohol use by the victim, perpetrator, or both, has been implicated in 46 to 75 percent of date rapes among college students.

- One survey of college students found that 78 percent of women had experienced sexual aggression (any type of sexual activity, including kissing, unwanted by the woman). Dates on which sexual aggression occurred were more likely to include heavy drinking or drug use than those dates that were not marked by sexually aggressive activity.

- While 93% of teenage women report that their first intercourse was voluntary, one-quarter of these young women report that it was unwanted. Seven out of ten women who first had intercourse before age 13 say it was unwanted or nonvoluntary.

- Compared with women in other age groups, women aged 19 to 29 report more violent incidents with intimate partners, for a rate of 21.3 violent victimizations per 1,000 women.

Chapter 50

Drug Abuse And HIV Infection

A 10-year study has found that the biggest predictor of HIV infection for both male and female injecting drug users (IDUs) is high-risk sexual behavior, not sharing needles used to inject drugs. High-risk homosexual activity was the most important factor in HIV transmission for men; high-risk heterosexual activity was most significant for women. Risky drug-use behaviors also were strong predictors of HIV transmission for men but were less significant for women, the study found.

"In the past, we assumed that IDUs who were HIV-positive had been infected with the virus through needle-sharing," says Dr. Steffanie Strathdee of the Johns Hopkins University Bloomberg School of Public Health in Baltimore, who conducted the NIDA-funded study. "Our analysis indicates that sexual behaviors, which we thought were less important among IDUs, really carry a heavy weight in terms of risks for HIV seroconversion for both men and women."

High-risk sexual behavior played the biggest role in HIV infection for both male and female injection drug users (IDUs) in this study of 1,800 IDUs. Significant risk factors for men were high-risk homosexual activity, using shooting galleries, and sharing needles used to inject drugs with multiple

About This Chapter: Information in this chapter is from "High-Risk Sex Is Main Factor in HIV Infection for Men and Women Who Inject Drugs," by Robert Mathias, NIDA Notes Staff Writer, *NIDA Notes*, National Institute on Drug Abuse, a component of the United States Department of Health and Human Services, May 2002.

partners. For women, high-risk heterosexual activity, as indicated by reporting a recent sexually transmitted disease (STD), was the most significant cause of HIV infection.

In the study, Dr. Strathdee led a team of researchers who analyzed data collected every 6 months from 1,800 IDUs in Baltimore from 1988 to 1998. Participants had to be at least 18 years of age when they entered the study, have a history of injection drug use within the previous 10 years, and not have HIV infection or AIDS. More than 90 percent of the participants said they had injected drugs in the 6 months prior to enrolling in the study. In their semiannual interviews, study participants reported their recent drug use and sexual behavior and submitted blood samples to determine if they had become HIV-positive since their last visit.

Researchers analyzed the role of homosexual activity in HIV seroconversions among male IDUs in the study, after taking into account other factors that increased their risk of acquiring HIV, such as their drug injection practices. This analysis revealed that the incidence of HIV infection among male IDUs who had engaged in homosexual activity within the previous 6 months was 10.44 percent a year, compared to 3.01 percent among men who did not report having homosexual sex.

Visiting "shooting galleries," where drug abusers gather to obtain and inject drugs, sharing needles used to inject drugs with multiple partners, and injecting drugs daily also were independently linked to significantly higher rates of HIV infection among men in the study. Men who said they had used shooting galleries had an HIV incidence rate of 6.28 percent per year, and men who shared needles with more than one partner had a rate of 5.52 percent per year. These infection rates were more than double those found among men who had not engaged in these behaviors. Men who injected drugs at least once a day had HIV

✎ What's It Mean?

Seroconversion: Development of antibodies in the blood of an individual who previously did not have detectable antibodies.

Source: "Glossary," National Immunization Program, Centers for Disease Control and Prevention, Department of Health and Human Services, July 2005.

infection rates of 4.68 percent, more than one and one-half times the rate among men who had injected less than once a day.

Sharing needles also increased risk of HIV infection among women IDUs. However, high-risk heterosexual activity was a much more important risk factor for these women, the study found. In fact, other than being younger than 30 years—which independently predicted HIV infection for both sexes—high-risk heterosexual activity was the main predictor of HIV seroconversion among women. Women who reported having a recent sexually transmitted disease (STD), an indicator of unprotected sex, had more than 2.5 times the rate of HIV infection of women who did not have an STD.

"Both homosexual men and heterosexual women IDUs appear to be at dual risk for becoming infected with HIV," Dr. Strathdee says. "In previous studies by our group, being a gay male IDU was closely linked to visiting shooting galleries and sharing needles. Heterosexual women IDUs tend to have more of an overlap in their sexual partners and their drug use than men do. This puts them at increased HIV risk because they are sharing needles and having unprotected sex with a partner who is more likely to be infected with the virus.

"HIV prevention programs have done a good job in reducing needle-sharing and other drug-use behaviors that spread the virus among IDUs," Dr. Strathdee says. "However, our study indicates that HIV prevention programs can achieve better results by also addressing sexual risk behaviors among IDUs. A multi-faceted approach is needed that screens both men and women IDUs for STDs at places where they go, such as needle-exchange programs and methadone treatment programs, and provides comprehensive treatment at those sites.

"HIV prevention efforts also should be gender-specific, targeting the important differences we have found in sexual and drug-use behaviors among men and women that increase their risk of acquiring and transmitting HIV," Dr. Strathdee says. "For example, women IDUs in stable relationships could be shown how to negotiate condom use with their partners and offered couple counseling to educate both partners about HIV risks associated with their drug use and sexual behaviors. We need more research to identify and evaluate HIV prevention approaches for male IDUs who have sex with men to determine what kinds of interventions might work."

♣ It's A Fact!!

NIDA Unveils Campaign To Send Teens The Message About The Link Between Drug Abuse And HIV

"*Drug Abuse and HIV: Learn the Link*" is the message of a public awareness campaign by the National Institute on Drug Abuse (NIDA), a component of the National Institutes of Health.

"Drug abuse prevention is HIV prevention," says NIDA Director Dr. Nora D. Volkow. "Research has shown that a significant proportion of young people are not concerned about becoming infected with HIV. In recent years, the number of young people in the United States diagnosed with AIDS rose substantially. Because drug use encourages risky behaviors that can promote HIV transmission, NIDA views drug abuse treatment as essential HIV prevention."

While research has shown that a large proportion of young people are not concerned about becoming infected with HIV, the reality is that there exists a very real danger for those engaged in risky behaviors. In addition, minority populations are disproportionately affected by the health consequences of drug abuse and HIV. For example, in 2004, black and Hispanic women represented about 25 percent of all U.S. women, yet they accounted for more than 80 percent of AIDS cases diagnosed in women that year. African-Americans, while they make up just 12 percent of the population, accounted for approximately half of the total AIDS cases diagnosed in 2004.

NIDA and partnering organizations—including the American Academy of Child and Adolescent Psychiatry (AACAP), the AIDS Alliance for Children, Youth & Families, and the United Negro College Fund Special Programs Corporation—are working together to get this important message about the link between drug abuse and HIV to teens and young adults.

In addition to public service announcements distributed to television stations across the country, NIDA has launched a website, www.hiv.drugabuse.gov that provides the latest scientific findings on the relationship between drug abuse and HIV. One item on the Institute's website is its HIV/AIDS Research Report which provides an overview of the latest NIDA-supported research into the multiple ways in which drugs of abuse contribute to the spread of HIV.

For example, the Research Report notes that studies supported by NIDA already have shown that drug abuse can interfere with the efficacy of highly active antiretroviral therapy (HAART), a treatment that can greatly extend the lives of people infected with HIV. Other research has shown that HIV can continue to replicate in people who abuse methamphetamine, despite taking HAART as prescribed.

Source: NIH News, National Institute on Drug Abuse (NIDA), a component of the National Institutes of Health, U.S. Department of Health and Human Services, November 2005.

Chapter 51

Drug Abuse And Hepatitis C

Viral Hepatitis Is An Important Health Issue For The Nation

Hepatitis, literally an "inflammation of the liver," has a number of causes. Viral infection is one of them. The most common types are hepatitis A, hepatitis B, and hepatitis C.

Hepatitis C virus (HCV) infection occurs when blood (or to a lesser extent, other body fluids such as semen or vaginal fluid) from an infected person enters the body of an uninfected person.

About 3.9 million Americans have been infected with HCV and 2.7 million have chronic HCV infection. Hepatitis C disproportionately affects people of color: 3.2% of African Americans and 2.1% of Mexican Americans are infected with HCV, compared to 1.5% of non-Hispanic whites. These numbers underestimate the actual impact because they do not include infections in prisoners or the homeless. In 2000, about 30,000 new infections occurred. Most of these infections occurred among young adults 20–39 years old.

Hepatitis B virus (HBV) infection occurs when blood or body fluids from an infected person enter the body of an uninfected person. High-risk

About This Chapter: Information in this chapter is excerpted from "Viral Hepatitis and Injection Drug Users," National Center for HIV, STD and TB Prevention, Centers for Disease Control and Prevention, September 2002.

sexual behaviors (unprotected sex with multiple partners) and injection drug use are the major risk factors. About 5% of people in the U.S. have evidence of past infection with HBV and approximately 1.25 million people have chronic HBV infection. Like hepatitis C, hepatitis B disproportionately affects people of color. An estimated 73,000 new HBV infections occurred in 2000. Most infections occurred in young adults, aged 20–39 years. Hepatitis B can be prevented through immunization.

Hepatitis A virus (HAV) is primarily transmitted through the fecal-oral route, when a person puts something in his or her mouth (such as food or a beverage) that has been contaminated with the feces of a person infected with HAV. Outbreaks occur more easily in overcrowded areas where poor sanitary conditions exist. Outbreaks of hepatitis A also have been reported among IDUs. About one-third of Americans have evidence of past infection with HAV. Hepatitis A can be prevented through immunization.

> ♣ **It's A Fact!!**
> Injection drug use is the major risk factor for hepatitis C virus infection.

Each year, 8,000 to 10,000 people die from the complications of liver disease caused by hepatitis C and about 5,000 die from complications caused by hepatitis B. Chronic liver disease is currently the 10th leading cause of death, and liver failure due to hepatitis C is the leading reason for liver transplants. Annual health care costs and lost wages associated with hepatitis-related liver disease are estimated to be $600 million for hepatitis C and $700 million for hepatitis B. The costs to individuals and society of illness related to hepatitis A are also substantial.

Viral hepatitis can be insidious. Frequently, symptoms of newly acquired (acute) infection are mild or nonexistent, so people may not even be diagnosed as having viral hepatitis. Those who do have symptoms might experience "flu-like" symptoms, fatigue, nausea, pain in the upper abdomen, and sometimes jaundice.

People who get HAV infection are able to clear the virus from their bodies and recover fully. They develop a lifelong immunity to the virus. The situation is different with hepatitis B and hepatitis C as indicated in the following:

- The majority of people who acquire HBV infection after age 5 are able to clear the virus from their bodies. However, about 2%–6% are not able to clear the virus and go on to become chronically infected. A much higher percentage of those who acquire HBV infection as infants (90%) or young children (30%) become chronically infected.

- About 75%–85% of people with HCV infection are unable to clear the virus and become chronically infected.

Many people with chronic infection—60% of those with HBV infection and 70% of those with HCV infection—develop chronic liver disease, a situation in which the virus damages the liver. The damage may progress to severe disease, including cirrhosis, liver cancer, and liver failure. This progressive liver disease usually develops slowly over 20 to 30 years. Because symptoms are so frequently mild or nonexistent, the majority of people with chronic HBV and HCV infections do not know they are infected and can unknowingly transmit the virus to others. For many, signs and symptoms appear only when liver disease is advanced and treatments are less effective.

Hepatitis C Is A Particular Concern

- So many people have been infected with HCV. During the 1960s, 1970s, and early 1980s, the number of new cases every year was very high, averaging an estimated 240,000 per year during the 1980s. Because many were unaware they were infected, the risks of transmitting the infection to others were extremely high. Since then, the incidence of HCV infection has declined dramatically (only 30,000 new infections estimated in 2000). Most of this decline has occurred among IDUs. The reasons are not fully understood but may be due to safer injection practices resulting from intensive HIV prevention programs and to the very high proportion of drug users already infected.

- Most people with HCV infection develop chronic infection, which frequently leads to chronic liver disease.

- The impact of HCV infection may explode over the next 10–20 years. Because it takes 20–30 years for chronic liver disease, cirrhosis, and liver cancer to develop, it is conservatively estimated that illness and deaths from HCV-related liver disease among the millions of people infected during earlier years will increase 2- to 3-fold over the next two decades. Direct medical costs may range from $6.5 to $13.6 billion, with even larger indirect and societal costs.

- No vaccine to prevent HCV infection is available.

> ♣ **It's A Fact!!**
>
> Hepatitis B virus and hepatitis C virus infections are acquired relatively rapidly among IDUs. Within 5 years of beginning injection drug use, 50%–70% of IDUs become infected with HBV. Between 50%–80% of IDUs become infected with HCV within 5 years of beginning injection drug use; it is usually the first blood borne virus they acquire.

Viral Hepatitis Is A Very Significant Problem Among IDUs

Because HBV and HCV are transmitted through exposure to infected blood and body fluids, IDUs are at very high risk of acquiring and transmitting both viruses. For example, it is estimated that 60%, or 17,000, of the 30,000 new cases of HCV that occurred in 2000 occurred among IDUs. It is estimated that 17%, or 13,000 of the 73,000 new cases of hepatitis B that occurred in 2000, occurred among IDUs.

Several factors favor the rapid spread of HCV infection among IDUs. They are as follows:

- Viral factors—HCV is transmitted efficiently through blood exposure.

- Host factors—A large number of individuals are infected and this provides multiple opportunities for transmission to others.

- IDU factors—IDUs often jointly purchase drugs and prepare the drug solution together; this solution is divided among users. Sharing the drug solution, syringes, or other drug preparation equipment (such as water, drug mixing containers, and cotton filters) all increase the risk of transmission if any of these components are infected with HCV.

- IDUs are at very high risk of co-infection with HIV and HCV.

- Many IDUs drink alcohol, which damages the liver and accelerates the progression of liver disease.

- HAV infection can be severe and very dangerous in those who already have liver disease from chronic hepatitis B or chronic hepatitis C.

- Treatment of chronic hepatitis B or chronic hepatitis C can be complicated and adherence difficult for infected IDUs because many have other conditions (HIV, mental illness, alcoholism, other illnesses), are poor, and have unstable living situations. The stigma surrounding injecting drugs also means that many IDUs are marginalized and have little or no contact with health care providers.

Chapter 52

Drug Use And Violence

Introduction

Teenagers abuse a variety of drugs, both legal and illegal. Some of the most commonly used drugs include alcohol, marijuana, inhalants, stimulants (cocaine, crack, and speed), LSD, PCP, prescription medications, opiates, heroin, steroids, tobacco, and club drugs, like Ecstasy (MDMA).

For Teenagers, There Is A Strong Relationship Between The Use Of Drugs And Violence

Teens who report engaging in violent behavior are also extremely likely to report using drugs. One national survey found that 85 percent of violent teens reported using marijuana, and 55 percent reported using several illegal drugs.

Do Drugs Cause Teens To Be Violent?

The relationship between drugs and violence is complicated.

Some teens may become violent under the influence of drugs. It is also likely that some teens engage in violence to get money to buy drugs. In most cases, however, it appears that the use of drugs does not cause violent behavior.

About This Chapter: Information in this chapter is from "Teen Drug Use and Violence," National Youth Violence Prevention Resource Center, sponsored by the Centers for Disease Control and Prevention and Federal Partners Working on Youth Violence, 2002.

Instead, it seems that violence and the use of drugs are both part of a lifestyle that involves antisocial and delinquent behavior. In many cases, the violent behavior actually comes before the drug use. The drug use is just one aspect of a risky and dangerous lifestyle.

♣ **It's A Fact!!**
Teens who engage in violent behavior are also extremely likely to be using drugs.

Teens Who Use Drugs Also Tend To Engage In Other Behaviors That Put Them At Risk

Almost 90 percent of the teens who use drugs also do other things that put them or those around them at risk for serious harm, including drinking heavily, fighting, carrying weapons, and having unsafe sex.

Children under the age of 12 that experiment with drugs are at a much greater risk than other children for engaging in serious violence during their teenage years, probably because the use of illegal drugs is an early sign of antisocial attitudes and involvement in delinquent behavior.

While the use of drugs does not generally cause teens to become involved in violence, those violent teens who do use illegal drugs tend to engage in violent behavior more frequently and to continue to engage in violence much longer than those violent teens who do not use drugs.

Teens That Use Drugs Are Also Much More Likely To Attempt And Die By Suicide.

Research has not proven that drug use actually causes suicidal behavior, only that the two behaviors are associated. It may be that teens who have emotional problems are more likely to use drugs and to contemplate suicide. Another possibility is that the use of drugs aggravates preexisting depression or other emotional problems. Drugs may also impair the judgment of teens considering suicide, making suicide attempts more likely.

What You Can Do

Get The Facts About Drugs

Many teens are not aware of basic facts about drugs and how drugs can affect their brains and bodies. For example, did you know these facts:

- Ecstasy, or MDMA, can affect users' brains, causing problems that interfere with normal learning and memory.

- Even first-time crack or cocaine users can have seizures or heart attacks, which can kill them.

- Marijuana damages the lungs and makes the body less able to resist illnesses.

Learn About Different Ways To Turn Down Drugs

Sometimes, watching TV or listening to people talk, it's easy to believe that everyone is smoking marijuana or trying other drugs. In fact, most teens haven't tried marijuana or other drugs, and using them doesn't make you "cool." If someone offers you drugs, just say, "No thanks," or "I'm not into that." You may want to try suggesting another activity instead.

Learn to recognize the signs of a drug problem in a friend (or yourself).

If a friend has one or more of the following warning signs, he or she may have a problem with drugs:

- Getting high on a regular basis

- Lying about the amount of drugs he or she is using

- Believing that drugs are necessary to have fun

- Constantly talking about using drugs

- Feeling run-down, depressed, or even suicidal

- Having problems at school or getting in trouble with the law

- Giving up activities he or she used to do, such as playing sports or doing homework, and shunning friends who don't use drugs.

If you recognize these signs in a friend or yourself, professional help may be necessary.

Don't try to handle this on your own. Talk with an adult you can trust, such as your parents or a trusted family member, a teacher, a school counselor, your clergy, or a professional at a mental health center.

Chapter 53

Drugs Linked To Sexual Assault

What is drug-facilitated sexual assault?

Drug-facilitated sexual assault involves the administration of an anesthesia-type drug to render a victim physically incapacitated or helpless and thus incapable of giving or withholding consent. Victims may be unconscious during all or parts of the sexual assault and, upon regaining consciousness, may experience anterograde amnesia—the inability to recall events that occurred while under the influence of the drug.

How prevalent are drug-facilitated sexual assaults?

There are no conclusive estimates as to the number of drug-facilitated sexual assaults that occur each year; however, nationwide law enforcement reporting indicates that the number of such assaults appears to be increasing. Many drug-facilitated sexual assaults are not reported. Victims often are reluctant to report incidents because of a sense of embarrassment, guilt, or perceived responsibility, or because they lack specific recall of the assault. Moreover, most of the drugs typically used in the commission of sexual assaults are rapidly absorbed and metabolized by the body, thereby rendering them undetectable in routine urine and blood drug screenings.

About This Chapter: Information in this chapter is from "Drug-Facilitated Sexual Assault Fast Facts," National Drug Intelligence Center, a component of the United States Department of Justice, Product No. 2004-L0559-004, April 2004.

What drugs are used in the commission of drug-facilitated sexual assaults?

Sexual assaults have long been linked to the abuse of substances, primarily alcohol, that may decrease inhibitions and render the user incapacitated. In addition to alcohol, the drugs most often implicated in the commission of drug-facilitated sexual assaults are GHB, Rohypnol (a benzodiazepine), ketamine, although others, including other benzodiazepines and other sedative hypnotics, are used as well. These drugs often render victims unconscious—an effect that is quickened and intensified when the drugs are taken with alcohol. A person also may become a victim after taking such a drug willingly. Because of the sedative properties of these drugs, victims often have no memory of an assault, only an awareness or sense that they were violated.

Where do perpetrators obtain drugs used to facilitate sexual assaults?

Drugs used in sexual assaults typically are distributed at raves, dance clubs, and bars, but they are increasingly being sold in schools, on college campuses, and at private parties. Some of these drugs also are purchased via the Internet while others, particularly prescription benzodiazepines, are often found in homes. Law enforcement reporting indicates that these drugs are widely available in most urban areas and are becoming increasingly available in suburban and rural communities.

> **✎ What's It Mean?**
>
> Benzodiazepines: A class of drugs used in medicine as minor tranquilizers, which is frequently prescribed to treat anxiety. They are central nervous system depressants.
>
> Source: "Glossary of Terms," U.S. Department of Labor, Office of the Assistant Secretary for Policy, cited January 2006.

Is drug-facilitated sexual assault illegal?

Yes, drug-facilitated sexual assault is illegal. Most of the drugs typically used to facilitate sexual assaults—GHB, ketamine, and Rohypnol—are designated as controlled substances under the Controlled Substances Act of 1970. The Drug-Induced Rape Prevention and Punishment Act of 1996 (Public Law 104-305) modified 21 U. S. C. § 841 to provide penalties of up to 20 years imprisonment and fines for persons who intend to commit a crime of violence (including rape) by distributing a controlled substance to another individual without that individual's knowledge.

Chapter 54

Drug-Facilitated Rape

Date rape drugs are substances used to increase the vulnerability of potential victims and decrease victims' ability to protect themselves. In the criminal justice community, assaults committed using these drugs are known as "drug-facilitated rapes". Many kinds of substances have been used as date rape drugs—everything from prescription drugs, illegal street drugs (including so-called "club drugs"), veterinary drugs, and alcoholic beverages. These substances can act in various ways, making victims confused, disoriented, helpless, unconscious, or even comatose. In a number of documented cases, the use of date rape drugs has ultimately resulted in death.

Three of the most commonly discussed date rape drugs are Rohypnol (flunitrazepam), GHB (gamma-hydroxybutyrate), and ketamine (ketamine hydrochloride). Rohypnol is a powerful benzodiazepine drug 10 to 20 times stronger than Valium. Rohypnol is widely used in Europe and Central and South America as a treatment for severe sleep disorders. Rohypnol cannot be legally distributed or possessed in the United States; however, illegal trafficking in Rohypnol tablets occurs nationwide. GHB can be produced in the form of a white powder, but it is more commonly encountered as an odorless, clear liquid. It is particularly dangerous because it is often given to victims in random, unmeasured doses (quickly squeezed into an unattended drink, for example).

About This Chapter: Information in this chapter is from "Drug Facilitated Rape." Reprinted with permission from the Butler County Rape Crisis Program, a service of the Community Counseling & Crisis Center, Oxford, Ohio. © 2005 Community Counseling & Crisis Center.

Ketamine, a veterinary tranquilizer and controlled substance, is another increasingly common date rape drug. When ingested by humans it is extremely dangerous and potentially lethal, and can result in hallucinations, paranoia, sensory distortions, and paralysis.

What is the number one date rape drug?

Across America, alcohol is by far the most common date rape drug. Although most of us are aware of dramatic media reports concerning GHB, Rohypnol, and other drugs, many people fail to realize that they are perhaps hundreds of times more likely to be victimized when under the influence of alcohol. Why? Because alcohol is readily available, and because it decreases your ability to think clearly, make good judgments, and protect yourself.

How can I tell if I may have been drugged?

Mixed with soft drinks, alcohol, or other beverages, a 2 mg tablet of Rohypnol or small amount of liquid or powder GHB can begin to affect the user within 15 minutes to one hour. Common effects of date rape drugs include the following:

- A drunken appearance

- Sedation

- Confusion

- Disinhibition

- Deep unresponsive sleep

- Respiratory and circulatory impairment

- Amnesia (memory loss of up to 24 hours)

☞ **Remember!!**
If you want to press charges against an assailant, you must report the crime to law enforcement officials in the jurisdiction where the crime occurred.

When administered in combination with alcohol, narcotics, or other central nervous system depressants, date rape drugs such as Rohypnol and GHB can cause seizures, cardiac and respiratory arrest, coma, or death.

In social situations, you should be concerned if you begin to feel confused, ill, or extremely intoxicated. Realize that a rapist who relies upon these drugs may offer to help when you begin to feel ill. Instead of leaving with a potential assailant, call 911 or ask a bartender or hotel clerk to call for emergency medical assistance. If you suspect that you or a friend may have been drugged, please realize how dangerous these drugs are and seek help immediately.

Can I prove that I was drugged? What are the penalties for using date rape drugs?

Although date rape drugs may make a rape victim unable to remember the assault, a wide variety of evidence is available, which can lead to arrest and conviction. If possible, victims should not change their clothing, eat, drink, bathe, or use the restroom until they have been examined in a hospital emergency department. Many date rape drugs are only detectable in the body for a few hours; for this reason, it is absolutely vital that you go to the emergency department of your local hospital as soon as possible if you think you or a friend may have been drugged. If possible, you should keep a sample of the beverage or the cup it was served in for analysis. A medical examination and consultation with law enforcement will help you to understand the legal options available in your unique situation.

It is against the law to have sexual intercourse with a person who has been drugged or is heavily intoxicated. Sexual assailants who possess, manufacture, or use date rape drugs to subdue their victims risk adding up to 20 years to their prison sentences. Possession of Rohypnol with no proven intent to use it in the commission of a violent crime carries a sentence of up to three years in prison.

How can I reduce the risk of drug-facilitated rape?

- Never leave your beverage unattended. If you need to leave your drink for any reason (getting up to dance, use the restroom, etc.), plan to finish it first or order a fresh drink when you return.

- At a bar or club, accept drinks only from the bartender, waiter, or waitress.

- At parties, do not accept open container drinks from anyone.

- Do not take any beverage, including soft drinks or alcohol, from someone you do not know well and trust. Don't be too quick to trust casual acquaintances. A friendly appearance can be deceiving; in fact, it may be a tool used by criminals to gain your trust.

- Use the buddy system and be alert to the behavior of your friends. Anyone who appears to be seriously intoxicated may be in danger.

Realize that rape is a crime of opportunity in which the assailant is looking for a vulnerable victim (one who is drugged, drunk, separated from friends, overly trusting, etc.). Do not allow anyone to take a person who appears to be intoxicated to an isolated area. If you believe that a friend may have been drugged, get medical attention immediately by going directly to the hospital, or by calling 911. Don't allow embarrassment (or concerns about underage drinking) to keep you from seeking help. And if possible, preserve the glass that your friend drank from—it may be important evidence of a crime.

What To Do If You Suspect You've Been Drugged And Sexually Assaulted

Remember, date rape drugs can cause serious medical problems with little warning, including seizures, cardiac and respiratory arrest, coma, and even death.

1. If you think that you or a friend may have been given a date rape drug, you are facing a potential medical emergency. Please go to your nearest hospital emergency department immediately for a medical evaluation. By acting quickly, you may save a life.

2. Trust yourself. It is hard to know what to do when you aren't sure what happened. But if your instincts tell you something is wrong, seek help. Don't delay.

3. Finally, if a crime did occur, it is important to preserve the evidence. You may not choose to press charges, but preserving evidence helps to keep your options open. If possible, don't shower, douche, change clothes, brush your teeth, eat, drink, or use the restroom. Go directly to your local emergency room. Some "date rape drugs" can only be detected in urine for about 12 hours after ingestion, while others can be detected for up to 72 hours. The sooner you get to the hospital, the more likely the drug will be found in your system.

☞ Remember!!

At least 80% of all rapes are committed by acquaintances.

Part Six

Treatment For Substance Abusers

Chapter 55

Signs Of Drug And Alcohol Use

If you notice unexplained changes in physical appearance or behavior, it may be a sign of substance use—or it could be a sign of another problem. You will not know definitively until a professional does a screening.

Physical Signs

- Change in sleeping patterns
- Bloodshot eyes
- Slurred or agitated speech
- Sudden or dramatic weight loss or gain
- Skin abrasions/bruises
- Neglected appearance/poor hygiene
- Sick more frequently
- Accidents or injuries

Behavioral Signs

- Hiding use; lying and covering up
- Sense that the person will "do anything" to use again regardless of consequences

About This Chapter: Information in this chapter is from "Signs Someone Is Using Drugs or Alcohol." © Partnership for Drug-Free America, 2004. Used with permission.

- Loss of control or choice of use (drug-seeking behavior)
- Loss of interest in previously enjoyed activities
- Emotional instability
- Hyperactive or hyper-aggressive
- Depression
- Missing school or work
- Failure to fulfill responsibilities at school or work
- Complaints from teachers or co-workers
- Reports of intoxication at school or work
- Furtive or secretive behavior
- Avoiding eye contact
- Locked doors
- Going out every night
- Change in friends or peer group
- Change in clothing or appearance
- Unusual smells on clothing or breath
- Heavy use of over-the-counter preparations to reduce eye reddening, nasal irritation, or bad breath
- Hidden stashes of alcohol
- Alcohol missing from supply
- Prescription medicine missing
- Money missing
- Valuables missing
- Disappearances for long periods of time
- Running away
- Secretive phone calls
- Unusual containers or wrappers

Chapter 56

Substance Abuse: Getting Help

Moving Forward With Your Life

You are probably already frightened, worried about your drinking or other drug taking, and afraid to ask for help. But it's one of the most courageous things you can do for yourself. It is difficult, but the sooner you do it, the easier it will be. It means that you have to start to value and care for yourself. It's the step to take so that all the other pieces can fall into place.

More than a million Americans of every possible description, who have found themselves struggling with a drinking or other drug problem, have taken charge of their lives and are free of these destructive dependencies. As you begin investigating the kinds of help available to you, you will discover that some people use one kind of help and others use a combination. Some people rely more on internal strengths and seek limited guidance from others, while many find the combined wisdom and experience of others with similar problems to be of priceless value. Still others benefit from the services of professional counselors and therapists; ministers, rabbis, and priests; community agencies. You might even want to take someone with you when seeking assistance.

About This Chapter: This chapter begins with excerpts from "Moving Forward With Your Life," National Clearinghouse for Alcohol and Drug Information (NCADI), Substance Abuse and Mental Health Services Administration (SAMHSA), 2002. Text under "Concerned about Your Drug Use," from the Partnership for Drug-Free America, is cited separately within the chapter.

You can find out what kind of help is available from a health care provider, clergy, or employee assistance program (EAP). Therapists, community health and social agencies, and alcohol/other drug treatment programs also can make useful suggestions.

♣ It's A Fact!!

More people in treatment for drug abuse, other than alcohol abuse, began using at least one of their problem drugs prior to the age of 13. A report by the Substance Abuse and Mental Health Services Administration (SAMHSA) states that the percentage of treatment admissions that initiated drug use before age 13 increased between 1993 and 2003 for marijuana and opiates. Opiates include prescription pain medications and heroin.

Source: Excerpted from "More People in Drug Abuse Treatment Began Drug Use Before Age 13," SAMHSA Advisory, Substance Abuse and Mental Health Services Administration (SAMHSA), January 26, 2006.

Concerned About Your Alcohol Or Drug Use?

© Partnership for Drug-Free America, 2004. Used with permission.

If you are concerned about your own drug or alcohol use, you may not need rehabilitation treatment or "rehab." There are other things you can do. Here are some ways to evaluate where you are and to help you figure out what you can do for your future:

- Recognize early signs if your drug or alcohol use is becoming a problem.

- Make an appointment with your doctor or other health professional, therapist or social worker to discuss the problem.

- Attend a meeting of Alcoholics Anonymous (AA), Narcotics Anonymous (NA), Smart Recovery or other anonymous self-help groups devoted to helping members get sober and stay that way.

✔ Quick Tip

Here are 12 questions to consider when selecting a treatment program:

1. Does the program accept your insurance? If not, will they work with you on a payment plan or find other means of support for you?

2. Is the program run by state-accredited, licensed and/or trained professionals?

3. Is the facility clean, organized, and well run?

4. Does the program encompass the full range of needs of the individual (medical: including infectious diseases; psychological: including co-occurring mental illness; social; vocational; legal; etc.)?

5. Does the treatment program also address sexual orientation and physical disabilities as well as provide age, gender, and culturally appropriate treatment services?

6. Is long-term aftercare support and/or guidance encouraged, provided, and maintained?

7. Is there ongoing assessment of an individual's treatment plan to ensure it meets changing needs?

8. Does the program employ strategies to engage and keep individuals in longer-term treatment, increasing the likelihood of success?

9. Does the program offer counseling (individual or group) and other behavioral therapies to enhance the individual's ability to function in the family/community?

10. Does the program offer medication as part of the treatment regimen, if appropriate?

11. Is there ongoing monitoring of possible relapse to help guide patients back to abstinence?

12. Are services or referrals offered to family members to ensure they understand addiction and the recovery process to help them support the recovering individual?

Source: "A Quick Guide to Finding Effective Alcohol and Drug Addiction Treatment," Center for Substance Abuse Treatment (CSAT), Substance Abuse and Mental Health Services Administration (SAMHSA), U.S. Department of Health and Human Services (DHHS), DHHS Publication No. (SMA) 02-3616, 2002.

It's easy to find an AA meeting or find an NA meeting in your area, as well as the most convenient locations and times. There are meetings all over and you can even sit in the back and just listen if you'd like.

- When the going gets tough, remember you can do it—you can give up alcohol and/or drugs. Talk to someone. Talk to anyone in your life who can give you encouragement, support or practical help, such as family or friends—the people who love you and want to help you in any way that they can. You might be surprised at how supportive they can be. If you feel like no one understands and you have no one to talk to about this, please know that there are many other people who do understand and can help you. Remember, you don't have to be alone in this.

Have faith in yourself and you will find a way. It takes courage and responsibility to be happy. It's not easy, but it is possible to recover and lead a healthy life.

Chapter 57

Substance Abuse Treatment: What Does It Mean?

What Is Treatment?

What is treatment? Is it a place? Is it a pill? Is it a therapy? Is it a religion?

Mention the word "treatment" in relation to substance use and many people think of long-term residential facilities or detox. In fact, treatment includes both of those options—and a variety of others. Treatment is actually a set of services.

There are many addictive drugs, and treatments for specific drugs can differ. Treatment also varies depending on the characteristics of the patient.

Problems associated with an individual's drug addiction can vary significantly. People who are addicted to drugs come from all walks of life. Many suffer from mental health, occupational, health, or social problems that make their addictive disorders much more difficult to treat. Even if there are few associated problems, the severity of addiction itself ranges widely among people.

Treatment addresses the individual's physical, psychological, emotional, and social conditions. Sustained reduction in alcohol or other drug use and sustained increases in personal health and social function are the primary goals.

About This Chapter: Information in this chapter is from "Treatment Intro," © Partnership for Drug-Free America, 2004. Used with permission.

A variety of scientifically based approaches to drug addiction treatment exists. Drug addiction treatment can include behavioral therapy (such as counseling, cognitive therapy, or psychotherapy), medications, or a combination of these. Behavioral therapies offer people strategies for coping with their drug cravings, teach them ways to avoid drugs and prevent relapse, and help them deal with relapse if it occurs. When a person's drug-related behavior places him or her at higher risk for AIDS or other infectious diseases, behavioral therapies can help to reduce the risk of disease transmission. Case management and referral to other medical, psychological, and social services are crucial components of treatment for many patients.

Treatment can occur in a variety of settings, in many different forms, and for different lengths of time. Because drug addiction is typically a chronic disorder characterized by occasional relapses, a short-term, one-time treatment often is not sufficient. For many, treatment is a long-term process that involves multiple interventions and attempts at abstinence.

♣ It's A Fact!!

Drug treatment programs in prisons can succeed in preventing patients' return to criminal behavior, particularly if they are linked to community-based programs that continue treatment when the client leaves prison. Some of the more successful programs have reduced the re-arrest rate by one-fourth to one-half. For example, the "Delaware Model," an ongoing study of comprehensive treatment of drug-addicted prison inmates, shows that prison-based treatment including a therapeutic community setting, a work release therapeutic community, and community-based aftercare reduces the probability of re-arrest by 57 percent and reduces the likelihood of returning to drug use by 37 percent.

Source: Excerpted from "NIDA InfoFacts: Drug Addiction Treatment Methods," National Institute on Drug Abuse, a component of the United States Department of Health and Human Services, March 2005.

If you or someone you care for is dependent on alcohol or drugs and needs treatment, it is important to know that no single treatment approach is appropriate for all individuals.

Finding the right treatment program involves careful consideration of such things as the setting, length of care, philosophical approach, and your or your loved one's needs.

The type of treatment needed is based on the severity of the problem. For those using in a risky way, treatment can be as simple as a screening and a brief intervention. For people exhibiting signs of dependence or addiction, a screening will probably lead to a referral for more intense attention.

Screening And Brief Intervention

All treatment starts with a screening, which is a series of questions about the amount and frequency of alcohol or other drug use and the consequences it may be causing. Many types of professionals, including a physician in a hospital or an office, a nurse, a clinical social worker, or a licensed substance abuse counselor can do screening.

After a screening, some people may need a brief intervention, usually done by a health professional. During a brief intervention, people receive feedback on their substance use based on the screening results. Frequently, people are asked to cut back or stop their use. If they are ready to cut down, the health care professional will work with them to set a goal based on lower consumption. They may also be encouraged to reflect on why they use and how their lives will change by lowering their use. People who want to stop substance use will most likely be referred for additional evaluation or treatment.

To help someone you know who you think may have a substance use problem, you first need to get him or her professionally screened. Your best bet is to talk to your own physician about referring you to someone who can help, such as a licensed substance abuse counselor or family therapist.

If Someone Needs Treatment

Formal treatment takes many forms, and no one type of treatment is best for everyone. There are many roads to recovery.

Experts believe that any of a number of programs can lead to success if the person is willing to accept help from others and invest energy in working on recovery. A physician or another health care professional can also help choose where someone should go for treatment.

How Effective Is Drug Addiction Treatment?

In addition to stopping drug use, the goal of treatment is to return the person so they can function productively in the family, school, workplace, and community. Measures of effectiveness typically include levels of criminal behavior, family functioning, employability, and medical condition. Overall, treatment of addiction is as successful as treatment of other chronic diseases, such as diabetes, hypertension, and asthma.

Treated Patients Show Far More Improvements Than Non-Treated Patients

According to several studies, drug treatment reduces drug use by 40 to 60 percent and significantly decreases criminal activity during and after treatment. Research also shows that drug addiction treatment reduces the risk of HIV infection and that interventions to prevent HIV are much less costly than treating HIV-related illnesses. Treatment can improve the prospects for employment, with gains of up to 40 percent after treatment.

Although these effectiveness rates hold in general, individual treatment outcomes depend on the extent and nature of the patient's presenting problems, the appropriateness of the treatment components and related services used to address those problems, and the degree of active engagement of the patient in the treatment process.

Be aware that there is no single approach to treatment that is successful for everyone. Like hypertension, diabetes, asthma or other chronic medical illnesses, different types of treatment are needed for different individuals. Treatment varies depending on the type of drug and the characteristics of the patient. The best programs provide a combination of therapies and other services to meet the needs of the individual patients.

> **☞ Remember!!**
>
> - Motivation is an important but not critical ingredient to effective treatment.
>
> - In order for a patient's symptoms to improve, their behavior needs to change.
>
> - Social and legal pressure can lead to changes in health.
>
> - Social support and counseling alone can improve symptoms and function.
>
> - Poor, psychiatrically ill, and criminal patients can improve.

The Three Stages Of Treatment

There are three stages of substance abuse treatments:

1. **Acute Care or Medical Detoxification/Stabilization.** Purpose: To safely and comfortably remove toxins from the body, to stabilize the patient, and to engage them into rehabilitation.

2. **Rehabilitation.** Purpose: To teach skills necessary to change behavior. To reduce threats to progress. To engage the patient in the next stage of treatment.

3. **Aftercare or Continuing Care.** Purpose: To maintain change behavior, support healthy living, and monitor threats to relapse. If relapse occurs, re-engage the patient and retain patient in continuing care.

Chapter 58

Principles Of Substance Abuse Treatment

1. **No single treatment is appropriate for all individuals.** Matching treatment settings, interventions, and services to each individual's particular problems and needs is critical to his or her ultimate success in returning to productive functioning in the family, workplace, and society.

2. **Treatment needs to be readily available.** Because individuals who are addicted to drugs may be uncertain about entering treatment, taking advantage of opportunities when they are ready for treatment is crucial. Potential treatment applicants can be lost if treatment is not immediately available or is not readily accessible.

3. **Effective treatment attends to multiple needs of the individual, not just his or her drug use.** To be effective, treatment must address the individual's drug use and any associated medical, psychological, social, vocational, and legal problems.

4. **An individual's treatment and services plan must be assessed continually and modified as necessary to ensure that the plan meets the person's changing needs.** A patient may require varying combinations of services

About This Chapter: Information in this chapter is from "Principles of Treatment," *Principles of Drug Addiction Treatment: A Research Based Guide*, Office of National Drug Control Policy, a component of the Executive Office of the President, 2000. Updated January 2006 by David A. Cooke, M.D., Diplomate, American Board of Internal Medicine.

and treatment components during the course of treatment and recovery. In addition to counseling or psychotherapy, a patient at times may require medication, other medical services, family therapy, parenting instruction, vocational rehabilitation, and social and legal services. It is critical that the treatment approach be appropriate to the individual's age, gender, ethnicity, and culture.

5. **Remaining in treatment for an adequate period of time is critical for treatment effectiveness.** The appropriate duration for an individual depends on his or her problems and needs. Research indicates that for most patients, the threshold of significant improvement is reached at about 3 months in treatment. After this threshold is reached, additional treatment can produce further progress toward recovery. Because people often leave treatment prematurely, programs should include strategies to engage and keep patients in treatment.

6. **Counseling (individual and/or group) and other behavioral therapies are critical components of effective treatment for addiction.** In therapy, patients address issues of motivation, build skills to resist drug use, replace drug-using activities with constructive and rewarding non-drug-using activities, and improve problem-solving abilities. Behavioral therapy also facilitates interpersonal relationships and the individual's ability to function in the family and community.

7. **Medications are an important element of treatment for many patients, especially when combined with counseling and other behavioral therapies.** Methadone and levo-alpha-acetylmethadol (LAAM) are very effective in helping individuals addicted to heroin or other opiates stabilize their lives and reduce their illicit drug use. A newly-available medication called buprenorphine (Suboxone®) is another option. Naltrexone is also an effective medication for some opiate addicts and some patients with co-occurring alcohol dependence. For persons addicted to nicotine, a nicotine replacement product (such as patches or gum) or an oral medication (such as bupropion) can be an effective component of treatment. For patients with mental disorders, both behavioral treatments and medications can be critically important.

8. **Addicted or drug-abusing individuals with coexisting mental disorders should have both disorders treated in an integrated way.** Because addictive disorders and mental disorders often occur in the same individual, patients presenting for either condition should be assessed and treated for the co-occurrence of the other type of disorder.

9. **Medical detoxification is only the first stage of addiction treatment and by itself does little to change long-term drug use.** Medical detoxification safely manages the acute physical symptoms of withdrawal associated with stopping drug use. While detoxification alone is rarely sufficient to help addicts achieve long-term abstinence, for some individuals it is a strongly indicated precursor to effective drug addiction treatment.

10. **Treatment does not need to be voluntary to be effective.** Strong motivation can facilitate the treatment process. Sanctions or enticements in the family, employment setting, or criminal justice system can increase significantly both treatment entry and retention rates and the success of drug treatment interventions.

11. **Possible drug use during treatment must be monitored continuously.** Lapses to drug use can occur during treatment. The objective monitoring of a patient's drug and alcohol use during treatment, such as through urinalysis or other tests, can help the patient withstand urges to use drugs. Such monitoring also can provide early evidence of drug use so that the individual's treatment plan can be adjusted. Feedback to patients who test positive for illicit drug use is an important element of monitoring.

12. **Treatment programs should provide assessment for HIV/AIDS, hepatitis B and C, tuberculosis and other infectious diseases, and counseling to help patients modify or change behaviors that place themselves or others at risk of infection.** Counseling can help patients avoid high-risk behavior. Counseling also can help people who are already infected manage their illness.

13. **Recovery from drug addiction can be a long-term process and frequently requires multiple episodes of treatment.** As with other chronic illnesses, relapses to drug use can occur during or after successful treatment episodes. Addicted individuals may require prolonged treatment and multiple

episodes of treatment to achieve long-term abstinence and fully restored functioning. Participation in self-help support programs during and following treatment often is helpful in maintaining abstinence.

Chapter 59

Types Of Substance Abuse Treatment

A variety of scientifically based approaches to drug addiction treatments exist. Drug addiction treatment can include behavioral therapy (such as counseling, cognitive therapy, or psychotherapy), medications, or their combination.

Agonist Maintenance Treatment for opiate addicts usually is conducted in outpatient settings, often called methadone treatment programs. These programs use a long-acting synthetic opiate medication, usually methadone or levo-alpha-acetylmethadol (LAAM), administered orally for a sustained period at a dosage sufficient to prevent opiate withdrawal, block the effects of illicit opiate use, and decrease opiate craving. Buprenorphine (Suboxone®) has been recently approved for similar use in doctors' offices by specially certified physicians. Patients stabilized on adequate, sustained dosages of methadone, LAAM, or buprenorphine can function normally. They can hold jobs, avoid the crime and violence of the street culture, and reduce their exposure to HIV by stopping or decreasing injection drug use and drug-related high-risk sexual behavior.

Patients stabilized on opiate agonists can engage more readily in counseling and other behavioral interventions essential to recovery and rehabilitation.

About This Chapter: Information in this chapter is from "Types of Treatment," *Principles of Drug Addiction Treatment: A Research Based Guide*, Office of National Drug Control Policy, a component of the Executive Office of the President, 2000. Updated January 2006 by David A. Cooke, M.D., Diplomate, American Board of Internal Medicine.

The best, most effective opiate agonist maintenance programs include individual and/or group counseling, as well as provision of, or referral to, other needed medical, psychological, and social services.

Narcotic Antagonist Treatment Using Naltrexone for opiate addicts usually is conducted in outpatient settings although initiation of the medication often begins after medical detoxification in a residential setting. Naltrexone is a long-acting synthetic opiate antagonist with few side effects that is taken orally either daily or three times a week for a sustained period of time. Individuals must be medically detoxified and opiate-free for several days before naltrexone can be taken to prevent precipitating an opiate abstinence syndrome. When used this way, all the effects of self-administered opiates, including euphoria, are completely blocked. The theory behind this treatment is that the repeated lack of the desired opiate effects, as well as the perceived futility of using the opiate, will gradually over time result in breaking the habit of opiate addiction. Naltrexone itself has no subjective effects or potential for abuse and is not addicting. Patient noncompliance is a common problem. Therefore, a favorable treatment outcome requires that there also be a positive therapeutic relationship, effective counseling or therapy, and careful monitoring of medication compliance.

Many experienced clinicians have found naltrexone most useful for highly motivated, recently detoxified patients who desire total abstinence because of external circumstances, including impaired professionals, parolees, probationers, and prisoners in work-release status. Patients stabilized on naltrexone can function normally. They can hold jobs, avoid the crime and violence of the street culture, and reduce their exposure to HIV by stopping injection drug use and drug-related high-risk sexual behavior.

Outpatient Drug-Free Treatment in the types and intensity of services offered. Such treatment costs less than residential or inpatient treatment and often is more suitable for individuals who are employed or who have extensive social supports. Low-intensity programs may offer little more than drug education and admonition. Other outpatient models, such as intensive day treatment, can be comparable to residential programs in services and effectiveness, depending on the individual patient's characteristics and needs.

In many outpatient programs, group counseling is emphasized. Some outpatient programs are designed to treat patients who have medical or mental health problems in addition to their drug disorder.

Long-Term Residential Treatment provides care 24 hours per day, generally in non-hospital settings. The best-known residential treatment model is the therapeutic community (TC), but residential treatment may also employ other models, such as cognitive-behavioral therapy. TCs are residential programs with planned lengths of stay of 6 to 12 months. TCs focus on the "re-socialization" of the individual and use the program's entire "community," including other residents, staff, and the social context, as active components of treatment. Addiction is viewed in the context of an individual's social and psychological deficits, and treatment focuses on developing personal accountability and responsibility and socially productive lives. Treatment is highly structured and can at times be confrontational, with activities designed to help residents examine damaging beliefs, self-concepts, and patterns of behavior and to adopt new, more harmonious and constructive ways to interact with others. Many TCs are quite comprehensive and can include employment training and other support services on site.

Compared with patients in other forms of drug treatment, the typical TC resident has more severe problems, with more co-occurring mental health problems and more criminal involvement. Research shows that TCs can be modified to treat individuals with special needs, including adolescents, women, those with severe mental disorders, and individuals in the criminal justice system.

Short-Term Residential Programs provide intensive but relatively brief residential treatment based on a modified 12-step approach. These programs were originally designed to treat alcohol problems, but during the cocaine epidemic of the mid-1980s, many began to treat illicit drug abuse and addiction. The original residential treatment model consisted of a 3 to 6 week hospital-based inpatient treatment phase followed by extended outpatient therapy and participation in a self-help group, such as Alcoholics Anonymous. Reduced health care coverage for substance abuse treatment has resulted in a diminished number of these programs, and the average length of stay under managed care review is much shorter than in early programs.

Medical Detoxification is a process whereby individuals are systematically withdrawn from addicting drugs in an inpatient or outpatient setting, typically under the care of a physician. Detoxification is sometimes called a distinct treatment modality but is more appropriately considered a precursor of treatment, because it is designed to treat the acute physiological effects of stopping drug use. Medications are available for detoxification from opiates, nicotine, benzodiazepines, alcohol, barbiturates, and other sedatives. In some cases, particularly for the last three types of drugs, detoxification may be a medical necessity, and untreated withdrawal may be medically dangerous or even fatal.

Detoxification is not designed to address the psychological, social, and behavioral problems associated with addiction and therefore does not typically produce lasting behavioral changes necessary for recovery. Detoxification is most useful when it incorporates formal processes of assessment and referral to subsequent drug addiction treatment.

Treating Criminal Justice-Involved Drug Abusers and Addicts. Research has shown that combining criminal justice sanctions with drug treatment can be effective in decreasing drug use and related crime. Individuals under

♣ It's A Fact!!

There are currently no medications approved by the Food and Drug Administration (FDA) for treating addiction to cocaine, LSD, PCP, marijuana, methamphetamine and other stimulants, inhalants, or anabolic steroids. There are medications, however, for treating the adverse health effects of these drugs, such as seizures or psychotic reactions, and for overdoses from opiates. Currently, the National Institute on Drug Abuse's (NIDA) top research priority is the development of a medication useful in treating cocaine addiction.

Source: Excerpted from "NIDA InfoFacts: Drug Addiction Treatment Medications," National Institute on Drug Abuse (NIDA), National Institutes of Health (NIH), a component of the U.S. Department of Health and Human Services, March 2005.

legal coercion tend to stay in treatment for a longer period of time and do as well as or better than others not under legal pressure. Often, drug abusers come into contact with the criminal justice system earlier than other health or social systems, and intervention by the criminal justice system to engage the individual in treatment may help interrupt and shorten a career of drug use. Treatment for the criminal justice-involved drug abuser or drug addict may be delivered prior to, during, after, or in lieu of incarceration.

- **Prison-Based Treatment Programs.** Offenders with drug disorders may encounter a number of treatment options while incarcerated, including didactic drug education classes, self-help programs, and treatment based on therapeutic community or residential milieu therapy models. The TC model has been studied extensively and can be quite effective in reducing drug use and recidivism to criminal behavior. Those in treatment should be segregated from the general prison population, so that the "prison culture" does not overwhelm progress toward recovery. As might be expected, treatment gains can be lost if inmates are returned to the general prison population after treatment. Research shows that relapse to drug use and recidivism to crime are significantly lower if the drug offender continues treatment after returning to the community.

- **Community-Based Treatment for Criminal Justice Populations.** A number of criminal justice alternatives to incarceration have been tried with offenders who have drug disorders, including limited diversion programs, pretrial release conditional on entry into treatment, and conditional probation with sanctions. The drug court is a promising approach. Drug courts mandate and arrange for drug addiction treatment, actively monitor progress in treatment, and arrange for other services to drug-involved offenders. Federal support for planning, implementation, and enhancement of drug courts is provided under the U.S. Department of Justice Drug Courts Program Office.

As a well-studied example, the Treatment Accountability and Safer Communities (TASC) program provides an alternative to incarceration by addressing the multiple needs of drug-addicted offenders in a community-based setting. TASC programs typically include counseling, medical care, parenting instruction, family counseling, school and job training, and legal and employment services. The key features of TASC include (1) coordination of criminal justice and drug treatment; (2) early identification, assessment, and referral of drug-involved offenders; (3) monitoring offenders through drug testing; and (4) use of legal sanctions as inducements to remain in treatment.

Chapter 60

Addiction And Recovery

As you learn about substance use disorders and how to treat them, you will probably hear the phrase "being in recovery."

What Happens To The Person With The Addiction In Recovery?

Recovery occurs over time—it is not a single moment in time. It is a constantly evolving period that requires work to maintain. Recovery is a new beginning and can be a time of great personal fulfillment and growth for people in recovery and their families.

Some addiction experts use the term "recovering" rather than "recovered." Although the person has made a commitment to abstinence and is moving in that direction, he or she continues to be vulnerable to relapse. Recovery requires sustained effort so some view it as if the work of recovery is never fully done, so they use the word "recovering."

Recovery requires that the person with the addiction repair relationships damaged through years of drinking and taking drugs. There may be feelings of shame and self-hatred. The person may have to give up the "addict mentality" that is suspicious, secretive, manipulative, and self-centered.

About This Chapter: Information in this chapter is from "Recovery Overview." © Partnership for Drug-Free America, 2004. Used with permission.

People in recovery abstain from substance use. By doing so, they regain their physical health and emotional well being. Once again, they are able to enjoy everyday activities with energy, enthusiasm, optimism, and confidence. Over time, people will return to being more loving spouses, happier kids, effective parents, good neighbors, and dedicated employees.

♣ **It's A Fact!!**
Signs of increasing health and wellness are that the person with the addiction improves physically and emotionally and in his or her relationship with others.

Recovering Or Recovered?

People who are in recovery have overcome the problems associated with their substance use. People do not have to be in the addiction stage of substance use to enter and appreciate recovery, and they don't have to enter a formal treatment program or attend a self-help group—they may have simply had a conversation with a family member and decided it was time to cut back on drinking or drug taking.

Relapsing

This time can also be challenging. People in recovery may feel shame or self-hatred. They might have to give up an "addict mentality" that is suspicious, secretive, manipulative, and self-centered. They may have to repair relationships damaged through years of substance use. Intense, painful memories and feelings stemming from anxiety, depression, school problems, sexual problems, neglect, loss, violence or other past trauma may come flooding back at unexpected times. With emotions already raw, the stresses and disappointments of daily living can feel intolerable. In the past, alcohol and drugs had provided relief from problems and trauma, but the recovering person now has to face these feelings with no "escape hatch."

Even Though The Person Is In Recovery, Relapse Is A Common Reaction To This Stress

Sometimes relapse occurs when the person is doing well with their recovery. He or she feels healthy, confident, and/or "cured" and believes that he or she is ready to go back to casual, regular or "controlled" use of alcohol or drugs. The person may remember the honeymoon period of their use (even though it may have been long ago) where his or her use didn't cause problems and may want to return to that place. But this is often impossible since addiction changes the physical makeup of the brain and therefore the person in recovery is not able to use drugs or alcohol in a controlled fashion.

Getting Help During Recovery

Medical professionals, particularly those who specialize in substance use disorders, are an extremely important asset during a time of relapse. They can help the person learn techniques for containing feelings, focusing on the present, and making use of support from others. Relying on group support from Twelve Step programs, engaging in prayer or meditation, and finding other ways to stay on an even keel can also be extremely helpful.

Chapter 61

Helping A Friend With A Substance Abuse Problem

This chapter will assist you in helping a friend who has a problem with alcohol or other drugs. Sometimes, being a good friend means you have to intervene, but before you get involved it is important to understand what is really going on with your friend.

How can I tell if my friend has a drinking or other drug problem?

Sometimes it's tough to tell. Most kids won't walk up to someone they're close to and ask for help. In fact, your friend will probably do everything possible to deny or hide the problem. But, there are signs you can look for. People with serious substance abuse problems say things like, "I can stop drinking or using other drugs any time I want to"— but they don't. They may be o.k. to hang around with, until they get high—then they often act like jerks or get into fights. No one is sure why some people get into trouble with alcohol or other drugs. There are signs, however, when substances are taking control of someone's life. Some of these signs are easy to see, others aren't, but if you see them happening over and over again, chances are your friend needs help.

About This Chapter: This text is excerpted from "A Guide for Teens: Does your friend have an alcohol or other drug problem? What can you do to help?" Produced and published by the Center for Health Communication of the Harvard School of Public Health. © Copyright 1994 President and Fellows of Harvard College. Reprinted with permission. Despite the older date of this document, the guidelines presented are still relevant.

If your friend has one or more of the following warning signs, he or she may have a problem with alcohol or other drugs:

- Getting drunk or high on drugs on a regular basis

- Lying about things, or about how much alcohol or other drugs he or she is using

- Avoiding you in order to get drunk or high

- Giving up activities he or she used to do, such as sports, homework, or hanging out with friends who don't drink or use other drugs

- Planning drinking in advance, hiding alcohol, drinking or using other drugs alone

- Having to drink more to get the same high

- Believing that in order to have fun you need to drink or use other drugs

- Frequent hangovers

- Pressuring others to drink or use other drugs

- Taking risks, including sexual risks

- Having "blackouts"—forgetting what he or she did the night before while drinking (if you tell your friend what happened, he or she might pretend to remember, or laugh it off as no big deal)

- Feeling run-down, hopeless, depressed, or even suicidal

- Sounding selfish and not caring about others

- Constantly talking about drinking or using other drugs

- Getting in trouble with the law

- Drinking and driving

- Suspension from school for an alcohol- or other drug-related incident

> **♣ It's A Fact!!**
> No matter what, in order to get better, your friend eventually has to admit that he or she has a problem and make an effort to get help. You can be the one that encourages and guides your friend to seek this help.

How serious can my friend's drinking or other drug problem be? What can it lead to?

Not all people who drink or use other drugs develop the same symptoms or consequences, but one thing is for sure: If your friend has a drinking or other drug problem and doesn't get help, things can get much worse. People with serious drinking or other drug problems don't like to admit it, even to themselves. In the beginning, they often say they feel great, that drinking or smoking pot or doing a few lines of cocaine is the best thing that ever happened to them. But then things change for the worse. Eventually, if they don't get help, they can develop serious psychological problems such as suicidal depression, and serious physical problems such as liver damage and brain damage; and some will die from an overdose. Getting drunk or high impairs judgment, and may lead to behaviors that people wouldn't do ordinarily if they weren't under the influence of these substances—such as having unsafe sex which could result in pregnancy, AIDS, or other sexually transmitted diseases. Substance abuse is dangerous; it can ruin your friend's health, cause your friend to drop out of school, lose friends, lose values, and even lose his or her self-respect.

Alcohol and other drugs don't care who you are, what color you are, if you're rich or poor, how old you are, your sex, or where you're from. They don't care if you're a jock, a cheerleader, or a genius.

What would cause my friend to have a serious drinking or other drug problem?

Lots of things lead to these problems. For one thing, these difficulties often run in families, just like heart disease and cancer. If your friend's parents are alcoholic, or there is a family history of alcoholism or other drug addiction, your friend is more likely to become alcoholic or drug dependent.

People often drink or use other drugs to avoid things that bother them— pressure from friends, stress in the family, hassles, the feeling that adults are on their case, the lousy feeling that they're different from everyone else in the world. They use these substances just to feel better. The problem is, drinking or using other drugs eventually makes things worse because all you care about is getting high, and once you start it's hard to stop; you need to use more just to feel normal. Alcohol and other substances change the way you think, and you start to believe things are better or worse than they really are. Alcohol and other drugs may make you feel good when you're high, but when they wear off, depression sets in.

Why is it so hard for individuals to get help for themselves?

It's tough for most people to admit that they have a serious substance abuse problem. It's especially hard to admit it when you're young because you think that kind of thing could never happen to you. Many people believe that alcoholics and other drug addicts are old people, or are street people, when, in reality, they can be anyone. People who have a serious problem with drinking or using other drugs might say that they are not using that much and that they won't get addicted. Denying that there's a problem is very common. In fact, this denial, along with hiding the substance abuse from friends, becomes almost as big a problem as the drinking or other drug use itself. Becoming dependent on alcohol or other drugs makes you want to cut off the people who care about you, and you can end up feeling lonely and afraid.

To avoid being found out, serious problem drinkers and other drug users often spend more and more time alone, and think they can solve their problem all by themselves, or that a boyfriend or girlfriend can solve it for them. Getting better doesn't work that way. What has to happen is that your friend has to admit that alcohol and/or other drugs are messing up his or her life. However, you can help even if your friend does not admit to having a problem.

What can I do to help my friend?

It is possible for you to help a friend who is in serious trouble with alcohol or other drugs. Whether or not your friend takes your advice and gets help is really your friend's decision and responsibility.

The first step in getting help is for your friend to talk to someone about his or her alcohol and drug use. Eventually, your friend will need to admit that there is a problem, and to agree to

> ✔ **Quick Tip**
> Sometimes, approaching the friend in trouble with another mutual friend can make your intervention easier since there is safety and support in numbers.

☞ Remember!!

You can't force a friend to get help, but you can encourage and support your friend to seek and find professional help.

stop drinking and/or using other drugs completely. Your friend needs support and understanding, and someone he or she can trust to talk to about the problem.

If you are worried about a friend, it is important for you to speak to someone in private who is knowledgeable and reassuring. Telling someone isn't being disloyal to your friend. It's important to know the facts about what's happening to your friend if you plan to help. Don't try to help your friend on your own until you have talked to someone you can trust—a counselor, teacher, doctor, nurse, parent, or someone at your church or synagogue. Ask this person to keep the conversation confidential. You don't have to mention your friend by name; you can just talk generally about the problem. Talking to a professional will help you figure out what the best steps are for you to take.

If you decide to speak to your friend, here are some guidelines that you and your advisor should consider in planning how and what you could do to help:

- Make sure the timing is right. Talk to your friend when he or she is sober or straight—before school is a good time.

- Never accuse your friend of being an alcoholic or a drug addict, but do express your concern. Try not to blame your friend for the problem; if you do, he or she might be turned off right away.

- Talk about your feelings. Tell your friend you're worried, and how it feels for you to see him or her drunk or high on other drugs.

- Tell your friend what you've seen him or her do when drinking or using other drugs. Give specific examples. Tell your friend you want to help.

- Speak in a caring and understanding tone of voice, not with pity but with friendship.

- Be prepared for denial and anger. Your friend may say there is nothing wrong and may get mad at you. Many people with alcohol and other drug problems react this way. When confronted, many users will defend their use, blame others for the problem, or give excuses for why they drink or use other drugs.

- Find out where help is available. You could offer to go with your friend to get help, but be prepared to follow through. This gesture will show your friend that you really care.

- You need to tell your friend that you are worried about him or her, and that someone who can help needs to be told. Your friend might get really mad at you, but if you say nothing, things may get worse and your friend may be in more danger.

- Your friend's problem is probably hard on you, too. The situation may have left you feeling lonely and afraid. Maybe you've thought, "What if I get my friend in trouble? What if I lose my friend over this? What if I don't do anything and something awful happens?" It's hard to keep all of these questions and feelings to yourself. It's important that you talk about them. You can share these feelings with the person that you go to for help about your friend's problem. There are also support groups for people like you who are trying to help a friend, such as Al-Anon or Alateen, where you can learn more about people's alcohol and other drug use problems. Your school may have a substance abuse prevention counselor as well.

What does my friend have to do to get help?

Probably the hardest decision your friend will be faced with is admitting that he or she has a problem. To get better and recover, your friend has to get some help to stop drinking or using other drugs.

Facing such a problem and asking for help can be a scary thing to do. Your friend will have to take an honest look at where drinking or other drug use has brought him or her, and admit that it has caused emotional and maybe physical pain. Your friend will have to see that it has robbed him or her of real friends, creativity, happiness, spirit, the respect of others, and even self-respect, and that it keeps your friend from growing up.

Your friend will not be able to solve this problem alone. He or she will need experienced help. A good counselor will support your friend and direct him or her to the kind of treatment and/or support groups that are most helpful.

Encourage your friend to talk to other people with drinking and other drug problems who are now in recovery, such as members of Alcoholics Anonymous (AA) and Narcotics Anonymous (NA). These groups are confidential, self-help organizations that offer assistance to anyone who has a drinking or other drug problem and wants to do something about it. AA and NA members are recovering alcoholics and addicts, so they have a special understanding of each other. Talking with others who have experienced similar problems is an important part of recovery. New members are encouraged to stay away from alcohol or other drugs "one day at a time." There is no fee for membership in these organizations. If your friend is afraid to go to a meeting alone, you can go along with him or her to an "open" meeting. Friends and family members are welcome to attend this type of meeting, and there are special meetings in most neighborhoods or communities. Local branches of AA and NA are listed in your phone directory.

If your friend has a drinking or other drug problem, you may be the only one willing to reach out and help. Your friend may not appreciate your help right away, or he or she may realize it means you really care. Ultimately, it's up to your friend to get help. It is not your responsibility to make that happen. In fact, you can't make that happen. All you can do is talk to your friend, show how much you care, and encourage him or her to get help. Your concern and support might be just what is needed to help your friend turn his or her life around.

However, if your friend is in serious trouble with alcohol or other drugs, and you have been unable to get your friend to get help on his or her own, you should consider speaking with your friend's parents or guardian. The potential consequences to your friend's life can be too severe to do nothing.

Chapter 62

If Your Parent Has A Substance Abuse Problem

If you are reading this, you might be wondering if your mom or dad has a problem with alcohol or other drugs. Or you might already know they do. In either case, the information in this chapter will help you think about what to do to help them and yourself.

How can I tell if my mom or dad has a problem with drinking or drugs?

Some people drink a lot of beer, wine, or hard alcohol like whisky or vodka. Some use other drugs like marijuana, cocaine, heroin, or pills. When they do, it can sometimes change the way they act and how other people act around them.

Maybe everyone gets tense when mom or dad is drinking or taking drugs. Maybe mom and dad fight a lot about how much the other person is drinking, or how often the other person is using drugs. "You've been drinking all day and that is not normal!" "Whenever you take those pills, you act crazy!"

Maybe family plans are always getting messed up. Did you ever miss out on a chance to go somewhere because your dad drank too much and forgot

About This Chapter: Information in this chapter is from "If You Are a Child Concerned about a Parent Q&A." © Partnership for Drug-Free America, 2004. Used with permission.

that you had plans? Or maybe your parent is having job problems. Does Mom ever call in sick to work after a night of drinking or taking drugs?

Maybe Mom or Dad changes into "a different person" after drinking or getting high on drugs. Sometimes people call this a "personality change" because a person who is quiet or calm gets loud, nasty, and maybe even violent. They might not remember things that happen, even if they seem to be okay.

People who act like this probably have a problem with alcohol or drugs. Sometimes a problem with alcohol is called alcoholism, and a problem with drugs is called drug addiction.

Why does my mom or dad have a problem with alcohol or drugs? Is it my fault?

No one knows why a person develops a problem with alcohol or drugs. Some people start drinking or taking drugs to avoid things that make them sad, angry, or worried. Others do it to relax. Pretty soon, they are not able to face their problems except by drinking or taking drugs.

☞ Remember!!
It is not your fault! You cannot make your parent have a problem with alcohol or drugs. Adults can't make other adults have these problems, either.

Their bodies are used to the feeling that alcohol and drugs gives them, and they feel like they need to keep drinking or using drugs. If they have to go without drinking for very long, they will feel shaky and may need to vomit. They may get a headache or even see things that aren't really there.

I want my parent to stop. What can I do?

You must remember, you did not cause the problem and you cannot make it go away. Your parent has an illness and needs help from other adults.

The first thing to do is to find an adult you trust and tell them you are worried. This person could be someone from school like a teacher, school nurse, coach, or guidance counselor. It could be your family doctor, or a minister, priest, or rabbi. The best people to talk to are people who work with children and understand problems like alcoholism and drug addiction. Find someone you can tell about what's going on.

You also need to take care of yourself. Get enough sleep, eat right, and have fun. Kids living with parents who have problems with alcohol or other drugs can forget to take care of themselves because they are so worried about their parents all the time. Remember, though, you are not alone. Telling someone else will help your parent and yourself.

Will my mom or dad get in trouble if I tell someone?

Your parent needs help from adults who understand alcoholism and drug addiction. That's the only way things will change.

If no one finds out, then your mom or dad could get worse and hurt himself or herself or someone else.

If you talk with an adult and you are worried about getting your parents or yourself into trouble, you could ask that person to keep the information private until the two of you can figure out what to do.

Will I get myself in trouble if I tell?

Your parents may be angry for a while, but if the family can get help, they may be glad someone else knows. Remember, it's not your fault. Your parent is sick. You didn't cause it, and you can't stop it by yourself.

Should I talk to my mom or dad about their behavior?

Definitely don't talk to your mom or dad when they are drinking or taking drugs. Your parent may become angry, lose control, and blame you. Wait until they are sober.

Start by trying to have an adult you trust with you when you talk to your mom or dad. If that cannot happen, get advice from an adult about what you should say to Mom or Dad.

If you do decide to talk to your mom or dad, try to tell them how you feel about their drinking or drug taking. It's okay to say that it upsets you, but don't tell them what they are doing is wrong or blame them for everything that isn't going right. When adults feel blamed, they get angry and it's hard for them to listen and stay calm. Talk about your own feelings.

What else can I do?

Try not to blurt out what you are feeling whenever you get upset. Ask your mom or dad if there is a quiet time when they can talk to you. That way they won't have to talk with you when they are in the middle of doing something else, and they won't get mad. Also, don't argue with your parent. It will not be helpful to you or them.

The most important thing to remember is that this is not your fault, and you cannot fix the problem. Your parent needs to get help.

Part Seven

Drug Policy Controversies

Chapter 63

The Controlled Substances Act

Controlling Drugs Or Other Substances

The Controlled Substances Act (CSA), Title II and Title III of the Comprehensive Drug Abuse Prevention and Control Act of 1970, is the legal foundation of the U.S. Government's fight against the abuse of drugs and other substances. This law is a consolidation of numerous laws regulating the manufacture and distribution of narcotics, stimulants, depressants, hallucinogens, anabolic steroids, and chemicals used in the illicit production of controlled substances.

Formal Scheduling

The Controlled Substances Act (CSA) places all substances, which were in some manner regulated under existing federal law, into one of five schedules. This placement is based upon the substance's medical use, potential for abuse, and safety or dependence liability. The Act also provides a mechanism for substances to be controlled, or added to a schedule; decontrolled, or removed from control; and rescheduled or transferred from one schedule to another. The procedure for these actions is found in Section 201 of the Act (21 U.S.C. 811).

About This Chapter: Information in this chapter is excerpted from "Chapter 1: The Controlled Substances Act," *Drugs of Abuse*, U.S. Drug Enforcement Administration, U.S. Department of Justice, 2005.

Proceedings to add, delete, or change the schedule of a drug or other substance may be initiated by the Drug Enforcement Administration (DEA), the Department of Health and Human Services (HHS), or by petition from any interested person: the manufacturer of a drug, a medical society or association, a pharmacy association, a public interest group concerned with drug abuse, a state or local government agency, or an individual citizen. When a petition is received by the DEA, the agency begins its own investigation of the drug.

The DEA also may begin an investigation of a drug at any time based upon information received from law enforcement laboratories, state and local law enforcement and regulatory agencies, or other sources of information.

Once the DEA has collected the necessary data, the DEA Administrator, by authority of the Attorney General, requests from HHS a scientific and medical evaluation and recommendation as to whether the drug or other substance should be controlled or removed from control. This request is sent to the Assistant Secretary of Health of HHS. HHS solicits information from the Commissioner of the Food and Drug Administration (FDA), evaluations and recommendations from the National Institute on Drug Abuse, and on occasion, from the scientific and medical community at large. The Assistant Secretary, by authority of the Secretary, compiles the information and transmits back to the DEA a medical and scientific evaluation regarding the drug or other substance, a recommendation as to whether the drug should be controlled, and in what schedule it should be placed.

The medical and scientific evaluations are binding on the DEA with respect to scientific and medical matters and form a part of the scheduling decision. The recommendation on the initial scheduling of a substance is binding only to the extent that if HHS recommends that the substance not be controlled, the DEA may not add it to the schedules.

Once the DEA has received the scientific and medical evaluation from HHS, the Administrator will evaluate all available data and make a final decision whether to propose that a drug or other substance should be removed or controlled and into which schedule it should be placed.

The threshold issue is whether the drug or other substance has potential for abuse. If a drug does not have a potential for abuse, it cannot be controlled. Although the term "potential for abuse" is not defined in the CSA, there is much discussion of the term in the legislative history of the Act. The following items are indicators that a drug or other substance has a potential for abuse:

1. There is evidence that individuals are taking the drug or other substance in amounts sufficient to create a hazard to their health or to the safety of other individuals or to the community; or

2. There is significant diversion of the drug or other substance from legitimate drug channels; or

3. Individuals are taking the drug or other substance on their own initiative rather than on the basis of medical advice from a practitioner licensed by law to administer such drugs; or

4. The drug is a new drug so related in its action to a drug or other substance already listed as having a potential for abuse to make it likely that the drug will have the same potential for abuse as such drugs, thus making it reasonable to assume that there may be significant diversions from legitimate channels, significant use contrary to or without medical advice, or that it has a substantial capability of creating hazards to the health of the user or to the safety of the community. Of course, evidence of actual abuse of a substance is indicative that a drug has a potential for abuse.

In determining into which schedule a drug or other substance should be placed, or whether a substance should be decontrolled or rescheduled, certain factors are required to be considered. Specific findings are not required for each factor. These factors are listed in Section 201 (c), [21 U.S.C. 811 (c)] of the CSA as follows:

1. **The drug's actual or relative potential for abuse.**

2. **Scientific evidence of the drug's pharmacological effects.** The state of knowledge with respect to the effects of a specific drug is, of course, a major consideration. For example, it is vital to know whether or not a drug has a hallucinogenic effect if it is to be controlled due to that effect. The best available knowledge of the pharmacological properties of a drug should be considered.

3. **The state of current scientific knowledge regarding the substance.** Criteria (2) and (3) are closely related. However, (2) is primarily concerned with pharmacological effects and (3) deals with all scientific knowledge with respect to the substance.

4. **Its history and current pattern of abuse.** To determine whether or not a drug should be controlled, it is important to know the pattern of abuse of that substance, including the socioeconomic characteristics of the segments of the population involved in such abuse.

5. **The scope, duration, and significance of abuse.** In evaluating existing abuse, the DEA Administrator must know not only the pattern of abuse, but also whether the abuse is widespread. In reaching a decision, the Administrator should consider the economics of regulation and enforcement attendant to such a decision. In addition, the Administrator should be aware of the social significance and impact of such a decision upon those people, especially the young that would be affected by it.

6. **What, if any, risk there is to the public health.** If a drug creates dangers to the public health, in addition to or because of its abuse potential, then the Administrator must also consider these dangers.

7. **The drug's psychic or physiological dependence liability.** There must be an assessment of the extent to which a drug is physically addictive or psychologically habit forming, if such information is known.

♣ It's A Fact!!

Here are some examples of drugs and the Schedules under which they are classified:

- **Schedule I:** heroin, LSD, marijuana, and methaqualone

- **Schedule II:** morphine, PCP, cocaine, methadone, and methamphetamine

- **Schedule III:** anabolic steroids, codeine and hydrocodone with aspirin or Tylenol®, and some barbiturates

- **Schedule IV:** Darvon®, Talwin®, Equanil®, Valium®, and Xanax®

- **Schedule V:** Cough medicines with codeine

8. **Whether the substance is an immediate precursor of a substance already controlled.** The CSA allows inclusion of immediate precursors on this basis alone into the appropriate schedule and thus safeguards against possibilities of clandestine manufacture.

After considering the above listed factors, the Administrator must make specific findings concerning the drug or other substance. This will determine into which schedule the drug or other substance will be placed. These schedules are established by the CSA. They are as follows:

Schedule I

- The drug or other substance has a high potential for abuse.

- The drug or other substance has no currently accepted medical use in treatment in the United States.

- There is a lack of accepted safety for use of the drug or other substance under medical supervision.

Schedule II

- The drug or other substance has a high potential for abuse.

- The drug or other substance has a currently accepted medical use in treatment in the United States or a currently accepted medical use with severe restrictions.

- Abuse of the drug or other substance may lead to severe psychological or physical dependence.

Schedule III

- The drug or other substance has less potential for abuse than the drugs or other substances in schedules I and II.

- The drug or other substance has a currently accepted medical use in treatment in the United States.

- Abuse of the drug or other substance may lead to moderate or low physical dependence or high psychological dependence.

Schedule IV

- The drug or other substance has a low potential for abuse relative to the drugs or other substances in Schedule III.

- The drug or other substance has a currently accepted medical use in treatment in the United States.

- Abuse of the drug or other substance may lead to limited physical dependence or psychological dependence relative to the drugs or other substances in Schedule III.

Schedule V

- The drug or other substance has a low potential for abuse relative to the drugs or other substances in Schedule IV.

- The drug or other substance has a currently accepted medical use in treatment in the United States.

- Abuse of the drug or other substances may lead to limited physical dependence or psychological dependence relative to the drugs or other substances in Schedule IV.

When the DEA Administrator has determined that a drug or other substance should be controlled, decontrolled, or rescheduled, a proposal to take action is published in the Federal Register. The proposal invites all interested persons to file comments with the DEA. Affected parties may also request a hearing with the DEA. If no hearing is requested, the DEA will evaluate all comments received and publish a final order in the Federal Register, controlling the drug as proposed or with modifications based upon the written comments filed. This order will set the effective dates for imposing the various requirements of the CSA.

If a hearing is requested, the DEA will enter into discussions with the party or parties requesting a hearing in an attempt to narrow the issue for litigation. If necessary, a hearing will then be held before an Administrative Law Judge. The judge will take evidence on factual issues and hear arguments on legal questions regarding the control of the drug. Depending on the scope and complexity of the issues, the hearing may be brief or quite extensive. The Administrative Law Judge, at the close of the hearing, prepares findings of fact and conclusions of law and a recommended decision, which is submitted to the DEA Administrator. The DEA Administrator will review these documents, as well as the underlying material, and prepare his/her own findings of fact and conclusions of law (which may or may not be the same as those drafted by the Administrative Law Judge). The DEA Administrator then publishes a final order in the Federal Register either scheduling the drug or other substance or declining to do so.

Once the final order is published in the Federal Register, interested parties have 30 days to appeal to a U.S. Court of Appeals to challenge the order. Findings of fact by the Administrator are deemed conclusive if supported by "substantial evidence." The order imposing controls is not stayed during the appeal, however, unless so ordered by the Court.

Emergency Or Temporary Scheduling

The Comprehensive Crime Control Act of 1984 amended the CSA. This Act included a provision, which allows the DEA Administrator to place a substance, on a temporary basis, into Schedule I when necessary to avoid an imminent hazard to the public safety.

This emergency scheduling authority permits the scheduling of a substance, which is not currently controlled, is being abused, and is a risk to the public health while the formal rule-making procedures described in the CSA are being conducted. This emergency scheduling applies only to substances with no accepted medical use. A temporary scheduling order may be issued for one year with a possible extension of up to six months if formal scheduling procedures have been initiated. The proposal and order are published in the Federal Register, as are the proposals and orders for formal scheduling. [21 U.S.C. 811 (h)]

Controlled Substance Analogues

The Anti-Drug Abuse Act of 1986 created a new class of substances. Controlled substance analogues are substances, which are not controlled substances, but may be found in the illicit traffic. They are structurally or pharmacologically similar to Schedule I or II controlled substances and have no legitimate medical use. A substance, which meets the definition of a controlled substance analogue and is intended for human consumption is treated under the CSA as if it were a controlled substance in Schedule I. [21U.S.C.802(32), 21U.S.C.813]

International Treaty Obligations

United States treaty obligations may require that a drug or other substance be controlled under the CSA, or rescheduled if existing controls are less stringent than those required by a treaty. The procedures for these scheduling actions are found in Section 201 (d) of the Act. [21 U.S.C. 811 (d)]

The United States is a party to the Single Convention on Narcotic Drugs of 1961, designed to establish effective control over international and domestic traffic in narcotics, coca leaf, cocaine, and cannabis. A second treaty, the Convention on Psychotropic Substances of 1971, which entered into force in 1976, is designed to establish comparable control over stimulants, depressants, and hallucinogens. Congress ratified this treaty in 1980.

☞ **Remember!!**

The CSA provides penalties for unlawful manufacturing, distribution, and dispensing of controlled substances. The penalties are basically determined by the schedule of the drug or other substance.

Chapter 64

Drug Testing In Schools

Drug Testing: An Overview

Why drug test students?

Thanks to advances in medical technology, researchers are now able to capture pictures of the human brain under the influence of drugs. These images clearly show the pleasurable sensations produced by some drugs are due to actual physical changes in the brain. Many of these changes are long lasting, and some are irreversible. Scientists have recently discovered that the brain is not fully developed in early childhood, as was once believed, but is in fact still growing even in adolescence. Introducing chemical changes in the brain through the use of illegal drugs can therefore have far more serious adverse effects on adolescents than on adults.

Even so-called soft drugs can take a heavy toll. Marijuana's effects, for example, are not confined to the "high"; the drug can also cause serious problems with memory and learning, as well as difficulty in thinking and problem solving. Use of methamphetamine or ecstasy (MDMA) may cause long-lasting damage to brain areas that are critical for thought and memory. In

About This Chapter: Information in this chapter is excerpted from "What You Need To Know About Drug Testing in Schools," Office of National Drug Control Policy, a component of the Executive Office of the President, September 2002.

animal studies, researchers found that four days of exposure to ecstasy caused damage that persisted for as long as six or seven years. Kids on drugs cannot perform as well in school as their drug-free peers of equal ability.

♣ **It's A Fact!!**
If testing can reduce students' use of illicit drugs, it will remove a significant barrier to academic achievement.

Substance abuse should be recognized for what it is—a major health issue—and dealt with accordingly. Like vision and hearing tests, drug testing can alert parents to potential problems that continued drug use might cause, such as liver or lung damage, memory impairment, addiction, overdose, even death. Once the drug problem has been identified, intervention and then treatment, if appropriate, can begin. Testing can also be an effective way to prevent drug use. The expectation that they may be randomly tested is enough to make some students stop using drugs—or never start in the first place.

That kind of deterrence has been demonstrated many times over in the American workplace. Employees in many national security and safety-sensitive positions—airline pilots, commercial truck drivers, school bus drivers, to name a few—are subject to pre-employment and random drug tests to ensure public safety. Employers who have followed the Federal model have seen a 67 percent drop in positive drug tests. Along with significant declines in absenteeism, accidents, and healthcare costs, they've also experienced dramatic increases in worker productivity.

While some students resist the idea of drug testing, many endorse it. For one thing, it gives them a good excuse to say "no" to drugs. Peer pressure among young people can be a powerful and persuasive force. Knowing they may have to submit to a drug test can help kids overcome the pressure to take drugs by giving them a convenient "out." This could serve them well in years to come: Students represent the workforce of tomorrow, and eventually many will need to pass a drug test to get a job.

It is important to understand that the goal of school-based drug testing is not to punish students who use drugs. Although consequences for illegal drug use should be part of any testing program—suspension from an athletic activity or revoked parking privileges, for example—the primary purpose is to deter use and guide those who test positive into counseling or treatment. In addition, drug testing in schools should never be undertaken as a stand-alone response to the drug problem. Rather, it should be one component of a broader program designed to reduce students' use of illegal drugs.

What are the benefits of drug testing?

Drug use can quickly turn to dependence and addiction, trapping users in a vicious cycle that destroys families and ruins lives. Students who use drugs or alcohol are statistically more likely to drop out of school than their peers who don't. Dropouts, in turn, are more likely to be unemployed, to depend on the welfare system, and to commit crimes. If drug testing deters drug use, everyone benefits—students, their families, their schools, and their communities.

Drug and alcohol abuse not only interferes with a student's ability to learn, it also disrupts the orderly environment necessary for all students to succeed. Studies have shown that students who use drugs are more likely to bring guns and knives to school, and that the more marijuana a student smokes, the greater the chances he or she will be involved in physical attacks, property destruction, stealing, and cutting classes. Just as parents and students can expect schools to offer protection from violence, racism, and other forms of abuse, so do they have the right to expect a learning environment free from the influence of illegal drugs.

What are the risks?

Schools should proceed with caution before testing students for drugs. Screenings are not 100 percent accurate, so every positive screen should be followed by a laboratory-based confirming test. Before going ahead with tests, schools should also have a good idea of precisely what drugs their students are using. Testing for just one set of illegal drugs when others pose an equal or greater threat would do little to address a school's drug problem.

Confidentiality is a major concern with students and their parents. Schools have a responsibility to respect students' privacy, so it is vital that only the people who need to know the test results see them—parents and school administrators, for example. The results should not be shared with anyone else, not even teachers.

Developing A Testing Program

What are the elements of a drug testing program?

Many workplaces have had drug testing programs in place for years, and recently some school districts have implemented programs for testing their athletes. Successful programs typically share a number of common elements, beginning with a clear written policy. Parents and teachers sign a statement declaring that they understand the policy, which is announced at least 90 days before testing begins. An effective policy addresses questions such as:

- Which students can be tested for drug use?

- What is the process for selecting students for testing?

- Who will conduct the test?

- What are the consequences of a positive drug test?

- Are steps clearly articulated for helping students who test positive for drugs?

- Will a second confirming test be done?

- Who pays for the test?

- Will subsequent positive tests result in suspension or expulsion from extracurricular activities?

- Are test results cumulative throughout a student's tenure at the school, or is the slate wiped clean each year?

- What happens if a student refuses to take the test? Will refusal be construed as a drug-positive test?

- Who will see the test results, and how will confidentiality be maintained?

- How will parents be informed about positive test results?

- How does a student contest the results of a positive test result? And what mechanism is in place for students whose prescription medication triggers a positive reading?

What kinds of tests are available?

Urinalysis, the most common drug testing method, has been studied exhaustively and used extensively, has undergone rigorous challenge in the courts, and has proved to be accurate and reliable. As a result, urinalysis currently is the only technique approved for drug testing in the Federal workforce. Some employers, however, have already begun using other types of drug tests—on hair, sweat, and oral fluids. Each of these new tests has benefits as well as drawbacks.

What does each test measure?

Drug tests are used to determine whether a person has used alcohol or illegal drugs. Some tests show recent use only, while others indicate use over a longer period. Each type of test has different applications and is used to detect a specific drug or group of drugs. The Federal Drug-Free Workplace program, which serves as a model for accuracy and quality assurance in drug testing, relies on a urine test designed to detect the use of marijuana, opiates, cocaine, amphetamines, and phencyclidine (PCP). Urine tests can also be used to detect alcohol, LSD, and cotinine, the major metabolite of nicotine.

The following are summaries of the most commonly used tests:

• **Urine:** Results of a urine test show the presence or absence of specific drugs or drug metabolites in the urine. Metabolites are drug residues that remain in the system for some time after the effects of the drug have worn off. A positive urine test does not necessarily mean the subject was under the influence of drugs at the time of the test. Rather, it detects and measures use of a particular drug within the previous few days.

• **Hair:** Analysis of hair may provide a much longer "testing window" for the presence of drugs and drug metabolites, giving a more complete drug use history that goes back as far as 90 days. Like urine testing, hair testing does not provide evidence of current impairment, only past use of a specific drug. Hair testing cannot be used to detect alcohol.

✎ What's It Mean?

Metabolites: Drug residues that remain in the system for some time after the effects of the drug have worn off.

- **Sweat Patch:** Another type of drug test consists of a skin patch that measures drugs and drug metabolites in perspiration. The patch, which looks like a large adhesive bandage, is applied to the skin and worn for some length of time. A gas-permeable membrane on the patch protects the tested area from dirt and other contaminants. The sweat patch is sometimes used in the criminal justice system to monitor drug use by parolees and probationers, but so far it has not been widely used in workplaces or schools.

- **Oral Fluids:** Traces of drugs, drug metabolites, and alcohol can be detected in oral fluids, the generic term for saliva and other material collected from the mouth. Oral fluids are easy to collect—a swab of the inner cheek is the most common way. They are harder to adulterate or substitute, and collection is less invasive than with urine or hair testing. Because drugs and drug metabolites do not remain in oral fluids as long as they do in urine, this method shows more promise in determining current use and impairment.

- **Breath Alcohol:** Unlike urine tests, breath alcohol tests do detect and measure current alcohol levels. The subject blows into a breath alcohol test device, and the results are given as a number, known as the Blood Alcohol Concentration, which shows the level of alcohol in the blood at the time the test was taken. In the U.S. Department of Transportation regulations, an alcohol level of 0.04 is high enough to stop someone from performing a safety-sensitive task for that day.

What do drug tests not measure?

The five-drug urine test used in the Federal Drug Free Workplace Program does not detect all drugs used by young people. For example, it does not detect so-called "club" drugs such as gamma hydroxybutyrate (GHB) and ecstasy, for example, although other urine tests can determine use of these drugs, and hair tests can easily detect ecstasy use. No standard test, however, can detect inhalant abuse, a problem that can have serious, even fatal, consequences. (Inhalant abuse refers to the deliberate inhalation or sniffing of common household products— gasoline, correction fluid, felt-tip markers, spray paint, air freshener, and cooking spray, to name a few—with the purpose of "getting high.")

Administering The Test

What can students expect?

Drug testing is commonly a four-step process: collection, screening, confirmation, and review. When called in to take a drug test, the student is met by a trained "collector," or test administrator, who gives instructions and receives the specimen. It is also the collector's job to complete the chain-of-custody form, which keeps track of where the specimen has been and who has handled it throughout the process. The form ensures that the specimen was handled properly and in such a way that does not call its source or the test results into question.

If the student is providing a urine sample, a temperature strip is put on the collection container to guard against a substitute sample. A tamper-evident tape is put over the specimen container, and then the student is asked to initial it and verify the chain-of-custody form.

Next, the specimen is screened for drugs or drug metabolites. If the screening test is positive, the test will be confirmed by a second, more exacting test. All confirmed positive tests should then be reviewed by a physician or nurse with knowledge of substance abuse disorders to rule out legitimate prescription drug use.

Some specimens are screened at the collection site, and the initial results are known within minutes; others are screened at a laboratory. All negative screens—those that show no drugs or drug metabolites—are eliminated from further consideration.

Specimens that test positive for drugs in the initial screen are examined further in the laboratory through a second analytic technique called gas chromatography/mass spectrometry (GC/MS), which is actually a combination of two specialized techniques. Technicians use gas chromatography to separate the various substances in the specimen, and then they make a positive identification through mass spectrometry.

Alcohol-specific tests may be performed entirely at the collection location if appropriate breath alcohol testing equipment and procedures are used. Some oral fluid tests can also be used to obtain an immediate initial test result, with the positive screen going on to a laboratory for confirmation.

♣ It's A Fact!!

The purpose of drug testing is to keep students from using drugs, and to help or refer to treatment those who may be drug dependent.

A positive test result does not automatically mean the student uses illegal drugs. In fact, other, legal substances sometimes trigger positive results. Certain over-the-counter medications, for example, can cause a positive reading for amphetamines. So when the GC/MS confirmation test comes back positive, it is important for a doctor, nurse, or other specialist to review the results and determine if illicit drugs are indeed the culprits.

In the Federal Drug-Free Workplace Program, a medical review officer is required to go over positive test results with the donor and determine if there could be a legitimate explanation. Everything is done confidentially, and safeguards are in place to make sure workers are not falsely labeled drug users when their positive test results are found to have a legitimate cause.

Schools should also take care that a student's confidentiality and privacy are not violated, and that students who test positive because they are taking prescription medications are not wrongly branded as drug users.

What happens if the test is positive?

Results of a positive drug test should not be used merely to punish a student. Drug and alcohol use can lead to addiction, and punishment alone may not necessarily halt this progression. However, the road to addiction can be blocked by timely intervention and appropriate treatment.

When a positive test result has been reviewed and confirmed for illegal drug use, the school's crucial next step is to contact the parents and help them stop their child's drug use. Parents play a key role in drug abuse prevention, so they need lots of guidance and support. They also need to know that anger, accusations, and harsh punishment could make the situation worse. The best approach for parents is usually to stay firm and to treat their child with respect as they work together as a family to change his or her behavior.

After involving the parents, school officials may refer the student to a trained substance abuse counselor, who can perform a drug assessment and determine whether the child needs treatment or other specialized help. For young people who use drugs occasionally, a few words from the counselor or parents—coupled with the prospect of future drug tests—may be enough to put an end to the drug use. For frequent users or those in danger of becoming drug dependent, treatment will likely be necessary.

♣ It's A Fact!!
Case History: A Reward For Staying Clean

In rural Autauga County, Alabama, students have a special incentive to stay off drugs. As part of a voluntary drug-testing program, participating students who test negative for drugs in random screenings receive discounts and other perks from scores of area businesses.

Community leaders and school officials, prompted by a growing concern about the use of drugs, alcohol, and cigarettes among students, launched the program in 2000 with the help of a local drug-free coalition called Peers Are Staying Straight (PASS).

The Independent Decision program began with just the 7th grade but expanded each year to include all grade levels. In the 2001–2002 school year, more than half of all 7th and 8th graders at public and private schools participated.

To enter the program, kids take a urine test for nicotine, cocaine, amphetamines, opiates, PCP, and marijuana. Those who test negative get a picture ID that entitles them to special deals at more than 55 participating restaurants and stores. Students keep the ID as long as they test negative in twice-yearly random drug tests.

Those who test positive (there have been only three) must relinquish their cards and any special privileges. The school counselor notifies the parents and, if appropriate, offers advice about where to find help. At that point, the matter is strictly in the parents' hands. If the child tests negative in a subsequent random test, his or her card is returned.

Surveys taken by PRIDE (the National Parents' Resource Institute for Drug Education) before the program began and again in 2002 showed significant reductions in drug use among Autauga County's 8th graders: from 35.9 percent to 24.4 percent for nicotine, 39.9 percent to 30 percent for alcohol, and 18.5 percent to 11.8 percent for marijuana.

Many schools require drug-positive students to enroll in a drug education course or activity. Some also offer Student Assistance Programs, whose trained counselors are linked to resources in the greater community and can help students cope with a variety of problems, including substance abuse. In any case, the school will want to perform follow-up drug tests on students with positive results to make sure they stay drug free.

Can students "beat" the tests?

Many drug-using students are aware of techniques that supposedly detoxify their systems or mask their drug use. Some drink large amounts of water just before the test to dilute their urine; others add salt, bleach, or vinegar to their sample. In some cases, users call on their drug-free friends to leave bottles of clean urine in the bathroom stalls.

Popular magazines and Internet sites give advice on how to dilute urine samples, and there are even companies that sell clean urine or products designed to distort test results. A number of techniques and products are focused on urine tests for marijuana, but masking products increasingly are becoming available for tests of hair, oral fluids, and multiple drugs.

Most of these masking products do not work, cost a lot of money, and are almost always easily identified in the testing process. But even if the specific drug is successfully masked, the product itself can be detected, in which case the student using it would become an obvious candidate for additional screening and attention.

Who does the testing?

Laboratories all over the country perform drug tests, but not all of them produce consistently accurate and reliable results. Many schools choose labs from among those certified by the Substance Abuse and Mental Health Services Administration (SAMHSA) to perform urine testing for Federal agencies.

Chapter 65

Opposing Drug Testing In Schools

While the U.S. Supreme Court has twice okayed the drug testing of school kids on the grounds that the invasion of their privacy is offset by the role of drug testing in preventing drug use, the first major study of the efficacy of drug testing in schools has found that it just isn't so. In fact, the study found that drug use is as frequent in schools with testing as in schools without it. The findings, which every activist faced with a proposal to institute school drug testing should have in hand, are a serious blow to the rationale behind school drug testing.

The federally financed survey of 76,000 students and 891 schools across the country, conducted by the social scientists at the University of Michigan who do the Monitoring the Future surveys of student drug use, came up with only statistically insignificant differences between schools, which subject their students to drug testing and those that don't. Among 12th graders, for example, 37% reported having smoked pot at schools that tested, while 36% reported doing so at schools that didn't. Similarly, 21% reported having used other drugs at schools that tested, while 19% reported doing so at schools that didn't. The findings hold true with other grades as well, the researchers reported.

The survey represents the only large or nationally representative sample of schools that has ever been used to evaluate the effectiveness of school drug testing.

About This Chapter: Information in this chapter is from "Drug Testing Has No Impact on Student Drug Use, Study Finds," *Drug War Chronicle* (May 2003), http://www.stopthe drugwar.org. © 2003 StoptheDrugWar.org: the Drug Reform Coordination Network.

"It suggests that there really isn't an impact from drug testing as practiced," said lead researcher Lloyd Johnston in announcing the study results. "We think the reason so few schools test their students for drugs is that it is an expensive undertaking. Schools are very pressed for funds, and I would say that the results of our investigation raise a serious question of whether drug testing is a wise investment of their resources. It's also very controversial with a lot of students and parents," Johnston added.

"The way that drug testing in the schools has been carried out looks very unpromising. I have no doubt one could design drug testing programs that could deter teen drug use, but at what monetary cost and what cost in terms of the intrusion into the privacy of our young people?" Johnston asked.

Some 19% of schools nationwide had some sort of drug testing program in place, the study found, but of those, the vast majority tested only "on suspicion," that is, when a student was already suspected of using drugs. Only 5% of schools test student athletes and only 4% test students involved in extracurricular activities, the two groups singled out by the Supreme Court for special attention. Another 4% of schools test students who volunteer to be tested. (Many of the schools that test athletes also test students in extracurricular activities or who volunteer, suggesting that rigorous drug testing programs are probably underway in less than 10% of all schools.)

The results of the study could put a damper on the use of drug testing in the schools, according to one attorney who has played a lead role in litigating school drug testing cases. "Now there should be no reason for a school to impose an intrusive or even insulting drug test when it's not going to do anything about student drug use," said Graham Boyd of the American Civil Liberties Union's Drug Policy Litigation Project, who argued the case against drug testing before the Supreme Court.

While the Supreme Court, in its two rulings allowing drug testing of student athletes (1995) and students involved in extracurricular activities (2002), may have allowed ideology to trump science in finding that drug testing prevents teen drug use, now the science is available to rebut that presumption. Battles to block student drug testing may have been lost at the high court, but this study provides powerful ammunition to win them at the school district level.

Chapter 66

Speaking Out Against Drug Legalization

In many circles, U.S. drug policy is under attack. Primarily those who favor a legalization agenda are criticizing it. It is also being challenged by those who encourage certain trends in European drug policy, like decriminalization of drug use, "harm reduction" programs, and distinctions between hard and soft drugs.

Proponents of legalization are spending huge amounts of money to encourage a greater tolerance for drug use. A number of states have passed referendums to permit their residents to use drugs for a variety of reasons. The citizens who vote in these referendums too often have to rely on the information, or rather, misinformation, being presented by the sponsors of these expensive campaigns to legalize drugs.

This chapter will cut through the fog of misinformation with hard facts. The ten facts, taken together, present an accurate picture of America's experience with drug use, the current state of the drug problem, and what might happen if America chooses to adopt a more permissive policy on drug abuse.

Drug abuse, and this nation's response to it, is one of the most important and potentially dangerous issues facing American citizens, and especially its youth, today. The unique freedoms of America have always depended on a well-informed citizenry.

About This Chapter: Information in this chapter is excerpted from "A Message from the Drug Enforcement Administration," U.S. Drug Enforcement Administration, U.S. Department of Justice, May 2003.

Fact 1: We have made significant progress in fighting drug use and drug trafficking in America. Now is not the time to abandon our efforts.

- Legalization advocates claim that the fight against drugs has not been won and is, in fact, unconquerable. They frequently state that people still take drugs, drugs are widely available, and that efforts to change this are futile. They contend that legalization is the only workable alternative.

- The facts are to the contrary to such pessimism. On the demand side, the U.S. has reduced casual use, chronic use and addiction, and prevented others from even starting using drugs. Overall drug use in the United States is down by more than a third since the late 1970s. That's 9.5 million fewer people using illegal drugs. We've reduced cocaine use by an astounding 70% during the last 15 years. That's 4.1 million fewer people using cocaine.

- The good news continues. According to the 2001–2002 National Parents' Resource Institute for Drug Education (PRIDE) survey, student drug use has reached the lowest level in nine years. According to the author of the study, "following 9/11, Americans seemed to refocus on family, community, spirituality, and nation." These statistics show that U.S. efforts to educate kids about the dangers of drugs are making an impact. Like smoking cigarettes, drug use is gaining a stigma, which is the best cure for this problem, as it was in the 1980s, when government, business, the media and other national institutions came together to do something about the growing problem of drugs and drug-related violence. This is a trend we should encourage and not send the opposite message of greater acceptance of drug use.

♣ **It's A Fact!!**
Almost two-thirds of teens say their schools are drug free, according to a new survey of teen drug use conducted by The National Center on Addiction and Substance Abuse (CASA) at Columbia University. This is the first time in the seven-year history of the study that a majority of public school students report drug-free schools.

- The crack cocaine epidemic of the 1980s and early 1990s has diminished greatly in scope. And we've reduced the number of chronic heroin users over the last decade. In addition, the number of new marijuana users and cocaine users continues to steadily decrease.

- The number of new heroin users dropped from 156,000 in 1976 to 104,000 in 1999, a reduction of 33 percent.

- Of course, drug policy also has an impact on general crime. In a 2001 study, the British Home Office found violent crime and property crime increased in the late 1990s in every wealthy country except the United States. Our murder rate is too high, and we have much to learn from those with greater success; but this reduction is due in part to a reduction in drug use.

- There is still much progress to make. There are still far too many people using cocaine, heroin, and other illegal drugs. In addition, there are emerging drug threats like ecstasy and methamphetamine. But the fact is that our current policies balancing prevention, enforcement, and treatment have kept drug usage outside the scope of acceptable behavior in the U.S.

- To put things in perspective, less than 5 percent of the population uses illegal drugs of any kind. Think about that: More than 95 percent of Americans do not use drugs. How could anyone but the most hardened pessimist call this a losing struggle?

Fact 2: A balanced approach of prevention, enforcement, and treatment is the key in the fight against drugs.

- Over the years, some people have advocated a policy that focuses narrowly on controlling the supply of drugs. Others have said that society should rely on treatment alone. Still others say that prevention is the only viable solution. As the 2002 National Drug Strategy observes, "What the nation needs is an honest effort to integrate these strategies."

- Drug treatment courts are a good example of this new balanced approach to fighting drug abuse and addiction in this country. These courts are given a special responsibility to handle cases involving drug-addicted offenders through an extensive supervision and treatment program. Drug court programs use the varied experience and skills of a wide variety of law enforcement and treatment professionals—judges, prosecutors, defense counsels, substance abuse treatment specialists, probation officers, law enforcement and correctional personnel, educational and vocational experts, community leaders and others—all focused on one goal to help cure addicts of their addiction, and to keep them cured.

• Drug treatment courts are working. Researchers estimate that more than 50 percent of defendants convicted of drug possession will return to criminal behavior within two to three years. Those who graduate from drug treatment courts have far lower rates of recidivism, ranging from 2 to 20 percent. That's very impressive when you consider that, for addicts who enter a treatment program voluntarily, 80 to 90 percent leave by the end of the first year. Among such dropouts, relapse within a year is generally the rule.

• What makes drug treatment courts so different? Graduates are held accountable for sticking with the program. Unlike other, purely voluntary treatment programs, the addict, who has a physical need for drugs, can't simply quit treatment whenever he or she feels like it.

• Law enforcement plays an important role in the drug treatment court program. It is especially important in the beginning of the process because it often triggers treatment for people who need it. Most people do not volunteer for drug treatment. It is more often an outside motivator, like an arrest, that gets, and keeps, people in treatment. And it is important for judges to keep people in incarceration if treatment fails.

• There are already more than 123,000 people who use heroin at least once a month, and 1.7 million who use cocaine at least once a month. For them, treatment is the answer. But for most Americans, particularly the young, the solution lies in prevention, which in turn is largely a matter of education and enforcement and which aims at keeping drug pushers away from children and teenagers.

• Enforcement of our laws creates risks that discourage drug use. Charles Van Deventer, a young writer in Los Angeles, wrote about this phenomenon in an article in *Newsweek*. He said that from his experience as a casual user—and he believes his experience with illegal drugs is "by far the most common"—drugs aren't nearly as easy to buy, as some critics would like people to believe. Being illegal, they are too expensive, their quality is too unpredictable, and their purchase entails too many risks. "The more barriers there are," he said, "be they the cops or the hassle or the fear of dying, the less likely you are to get addicted....The road to addiction was just bumpy enough," he concluded, "that I chose not to go down it. In this sense, we are winning the war on drugs just by fighting them."

• The element of risk, created by strong drug enforcement policies, raises the price of drugs, and therefore lowers the demand. A research paper, Marijuana and Youth, funded by the Robert Wood Johnson Foundation, concludes that changes in the price of marijuana "contributed significantly to the trends in youth marijuana use between 1982 and 1998, particularly during the contraction in use from 1982 to 1992." That contraction was a product of many factors, including a concerted effort among federal agencies to disrupt domestic production and distribution; these factors contributed to a doubling of the street price of marijuana in the space of a year.

• The 2002 National Drug Control Strategy states that drug control policy has just two elements—modifying individual behavior to discourage and reduce drug use and addiction, and disrupting the market for illegal drugs. Those two elements call for a balanced approach to drug control, one that uses prevention, enforcement, and treatment in a coordinated policy. This is a simple strategy and an effective one. The enforcement side of the fight against drugs, then, is an integrated part of the overall strategy.

Fact 3: Illegal drugs are illegal because they are harmful.

- There is a growing misconception that some illegal drugs can be taken safely, with many advocates of legalization going so far as to suggest it can serve as medicine to heal anything from headaches to bipolar diseases. Today's drug dealers are savvy businessmen. They know how to market to kids. They imprint ecstasy pills with cartoon characters and designer logos. They promote parties as safe and alcohol-free. Meanwhile, the drugs can flow easier than water. Many young people believe the new "club drugs," such as ecstasy, are safe, and tablet testing at raves has only fueled this misconception.

- Because of the new marketing tactics of drug promoters, and because of a major decline in drug use in the 1990s, there is a growing perception among young people today that drugs are harmless. A decade ago, for example, 79 percent of 12th graders thought regular marijuana use was harmful—only 58 percent do so today. Because peer pressure is so important in inducing kids to experiment with drugs, the way kids perceive the risks of drug use is critical. There always have been, and there continues to be, real health risks in using illicit drugs.

- Drug use can be deadly—far more deadly than alcohol. Although alcohol is used by seven times as many people as drugs, the number of deaths induced by those substances is not far apart. According to the Centers for Disease Control and Prevention (CDC), during 2000, there were 15,852 drug-induced deaths—only slightly less than the 18,539 alcohol-induced deaths.

- Ecstasy has rapidly become a favorite drug among young party goers in the U.S. and Europe, and it is now being used within the mainstream as well. According to the 2001 National Household Survey on Drug Abuse, ecstasy use tripled among Americans between 1998 and 2001. Many people believe, incorrectly, that this synthetic drug is safer than cocaine and heroin. In fact, the drug is addictive and can be deadly.

- The misconception about the safety of club drugs, like ecstasy, is often fueled by some governments' attempts to reduce the harm of mixing drugs. Some foreign governments and private organizations in the U.S. have established ecstasy testing at rave parties. Once the drug is tested, it is returned to the partygoers. This process leads partygoers to believe that the government has declared their pill safe to consume. But the danger of ecstasy is the drug itself, not simply its purity level.

- Cocaine is a powerfully addictive drug. Compulsive cocaine use seems to develop more rapidly when the substance is smoked rather than snorted. A tolerance to the cocaine high may be developed, and many addicts report that they fail to achieve as much pleasure as they did from their first cocaine exposure.

- Drug legalization advocates in the United States single out marijuana as a different kind of drug, unlike cocaine, heroin, and methamphetamine. They say it's less dangerous. Several European countries have lowered the classification of marijuana. However, as many people are realizing, marijuana is not as harmless as some would have them believe. Marijuana is far more powerful than it used to be. In 2000, there were six times as many emergency room mentions of marijuana use as there were in 1990, despite the fact that the number of people using marijuana is roughly the same. In 1999, a record 225,000 Americans entered substance abuse treatment primarily for marijuana dependence, second only to heroin—and not by much.

- At a time of great public pressure to curtail tobacco because of its effects on health, advocates of legalization are promoting the use of marijuana. Yet, according to the National Institute on Drug Abuse, "Studies show that someone who smokes five joints per week may be taking in as many cancer-causing chemicals as someone who smokes a full pack of cigarettes every day." Marijuana contains more than 400 chemicals, including the most harmful substances found in tobacco smoke. For example, smoking one marijuana cigarette deposits about four times more tar into the lungs than a filtered tobacco cigarette.

Fact 4: Smoked marijuana is not scientifically approved medicine. Marinol®, the legal version of medical marijuana, is approved by science.

- Medical marijuana already exists. It's called Marinol®.

- A pharmaceutical product, Marinol®, is widely available through prescription. It comes in the form of a pill and is also being studied by researchers for suitability via other delivery methods, such as an inhaler or patch. The active ingredient of Marinol® is synthetic THC, which has been found to relieve the nausea and vomiting associated with chemotherapy for cancer patients and to assist with loss of appetite with AIDS patients.

- Unlike smoked marijuana, which contains more than 400 different chemicals, including most of the hazardous chemicals found in tobacco smoke, Marinol® has been studied and approved by the medical community and the Food and Drug Administration (FDA), the nation's watchdog over unsafe and harmful food and drug products. Since the passage of the 1906 Pure Food and Drug Act, any drug that is marketed in the United States must undergo rigorous scientific testing. The approval process mandated by this act ensures that claims of safety and therapeutic value are supported by clinical evidence and keeps unsafe, ineffective, and dangerous drugs off the market.

- There are no FDA-approved medications that are smoked. For one thing, smoking is generally a poor way to deliver medicine. It is difficult to administer safe, regulated dosages of medicines in smoked form. Secondly, the harmful chemicals and carcinogens that are byproducts of smoking create entirely new health problems. There is four times the level of tar in a marijuana cigarette, for example, than in a tobacco cigarette.

- Morphine, for example, has proven to be a medically valuable drug, but the FDA does not endorse the smoking of opium or heroin. Instead, scientists have extracted active ingredients from opium, which are sold as pharmaceutical products like morphine, codeine, hydrocodone or oxycodone. In a similar vein, the FDA has not approved smoking marijuana for medicinal purposes, but has approved the active ingredient THC in the form of scientifically regulated Marinol®.

- The U.S. Drug Enforcement Administration (DEA) helped facilitate the research on Marinol®. The National Cancer Institute approached the DEA in the early 1980s regarding their study of THC in relieving nausea and vomiting. As a result, the DEA facilitated the registration and provided regulatory support and guidance for the study. California researchers are studying the potential use of marijuana and its ingredients on conditions such as multiple sclerosis and pain. At this time, however, neither the medical community nor the scientific community has found sufficient data to conclude that smoked marijuana is the best approach to dealing with these important medical issues.

- The most comprehensive, scientifically rigorous review of studies of smoked marijuana was conducted by the Institute of Medicine, an organization chartered by the National Academy of Sciences. In a report released in 1999, the Institute did not recommend the use of smoked marijuana, but did conclude that active ingredients in marijuana could be isolated and developed into a variety of pharmaceuticals, such as Marinol®.

- In the meantime, the DEA is working with pain management groups to make sure that those who need access to safe, effective pain medication can get the best medication available.

Fact 5: Drug control spending is a minor portion of the U.S. budget. Compared to the social costs of drug abuse and addiction, government spending on drug control is minimal.

- Legalization advocates claim that the United States has spent billions of dollars to control drug production, trafficking, and use, with few, if any, positive results. The fact is that the results of the American drug strategy have been positive indeed, with a 95 percent rate of Americans who do not use drugs. If the number of drug abusers doubled or tripled, the social costs would be enormous.

- Legalization would result in skyrocketing costs that would be paid by American taxpayers and consumers. Legalization would significantly increase drug use and addiction and all the social costs that go with it. With the removal of the social and legal sanctions against drugs, many experts estimate the user population would at least double. For example, a 1994 article in the *New England Journal of Medicine* stated that it was probable, that if cocaine were legalized, the number of cocaine addicts in America would increase from 2 million to at least 20 million.

• Drug abuse drives some of America's most costly social problems including domestic violence, child abuse, chronic mental illness, the spread of AIDS, and homelessness. Drug treatment costs, hospitalization for long-term drug-related disease, and treatment of the consequences of family violence burden our already strapped health care system. In 2000, there were more than 600,000 hospital emergency department drug episodes in the United States. Health care costs for drug abuse alone were about $15 billion.

• Drug abuse among the homeless has been conservatively estimated at better than 50 percent. Chronic mental illness is inextricably linked with drug abuse. In Philadelphia, nearly half of the VA's mental patients abused drugs. The Centers for Disease Control and Prevention has estimated that 36 percent of new HIV cases are directly or indirectly linked to injecting drug users.

• In 1998, Americans spent $67 billion for illegal drugs, a sum of money greater than the amount spent that year to finance public higher education in the United States. If the money spent on illegal drugs were devoted instead to public higher education, for example, public colleges would have the financial ability to accommodate twice as many students as they already do.

• In addition, legalization, and the increased addiction it would spawn, would result in lost workforce productivity and the unpredictable damage that it would cause to the American economy. The latest drug use surveys show that about 75% of adults who reported current illicit drug use, which means they've used drugs once in the past month, are employed either full or part-time. In 2000, productivity losses due to drug abuse cost the economy $110 billion. Drug use by workers leads not only to more unexcused absences and higher turnover, but also

♣ It's A Fact!!

In the year 2000, drug abuse cost American society an estimated $160 billion. More important were the concrete losses that are imperfectly symbolized by those billions of dollars—the destruction of lives, the damage of addiction, fatalities from car accidents, illness, and lost opportunities and dreams.

presents an enormous safety problem in the workplace. Studies have confirmed what common sense dictates: Employees who abuse drugs are five times more likely than other workers to injure themselves or coworkers and they cause 40% of all industrial fatalities. They were more likely to have worked for three or more employers and to have voluntarily left an employer in the past year.

• Legalization would also result in a huge increase in the number of traffic accidents and fatalities. Drugs are already responsible for a significant number of accidents. Marijuana, for example, impairs the ability of drivers to maintain concentration and show good judgment. A study by the National Institute on Drug Abuse surveyed 6,000 teenage drivers. It studied those who drove more than six times a month after using marijuana. The study found that they were about two-and-a-half times more likely to be involved in a traffic accident than those who didn't smoke before driving.

• Will the right to use drugs imply a right to the access of drugs? One of the arguments for legalization is that it will end the need for drug trafficking cartels. If so, who will distribute drugs? Government employees? The local supermarket? The college bookstore? In view of the huge settlement agreed to by the tobacco companies, what marketer would want the potential liability for selling a product as harmful as cocaine or heroin, or even marijuana?

• Advocates also argue that legalization will lower prices. But that raises a dilemma: If the price of drugs is low, many more people will be able to afford them and the demand for drugs will explode. For example, the cost of cocaine production is now as low as $3 per gram. At a market price of, say, $10 a gram, cocaine could retail for as little as ten cents a hit. That means a young person could buy six hits of cocaine for the price of a candy bar. On the other hand, if legal drugs are priced too high, through excise taxes, for example, illegal traffickers will be able to undercut it.

• Advocates of legalization also argue that the legal market could be limited to those above a certain age level, as it is for alcohol and cigarettes. Those under the age limits would not be permitted to buy drugs at authorized outlets. But teenagers today have found many ways to circumvent the age restrictions, whether by using false identification or by buying liquor and cigarettes from older friends. According to the 2001 National Household Survey on Drug Abuse, approximately 10.1 million young people aged 12–20 reported past month alcohol use (28.5 percent of this age group). Of these, nearly 6.8 million (19 percent) were binge drinkers. With drugs, teenagers would have an additional outlet, the highly organized illegal trafficking networks that exist today. They would undoubtedly concentrate their marketing efforts on young people to make up for the business they lost to legal outlets.

Fact 6: Legalization of drugs will lead to increased use and increased levels of addiction. Legalization has been tried before, and failed miserably.

• Legalization proponents claim, absurdly, that making illegal drugs legal would not cause more of these substances to be consumed, nor would addiction increase. They claim that many people can use drugs in moderation and that many would choose not to use drugs, just as many abstain from alcohol and tobacco now. Yet how much misery can already be attributed to alcoholism and smoking? Is the answer to just add more misery and addiction?

♣ It's A Fact!!
It's clear from history that periods of lax controls are accompanied by more drug abuse and that periods of tight controls are accompanied by less drug abuse.

- During the 19th Century, morphine was legally refined from opium and hailed as a miracle drug. Many soldiers on both sides of the Civil War who were given morphine for their wounds became addicted to it, and this increased level of addiction continued throughout the nineteenth century and into the twentieth. In 1880, many drugs, including opium and cocaine, were legal; and, like some drugs today, seen as benign medicine not requiring a doctor's care and oversight. Addiction skyrocketed. There were over 400,000 opium addicts in the U.S. That is twice as many per capita as there are today.

- By 1900, about one American in 200 was either a cocaine or opium addict. Among the reforms of this era was the Federal Pure Food and Drug Act of 1906, which required manufacturers of patent medicines to reveal the contents of the drugs they sold. In this way, Americans learned which of their medicines contained heavy doses of cocaine and opiates—drugs they had now learned to avoid.

- Specific federal drug legislation and oversight began with the 1914 Harrison Act, the first broad anti-drug law in the United States. Enforcement of this law contributed to a significant decline in narcotic addiction in the United States. Addiction in the United States eventually fell to its lowest level during World War II, when the number of addicts is estimated to have been somewhere between 20,000 and 40,000. Many addicts, faced with disappearing supplies, were forced to give up their drug habits.

- What was virtually a drug-free society in the war years remained much the same way in the years that followed. In the mid-1950s, the Federal Bureau of Narcotics estimated the total number of addicts nationwide at somewhere between 50,000 to 60,000. The former chief medical examiner of New York City, Dr. Milton Halpern, said in 1970 that the number of New Yorkers who died from drug addiction in 1950 was 17. By comparison, in 1999, the New York City medical examiner reported 729 deaths involving drug abuse.

- The consequences of legalization became evident when the Alaska Supreme Court ruled in 1975 that the state could not interfere with an adult's possession of marijuana for personal consumption in the home. The court's ruling became a green light for marijuana use. Although the ruling was limited to persons 19 and over, teens were among those increasingly using marijuana. According to a 1988 University of Alaska study, the state's 12 to 17-year-olds used marijuana at more than twice the national average for their age group. Alaska's residents voted in 1990 to re-criminalize possession of marijuana, demonstrating their belief that increased use was too high a price to pay.

• By 1979, after 11 states decriminalized marijuana and the Carter administration had considered federal decriminalization, marijuana use shot up among teenagers. That year, almost 51 percent of 12th graders reported they used marijuana in the last 12 months. By 1992, with tougher laws and increased attention to the risks of drug abuse, that figure had been reduced to 22 percent, a 57 percent decline.

• Other countries have also had this experience. The Netherlands has had its own troubles with increased use of cannabis products. From 1984 to 1996, the Dutch liberalized the use of cannabis. Surveys reveal that lifetime prevalence of cannabis in Holland increased consistently and sharply. For the age group 18–20, the increase is from 15 percent in 1984 to 44 percent in 1996.

• The Netherlands is not alone. Switzerland, with some of the most liberal drug policies in Europe, experimented with what became known as Needle Park. Needle Park became the Mecca for drug addicts throughout Europe, an area where addicts could come to openly purchase drugs and inject heroin without police intervention or control. The rapid decline in the neighborhood surrounding Needle Park, with increased crime and violence, led authorities to finally close Needle Park in 1992.

• The British have also had their own failed experiments with liberalizing drug laws. England's experience shows that use and addiction increase with "harm reduction" policy. Great Britain allowed doctors to prescribe heroin to addicts, resulting in an explosion of heroin use, and by the mid-1980s, known addiction rates were increasing by about 30 percent a year.

- The relationship between legalization and increased use becomes evident by considering two current "legal drugs," tobacco and alcohol. The number of users of these "legal drugs" is far greater than the number of users of illegal drugs. The numbers were explored by the 2001 National Household Survey on Drug Abuse. Roughly 109 million Americans used alcohol at least once a month. About 66 million Americans used tobacco at the same rate. But less than 16 million Americans used illegal drugs at least once a month.

Fact 7: Crime, violence, and drug use go hand-in-hand.

- Proponents of legalization have many theories regarding the connection between drugs and violence. Some dispute the connection between drugs and violence, claiming that drug use is a victimless crime and users are putting only themselves in harm's way and therefore have the right to use drugs. Other proponents of legalization contend that if drugs were legalized, crime and violence would decrease, believing that it is the illegal nature of drug production, trafficking, and use that fuels crime and violence, rather than the violent and irrational behavior that drugs themselves prompt.

- Yet, under a legalization scenario, a black market for drugs would still exist. And it would be a vast black market. If drugs were legal for those over 18 or 21, there would be a market for everyone under that age. People under the age of 21 consume the majority of illegal drugs, and so an illegal market and organized crime to supply it would remain, along with the organized crime that profits from it. After Prohibition ended, did the organized crime in our country go down? No. It continues today in a variety of other criminal enterprises. Legalization would not put the cartels out of business; cartels would simply look to other illegal endeavors.

- If only marijuana were legalized, drug traffickers would continue to traffic in heroin and cocaine. In either case, traffic-related violence would not be ended by legalization.

- If only marijuana, cocaine, and heroin were legalized, there would still be a market for PCP and methamphetamine. Where do legalizers want to draw the line? Or do they support legalizing all drugs, no matter how addictive and dangerous?

- In addition, any government agency assigned to distribute drugs under a legalization scenario would, for safety purposes, most likely not distribute the most potent drug. The drugs may also be more expensive because of bureaucratic costs of operating such a distribution system. Therefore, until 100 percent pure drugs are given away to anyone, at any age, a black market will remain.

- The greatest weakness in the logic of legalizers is that the violence associated with drugs is simply a product of drug trafficking. That is, if drugs were legal, then most drug crime would end. But most violent crime is committed not because people want to buy drugs, but because people are on drugs. Drug use changes behavior and exacerbates criminal activity, and there is ample scientific evidence that demonstrates the links between drugs, violence, and crime. Drugs often cause people to do things they wouldn't do if they were rational and free of the influence of drugs.

- According to the 1999 Arrestee Drug Abuse Monitoring (ADAM) study, more than half of arrestees for violent crimes test positive for drugs at the time of their arrest.

Fact 8: Alcohol has caused significant health, social, and crime problems in this country, and legalized drugs would only make the situation worse.

- Drugs are far more addictive than alcohol. Only 10 percent of drinkers become alcoholics, while up to 75 percent of regular illicit drug users become addicted.

- According to the Centers for Disease Control and Prevention (CDC), during 2000, there were 15,852 drug-induced deaths, only slightly less than the 18,539 alcohol-induced deaths. Yet the personal costs of drug use are far higher. According to a 1995 article by Dr. Robert L. DuPont, an expert on drug abuse, the health-related costs per person is more than twice as high for drugs as it is for alcohol—$1,742 for users of illegal drugs and $798 for users of alcohol. Legalization of drugs would compound the problems in the already overburdened health care, so-cial service, and criminal justice systems. And it would demand a stag-gering new tax burden on the public to pay for the costs. The cost to families affected by addiction is incalculable.

✦ It's A Fact!!

According to the 1998 National Household Survey on Drug Abuse, teenage drug users are five times far more likely to attack some-one than those who don't use drugs. About 20 percent of the 12–17 year olds reporting use of an illegal drug in the past year attacked someone with the intent to seriously hurt them, compared to 4.3 percent of the non-drug users.

Fact 9: Europe's more liberal drug policies are not the right model for America.

- Drug abuse has increased in the Netherlands. From 1984 to 1996, marijuana use among 18–25 year olds in Holland increased twofold. Since legalization of marijuana, heroin addiction levels in Holland have tripled and perhaps even quadrupled by some estimates.

- The increasing use of marijuana is responsible for more than increased crime. It has widespread social implications as well. The head of Holland's best-known drug abuse rehabilitation center has described what the new drug culture has created: The strong form of marijuana that most of the young people smoke, he says, produces "a chronically passive individual, someone who is lazy, who doesn't want to take initiatives, doesn't want to be active, the kid who'd prefer to lie in bed with a joint in the morning rather than getting up and doing something."

- The United Kingdom has also experimented with the relaxation of drug laws. Until the mid-1960s, British physicians were allowed to prescribe heroin to certain classes of addicts. According to political scientist James Q. Wilson, "a youthful drug culture emerged with a demand for drugs far different from that of the older addicts." Many addicts chose to boycott the program and continued to get their heroin from illicit drug distributors. The British Government's experiment with controlled heroin distribution, says Wilson, resulted in, at a minimum, a 30-fold increase in the number of addicts in ten years.

- Not all of Europe has been swept up in the trend to liberalize drug laws. Sweden, Finland, and Greece have the strictest policies against drugs in Europe. Sweden's zero-tolerance policy is widely supported within the country and among the various political parties. Drug use is relatively low in the Scandinavian countries.

Fact 10: Most non-violent drug users get treatment, not just jail time.

- There has been a shift in the U.S. criminal justice system to provide treatment for non-violent drug users with addiction problems, rather than incarceration. The criminal justice system actually serves as the largest referral source for drug treatment programs.

- Any successful treatment program must also require accountability from its participants. Drug treatment courts are a good example of combining treatment with such accountability. These courts are given a special responsibility to handle cases involving drug-addicted offenders through an extensive supervision and treatment program. Drug treatment court programs use the varied experience and skills of a wide variety of law enforcement and treatment professionals—judges, prosecutors, defense counsels, substance abuse treatment specialists, probation officers, law enforcement and correctional personnel, educational and vocational experts, community leaders and others. They are all focused on one goal—to help cure addicts of their addiction, and to keep them cured.

- Drug treatment courts are working. Researchers estimate that more than 50 percent of defendants convicted of drug possession will return to criminal behavior within two to three years. Those who graduate from drug treatment courts have far lower rates of recidivism, ranging from 2 to 20 percent.

- What makes drug treatment courts so different? Graduates are held accountable to the program. Unlike purely voluntary treatment programs, the addict, who has a physical need for drugs, can't simply quit treatment whenever he or she feels like it.

Chapter 67

An Opposing Point Of View:
Against Drug Prohibition

More and more ordinary people, elected officials, newspaper columnists, economists, doctors, judges, and even the Surgeon General of the United States are concluding that the effects of our drug control policy are at least as harmful as the effects of drugs themselves.

After decades of criminal prohibition and intensive law enforcement efforts to rid the country of illegal drugs, violent traffickers still endanger life in our cities, a steady stream of drug offenders still pours into our jails and prisons, and tons of cocaine, heroin and marijuana still cross our borders unimpeded.

Currently Illegal Drugs Have Not Always Been Illegal

During the Civil War, morphine (an opium derivative and cousin of heroin) was found to have pain-killing properties and soon became the main ingredient in several patent medicines. In the late 19th century, marijuana and cocaine were put to various medicinal uses—marijuana to treat migraines, rheumatism, and insomnia, and cocaine to treat sinusitis, hay fever, and chronic fatigue. All of these drugs were also used recreationally, and cocaine, in particular, was a common ingredient in wines and soda pop—including the popular Coca Cola.

At the turn of the century, many drugs were made illegal when a mood of temperance swept the nation. In 1914, Congress passed the Harrison Act, banning opiates and cocaine. Alcohol prohibition quickly followed, and by 1918 the U.S. was officially a "dry" nation. That did not mean, however, an end to drug use. It meant that, suddenly, people were arrested and jailed for doing what they had previously done without government interference. Prohibition also meant the emergence of a black market, operated by criminals and marked by violence.

> ♣ **It's A Fact!!**
> The American Civil Liberties Union (ACLU) opposes criminal prohibition of drugs. Not only is prohibition a proven failure as a drug control strategy, but it subjects otherwise law-abiding citizens to arrest, prosecution, and imprisonment for what they do in private. In trying to enforce the drug laws, the government violates the fundamental rights of privacy and personal autonomy that are guaranteed by our Constitution. The ACLU believes that unless they do harm to others, people should not be punished—even if they do harm to themselves. There are better ways to control drug use, ways that will ultimately lead to a healthier, freer, and less crime-ridden society.

In 1933, because of concern over widespread organized crime, police corruption, and violence, the public demanded repeal of alcohol prohibition and the return of regulatory power to the states. Most states immediately replaced criminal bans with laws regulating the quality, potency, and commercial sale of alcohol; as a result, the harms associated with alcohol prohibition disappeared. Meanwhile, federal prohibition of heroin and cocaine remained, and with passage of the Marijuana Stamp Act in 1937, marijuana was prohibited as well. Federal drug policy has remained strictly prohibitionist to this day.

Decades Of Drug Prohibition: A History Of Failure

Criminal prohibition, the centerpiece of U.S. drug policy, has failed miserably. Since 1981, tax dollars to the tune of $150 billion have been spent trying to prevent Colombian cocaine, Burmese heroin, and Jamaican marijuana from penetrating our borders. Yet the evidence is that for every ton seized, hundreds more get through. Hundreds of thousands of otherwise law-abiding people have been arrested and jailed for drug possession. Between 1968 and 1992, the annual number of drug-related arrests increased from 200,000 to over 1.2 million. One-third of those were marijuana arrests, most for mere possession.

The best evidence of prohibition's failure is the government's current war on drugs. This war, instead of employing a strategy of prevention, research, education, and social programs designed to address problems such as permanent poverty, long term unemployment, and deteriorating living conditions in our inner cities, has employed a strategy of law enforcement. While this military approach continues to devour billions of tax dollars and sends tens of thousands of people to prison, illegal drug trafficking thrives, violence escalates and drug abuse continues to debilitate lives. Compounding these problems is the largely unchecked spread of the AIDS virus among drug users, their sexual partners and their offspring.

Those who benefit the most from prohibition are organized crime barons, who derive an estimated $10 to $50 billion a year from the illegal drug trade. Indeed, the criminal drug laws protect drug traffickers from taxation, regulation, and quality control. Those laws also support artificially high prices and assure that commercial disputes among drug dealers and their customers will be settled not in courts of law, but with automatic weapons in the streets.

Drug Prohibition Is A Public Health Menace

Drug prohibition promises a healthier society by denying people the opportunity to become drug users and, possibly, addicts. The reality of prohibition belies that promise.

No quality control. When drugs are illegal, the government cannot enact standards of quality, purity, or potency. Consequently, street drugs are often contaminated or extremely potent, causing disease and sometimes death to those who use them.

Dirty needles. Unsterilized needles are known to transmit HIV among intravenous drug users. Yet drug users share needles because laws prohibiting possession of drug paraphernalia have made needles a scarce commodity. These laws, then, actually promote epidemic disease and death. In New York City, more than 60 percent of intravenous drug users are HIV positive. By contrast, the figure is less than one percent in Liverpool, England, where clean needles are easily available.

Scarce treatment resources. The allocation of vast sums of money to law enforcement diminishes the funds available for drug education, preventive social programs and treatment. As crack use rose during the late 1980s, millions of dollars were spent on street-level drug enforcement and on jailing tens of thousands of low level offenders, while only a handful of public drug treatment slots were created. An especially needy group—low-income pregnant women who abused crack—often had no place to go at all because Medicaid would not reimburse providers. Instead, the government prosecuted and jailed such women without regard to the negative consequences for their children.

Drug Prohibition Creates More Problems Than It Solves

Drug prohibition has not only failed to curb or reduce the harmful effects of drug use, it has created other serious social problems.

Caught in the crossfire. In the same way that alcohol prohibition fueled violent gangsterism in the 1920s, today's drug prohibition has spawned a culture of drive-by shootings and other gun-related crimes. And just as people who were drunk did not commit most of the 1920s violence, most of the drug-related violence today is not committed by people who are high on drugs. The killings, then and now, are based on rivalries: Al Capone ordered the executions of rival bootleggers, and drug dealers kill their rivals today. A 1989 government study of all 193 "cocaine-related" homicides in New York City found that 87 percent grew out of rivalries and disagreements related to doing business in an illegal market. In only one case was the perpetrator actually under the influence of cocaine.

A nation of jailers. The "lock 'em up" mentality of the war on drugs has burdened our criminal justice system to the breaking point. Today, drug-law enforcement consumes more than half of all police resources nationwide, resources that could be better spent fighting violent crimes like rape, assault, and robbery.

The recent steep climb in our incarceration rate has made the U.S. the world's leading jailer, with a prison population that now exceeds one million people, compared to approximately 200,000 in 1970. Nonviolent drug offenders make up 58 percent of the federal prison population, a population that is extremely costly to maintain. In 1990, the states alone paid $12 billion, or $16,000 per prisoner. While drug imprisonments are a leading cause of rising local tax burdens, they have neither stopped the sale and use of drugs nor enhanced public safety.

Not drug free—just less free. We now have what some constitutional scholars call "the drug exception to the Bill of Rights." Random drug testing without probable cause, the militarization of drug law enforcement, heightened wiretapping and other surveillance, the enactment of vaguely worded loitering laws and curfews, forfeiture of people's homes and assets, excessive and mandatory prison terms—these practices and more have eroded the constitutional rights of all Americans.

♣ It's A Fact!!
The ACLU Suggests That Prohibition Is A Destructive Force In Inner City Communities

Inner city communities suffer most from both the problem of drug abuse and the consequences of drug prohibition.

Although the rates of drug use among white and non-white Americans are similar, African Americans and other racial minorities are arrested and imprisoned at higher rates. For example, according to government estimates only 12 percent of drug users are black, but nearly 40 percent of those arrested for drug offenses are black. Nationwide, one-quarter of all young African American men are under some form of criminal justice supervision, mostly for drug offenses. This phenomenon has had a devastating social impact in minority communities. Moreover, the abuse of drugs, including alcohol, has more dire consequences in impoverished communities where good treatment programs are least available.

Finally, turf battles and commercial disputes among competing drug enterprises, as well as police responses to those conflicts, occur disproportionately in poor communities, making our inner cities war zones and their residents the war's primary casualties.

Drugs Are Here to Stay—Let's Reduce Their Harm

The universality of drug use throughout human history has led some experts to conclude that the desire to alter consciousness, for whatever reasons, is a basic human drive. People in almost all cultures, in every era, have used psychoactive drugs. Native South Americans take coca breaks the way we, in this country, take coffee breaks. Native North Americans use peyote and tobacco in their religious ceremonies the way Europeans use wine. Alcohol is the drug of choice in Europe, the U.S., and Canada, while many Muslim countries tolerate the use of opium and marijuana.

A "drug free America" is not a realistic goal, and by criminally banning psychoactive drugs, the government has ceded all control of potentially dangerous substances to criminals. Instead of trying to stamp out all drug use, our government should focus on reducing drug abuse and prohibition-generated crime. This requires a fundamental change in public policy: repeal of criminal prohibition and the creation of a reasonable regulatory system.

Ending Prohibition Would Not Necessarily Increase Drug Abuse

While it is impossible to predict exactly how drug use patterns would change under a system of regulated manufacture and distribution, the iron rules of prohibition are that 1) illegal markets are controlled by producers, not consumers, and 2) prohibition fosters the sale and consumption of more potent and dangerous forms of drugs.

During alcohol prohibition in the 1920s, bootleggers marketed small bottles of 100-plus proof liquor because they were easier to conceal than were large, unwieldy kegs of beer. The result: Consumption of beer and wine went down while consumption of hard liquor went up. Similarly, contemporary drug smugglers' preference for powdered cocaine over bulky, pungent coca leaves encourages use of the most potent and dangerous cocaine products. In contrast, under legal conditions, consumers—most of whom do not wish to harm themselves—play a role in determining the potency of marketed products, as indicated by the popularity of today's light beers, wine coolers and decaffeinated coffees. Once alcohol prohibition was repealed, consumption increased somewhat, but the rate of liver cirrhosis went down because people tended to choose beer and wine over the more potent, distilled spirits previously promoted by bootleggers. So, even though the number of drinkers went up, the health risks of drinking went down. The same dynamic would most likely occur with drug legalization: some increase in drug use, but a decrease in drug abuse.

Another factor to consider is the lure of forbidden fruit. For young people, who are often attracted to taboos, legal drugs might be less tempting than they are now. That has been the experience of The Netherlands: After the Dutch government decriminalized marijuana in 1976, allowing it to be sold and consumed openly in small amounts, usage steadily declined—particularly among teenagers and young adults. Prior to decriminalization, 10 percent of Dutch 17- and 18-year-olds used marijuana. By 1985, that figure had dropped to 6.5 percent.

What The United States Would Look Like After Repeal

Some people, hearing the words "drug legalization," imagine pushers on street corners passing out cocaine to anyone—even children. But that is what exists today under prohibition. Consider the legal drugs, alcohol and tobacco: Their potency, time and place of sale, and purchasing age limits are set by law. Similarly, warning labels are required on medicinal drugs, and some of these are available by prescription only.

After federal alcohol prohibition was repealed, each state developed its own system for regulating the distribution and sale of alcoholic beverages. The same could occur with currently illegal drugs. For example, states could create different regulations for marijuana, heroin, and cocaine.

Ending prohibition is not a panacea. It will not by itself end drug abuse or eliminate violence. Nor will it bring about the social and economic revitalization of our inner cities. However, ending prohibition would bring one very significant benefit: It would sever the connection between drugs and crime that today blights so many lives and communities. In the long run, ending prohibition could foster the redirection of public resources toward social development, legitimate economic opportunities, and effective treatment, thus enhancing the safety, health, and well being of the entire society.

♣ It's A Fact!!
Would drugs be more available
once prohibition is repealed?

According to the ACLU, it is hard to imagine drugs being more available than they are today. Despite efforts to stem their flow, drugs are accessible to anyone who wants them. In a recent government-sponsored survey of high school seniors, 55 percent said it would be "easy" for them to obtain cocaine, and 85 percent said it would be "easy" for them to obtain marijuana. In our inner cities, access to drugs is especially easy, and the risk of arrest has proven to have a negligible deterrent effect. What would change under decriminalization is not so much drug availability as the conditions under which drugs would be available. Without prohibition, providing help to drug abusers who wanted to kick their habits would be easier because the money now being squandered on law enforcement could be used for preventive social programs and treatment.

Chapter 68

Medical Marijuana Should Not Be Legalized

Myth Vs. Reality

When 14-year-old Irma Perez of Belmont, California, took a single ec-stasy pill one evening, she had no idea she would become one of the 26,000 people who die every year from drugs. Irma took ecstasy with two of her 14-year-old friends in her home. Soon after taking the tiny blue pill, Irma com-plained of feeling awful and said she felt like she was "going to die." Instead of seeking medical care, her friends called the 17-year-old dealer who supplied the pills and asked for advice. The friends tried to get Irma to smoke marijuana, but when she couldn't because she was vomiting and lapsing into a coma, they stuffed marijuana leaves into her mouth because, according to news sources, "they knew that drug is sometimes used to treat cancer patients."

Irma Perez died from taking ecstasy, but compounding that tragedy was the deadly decision to use marijuana to "treat" her instead of making what could have been a lifesaving call to 911. Irma was a victim of our society's stunning misinformation about marijuana—a society that has come to be-lieve that marijuana use is not only an individual's free choice but also is good medicine, a cure-all for a variety of ills. A recent poll showed that nearly three-fourths of Americans over the age of 45 support legalizing marijuana for medical use.

The natural extension of this myth is that, if marijuana is medicine, it must also be safe for recreational use. This pervasive mindset has even reached our courts. In January 2005, for example, Governor Frank Murkowski of Alaska had to ask the legislature "to overrule a court ruling that adult Alaskans have the right to possess marijuana for personal use in their homes." There was no pretense of medical use in this ruling; it gave Alaskans the legal right to smoke marijuana for any reason, lending credence to the belief that marijuana is not only safe to treat serious illness but somehow safe for general use and for all society.

Myth: Marijuana Is Medicine

Reality: Smoked marijuana is not medicine. The scientific and medical communities have determined that smoked marijuana is a health danger, not a cure. There is no medical evidence that smoking marijuana helps patients. In fact, the Food and Drug Administration (FDA) has approved no medications that are smoked, primarily because smoking is a poor way to deliver medicine. Morphine, for example has proven to be a medically valuable drug, but the FDA does not endorse smoking opium or heroin.

Congress enacted laws against marijuana in 1970 based in part on its conclusion that marijuana has no scientifically proven medical value, which the U.S. Supreme Court affirmed more than 30 years later in United States v. Oakland Cannabis Buyers' Cooperative, et al., 532 U.S. 483 (2001). Marijuana remains in schedule 1 of the Controlled Substances Act because it has a high potential for abuse, a lack of accepted safety for use under medical supervision, and no currently accepted medical value.

The American Medical Association has rejected pleas to endorse marijuana as medicine, and instead urged that marijuana remain a prohibited schedule 1 drug at least until the results of controlled studies are in. The National Multiple Sclerosis Society stated that studies done to date "have not provided convincing evidence that marijuana benefits people with MS" and does not recommend it as a treatment. Further, the MS Society states that for people with MS "long-term use of marijuana may be associated with significant serious side effects."

The British Medical Association has taken a similar position, voicing "extreme concern" that downgrading the criminal status of marijuana would "mislead" the public into thinking that the drug is safe to use when, "in fact, it has been linked to greater risk of heart disease, lung cancer, bronchitis, and emphysema."

In 1999 the Institute of Medicine (IOM) undertook a landmark study reviewing the alleged medical properties of marijuana. Advocates of so-called medical marijuana frequently tout this study, but the study's findings decisively undercut their arguments. In truth, the IOM explicitly found that marijuana is not medicine and expressed concern about patients' smoking it because smoking is a harmful drug-delivery system. The IOM further found that there was no scientific evidence that smoked marijuana had medical value, even for the chronically ill, and concluded "there is little future in smoked marijuana as a medically approved medication." In fact, the researchers who conducted the study could find no medical value to marijuana for virtually any ailment they examined, including the treatment of wasting syndrome in AIDS patients, movement disorders such as Parkinson's disease and epilepsy, or glaucoma.

The IOM found that THC (the primary psychoactive ingredient in marijuana) in smoked marijuana provides only temporary relief from intraocular pressure (IOP) associated with glaucoma and would have to be smoked 8 to 10 times a day to achieve consistent results. And there exists another treatment for IOP, as the availability of medically approved once- or twice-a-day eye drops makes IOP control a reality for many patients and provides round-the-clock IOP reduction. For two other conditions, nausea and pain, the report recommended against marijuana use, while suggesting further research in limited circumstances for THC but not smoked marijuana.

Before any drug can be marketed in the United States, it must undergo rigorous scientific scrutiny and clinical evaluation overseen by the FDA. For example, the FDA has approved Marinol® (dronabinol), a safe capsule form of synthetic THC that meets the standard of accepted medicine and has the same properties as cultivated marijuana without the high, for the treatment of nausea and vomiting associated with cancer chemotherapy and for the treatment of wasting syndrome in AIDS patients.

The federal government has approved and continues to approve research into the possible use of marijuana as medicine and any new delivery systems of marijuana's active ingredients. Proving that the regulatory process does work, DEA has registered every researcher who meets FDA standards to use marijuana in scientific studies. Since 2000, for example, the California-based Center for Medicinal Cannabis Research (CMCR) has gained approval for 14 trials using smoked marijuana in human beings and three trials in laboratory and animal models. This CMCR research is the first effort to study the medical efficacy of marijuana.

♣ **It's A Fact!!**
Researchers have not endorsed smoking marijuana and instead are attempting to isolate marijuana's active ingredients to develop alternative delivery systems to smoking. Not one of these researchers has found scientific proof that smoking marijuana is medicine.

Source: Excerpted from "Marijuana: The Myths Are Killing Us," U.S. Drug Enforcement Administration, U.S. Department of Justice, April 2005.

Myth: Legalization Of Marijuana In Other Countries Has Been A Success

Reality: Liberalization of drug laws in other countries has often resulted in higher use of dangerous drugs. Over the past decade, drug policy in some foreign countries, particularly those in Europe, has gone through some dramatic changes toward greater liberalization with failed results. Consider the experience of the Netherlands, where the government reconsidered its legalization measures in light of that country's experience. After marijuana use became legal, consumption nearly tripled among 18- to 20-year-olds. As awareness of the harm of marijuana grew, the number of cannabis coffeehouses in the Netherlands decreased 36 percent in six years. Almost all Dutch towns have a cannabis policy, and 73 percent of them have a no-tolerance policy toward the coffeehouses.

In 1987 Swiss officials permitted drug use and sales in a Zurich park, which was soon dubbed Needle Park, and Switzerland became a magnet for drug users the world over. Within five years, the number of regular drug users at the park had reportedly swelled from a few hundred to 20,000. The area around the park became crime-ridden to the point that the park had to be shut down and the experiment terminated.

Myth: Marijuana Is Harmless

Reality: Marijuana is dangerous to the user. Use of marijuana has adverse health, safety, social, academic, economic, and behavioral consequences; and children are the most vulnerable to its damaging effects. Marijuana is the most widely used illicit drug in America and is readily available to kids. Compounding the problem is that the marijuana of today is not the marijuana of the baby boomers 30 years ago. Average THC levels rose from less than 1 percent in the mid-1970s to more than 8 percent in 2004. And the potency of B.C. Bud, a popular type of marijuana cultivated in British Columbia, Canada, is roughly twice the national average, ranging from 15 percent THC content to 20 percent or even higher.

Marijuana is a gateway drug. In drug law enforcement, rarely do we meet heroin or cocaine addicts who did not start their drug use with marijuana. Scientific studies bear out our anecdotal findings. For example, the Journal of the American Medical Association reported, based on a study of 300 sets of twins, that marijuana-using twins were four times more likely than their siblings to use cocaine and crack cocaine, and five times more likely to use hallucinogens such as LSD.

♣ It's A Fact!!

Marijuana use by Canadian teenagers is at a 25-year peak in the wake of an aggressive decriminalization movement. At the very time a decriminalization bill was before the House of Commons, the Canadian government released a report showing that marijuana smoking among teens is "at levels that we haven't seen since the late '70s when rates reached their peak." After a large decline in the 1980s, marijuana use among teens increased during the 1990s, as young people apparently became "confused about the state of federal pot laws."

Source: Excerpted from "Marijuana: The Myths Are Killing Us," U.S. Drug Enforcement Administration, U.S. Department of Justice, April 2005.

Smoking marijuana can cause significant health problems. Marijuana contains more than 400 chemicals, of which 60 are cannabinoids. Smoking a marijuana cigarette deposits about three to five times more tar into the lungs than one filtered tobacco cigarette. Consequently, regular marijuana smokers suffer from many of the same health problems as tobacco smokers, such as chronic coughing and wheezing, chest colds, and chronic bronchitis. In fact, studies show that smoking three to four joints per day causes at least as much harm to the respiratory system as smoking a full pack of cigarettes every day. Marijuana smoke also contains 50 to 70 percent more carcinogenic hydrocarbons than tobacco smoke and produces high levels of an enzyme that converts certain hydrocarbons into malignant cells.

> ### ♣ It's A Fact!!
> Marijuana use can lead to dependence and abuse. Marijuana was the second most common illicit drug responsible for drug treatment admissions in 2002—outdistancing crack cocaine, the next most prevalent cause. Shocking to many is that more teens are in treatment each year for marijuana dependence than for alcohol and all other illegal drugs combined. This is a trend that has been increasing for more than a decade. In 2002, 64 percent of adolescent treatment admissions reported marijuana as their primary substance of abuse, compared to 23 percent in 1992.
>
> Source: Excerpted from "Marijuana: The Myths Are Killing Us," U.S. Drug Enforcement Administration, U.S. Department of Justice, April 2005.

In addition, smoking marijuana can lead to increased anxiety, panic attacks, depression, social withdrawal, and other mental health problems, particularly for teens. Research shows that kids aged 12 to 17 who smoke marijuana weekly are three times more likely than nonusers to have suicidal thoughts. Marijuana use also can cause cognitive impairment, to include such short-term effects as distorted perception, memory loss, and trouble with thinking and problem solving.

Myth: Smoking Marijuana Harms Only The Smokers

Reality: Marijuana use harms nonusers. We need to put to rest the thought that there is such a thing as a lone drug user, a person whose habits affect only himself or herself. Drug use, including marijuana use, is not a victimless crime. Some in your communities may resist involvement because they think someone else's drug use is not hurting them. But this kind of not-my-problem thinking is tragically misguided. Ask those same people about secondhand smoke from cigarettes, and they'll quickly acknowledge the harm that befalls nonsmokers. Secondhand smoke is a well-known problem, one that Americans are becoming more unwilling to bear. We need to apply the same common-sense thinking to the even more pernicious secondhand effects of drug use.

Take for instance the disastrous effects of marijuana smoking on driving. As the National Highway Traffic Safety Administration (NHTSA) noted, "Epidemiology data from . . . traffic arrests and fatalities indicate that after alcohol, marijuana is the most frequently detected psychoactive substance among driving populations." Marijuana causes drivers to experience decreased car handling performance, increased reaction times, distorted time and distance estimation, sleepiness, impaired motor skills, and lack of concentration.

The extent of the problem of marijuana-impaired driving is startling. One in six (or 600,000) high school students drive under the influence of marijuana, almost as many as drive under the influence of alcohol, according to estimates released in September 2003 by the Office of National Drug Control Policy (ONDCP). A study of motorists pulled over for reckless driving showed that, among those who were not impaired by alcohol, 45 percent tested positive for marijuana.

The consequences of marijuana-impaired driving can be tragic. For example, four children and their van driver, nicknamed Smokey by the children for his regular marijuana smoking, died in April 2002 when a Tippy Toes

♣ It's A Fact!!

The younger a person is when he or she first uses marijuana, the more likely that person is to use cocaine and heroin and become drug-dependent as an adult. One study found that 62 percent of the adults who first tried marijuana before they were 15 were likely to go on to use cocaine. In contrast, only 1 percent or less of adults who never tried marijuana used heroin or cocaine.

Source: Excerpted from "Marijuana: The Myths Are Killing Us," U.S. Drug Enforcement Administration, U.S. Department of Justice, April 2005.

Learning Academy van veered off a freeway and hit a concrete bridge abut-
ment. He was found at the crash scene with marijuana in his pocket.

If we are to bolster cases against drugged drivers, greater protection for
innocents on the road requires the development of affordable roadside drug
detection tests, and some are in the testing phase now.

Secondhand smoke from marijuana kills other innocents as well. Last
year, two Philadelphia firefighters were killed when they responded to a residential fire stemming from an indoor marijuana grow. In New York City, an
eight-year-old boy, Deasean Hill, was killed by a stray bullet just steps from
his Brooklyn home after a drug dealer sold a dime bag of marijuana on another dealer's turf.

Medical Marijuana And The Supreme Court

Angel McClary Raich, a California woman at the center a Supreme Court
case on medical marijuana, hasn't changed her treatment regimen since the Court
ruled in June [2005] that patients who take the drug in states where its medicinal
use is legal are not shielded from federal prosecution. A thin woman with long,
dark hair and an intense gaze, Raich takes marijuana, or cannabis as she prefers
to call it, about every two waking hours by smoking it, by inhaling it as a vapor,
by eating it in foods, or by applying it topically as a balm. She says that it relieves
her chronic pain and boosts her appetite, preventing her from becoming emaci-
ated because of a mysterious wasting syndrome. Raich and her doctor maintain
that without access to the eight or nine pounds of privately grown cannabis that
she consumes each year, she would die.

Although Raich has embraced a public role advocating the medicinal use of marijuana, she says that her health suffered during the hectic days following the announcement of the Court's decision, when a whirlwind schedule of press conferences and congressional meetings in Washington prevented her from medicating herself with cannabis as regularly as she needed to. "My body was shutting down on me," she said in an interview from her Oakland home. "I'm scared of my health failing. I'm scared of the federal government coming in and doing more harm. [Recently,] the city of Oakland warned there were going to be some raids" on marijuana dispensaries. "We're all just waiting. Sitting on the frontline is extremely stressful."

In the Supreme Court case Gonzales v. Raich, the justices ruled 6 to 3 that the federal government has the power to arrest and prosecute patients and their suppliers even if the marijuana use is permitted under state law, because of its authority under the federal Controlled Substances Act to regulate interstate commerce in illegal drugs. In practical terms, it is not yet clear what effect the Court's decision will have on patients. An estimated 115,000 people have obtained recommendations for marijuana from doctors in the 10 states that have legalized the cultivation, possession, and use of marijuana for medicinal purposes. Besides California, those states are Alaska, Colorado, Hawaii, Maine, Montana, Nevada, Oregon, Vermont, and Washington. (Three weeks after the decision was announced, Rhode Island's legislature passed a similar law and soon afterward overrode a veto by the state's governor.)

Immediately after the news of the high court's ruling, attorneys general in the states that have approved the use of medical marijuana emphasized that the practice remained legal under their state laws, and a telephone survey of a random national sample of registered voters, commissioned by the Washington-based Marijuana Policy Project, indicated that 68 percent of respondents opposed federal prosecution of patients who use marijuana for medical reasons. Nationally, most marijuana arrests are made by state and local law-enforcement agencies, with federal arrests accounting for only about 1 percent of cases. However, soon after the decision was announced, federal agents raided 3 of San Francisco's more than 40 medical marijuana dispensaries. Nineteen people were charged with running an international drug ring. They allegedly were using the dispensaries as a front for trafficking in marijuana and in the illegal amphetamine "ecstasy."

In California, the raids were widely viewed as a signal that federal drug enforcement agents intended to crack down on abuse of the state's medical marijuana program. California has an estimated 100,000 medical marijuana users. Its 1996 law grants doctors much greater latitude in recommending the drug than do similar laws in other states, and the U.S. District Court for the Northern District of California ruled in 2000 that doctors who prescribe marijuana are protected from federal prosecution under the First Amendment, provided that they do not help their patients obtain the drug. In San Francisco, some journalists or investigators who posed as patients have reported that they had little difficulty obtaining a recommendation for medical marijuana, which allows the holder to purchase the drug from a dispensary. "We're empathetic to the sick," the Drug Enforcement Administration's Javier Pena told reporters after the raids, "but we can't disregard the federal law."

Even before the Supreme Court decision, many Californians had been calling for stricter state regulation of medical marijuana. Some cities have banned marijuana dispensaries, and many counties and cities, including San Francisco, have imposed moratoriums on the opening of new ones. Some local jurisdictions register and issue identification cards to patients who use marijuana for medical reasons, and state officials have been working on a voluntary statewide registration program. However, the officials recently put the program on hold, citing concern that the issuance of identification cards to patients might put state health officials at risk of prosecution for aiding a federal crime and that federal drug enforcement agents might seek state records in order to identify medical marijuana users. Registration of patients and the issuance of identification cards by the state are required in seven other states that have legalized the medical use of marijuana. Patients can show the card as a defense against arrest by local or state police for possession of the drug. Maine and Washington do not issue identification cards to patients.

Conditions for which marijuana is commonly recommended include nausea caused by cancer chemotherapy; anorexia or wasting due to cancer, AIDS, or other diseases; chronic pain; spasticity caused by multiple sclerosis or other neurologic disorders; and glaucoma. Frank Lucido, a Berkeley family practitioner who is Raich's doctor, said that so far, the Court ruling appears to have had little effect on his patients who use medical marijuana. About 30 percent of Lucido's practice consists of evaluating patients who want a recommendation for the drug. He said in an interview that he would not issue such a recommendation unless a patient has a primary care physician and has a condition serious enough to require follow-up at least annually. About 80 percent of his patients who use medical cannabis have chronic pain; a smaller number take the drug for muscle spasms, mood disorders, migraine, AIDS, or cancer. "My patients probably average in their 30s," Lucido said. "I have had probably five patients who are under 18. These are people with serious illnesses, where parents were very clear that this would be a good medication for them."

Peter A. Rasmussen, an oncologist in Salem, Oregon, said he discusses the option of trying marijuana with about 1 in 10 patients in his practice. "It's not my first choice for any symptom," he said in an interview. "I only talk about it with people if my first-line treatment doesn't work." Rasmussen said marijuana has helped stimulate appetite or reduce nausea in a number of his patients with cancer, but its psychological effects have distressed others. Some express interest in trying marijuana but have difficulty getting the drug. "Most of my patients who use it, I think, just buy the drug illegally," he said. "But a lot of my patients, they're older, they don't know any kids, they don't hang out on the street. They just don't know how to get it."

In a report published in 1999, an expert committee of the Institute of Medicine expressed concern about the adverse health effects of smoking marijuana, particularly on the respiratory tract. The report called for expanded research on marijuana's active components, known as cannabinoids, including studies to explore the chemicals' potential therapeutic effects and to develop safe, reliable, rapid-onset delivery systems. It also recommended short-term clinical trials of marijuana "in patients with conditions for which there is reasonable expectation of efficacy."

There has been some progress toward those goals. The Center for Medicinal Cannabis Research (CMCR), a three-year research initiative established in 1999 by the California state legislature, has funded several placebo-controlled clinical trials of smoked marijuana to treat neuropathic pain,

pain from other causes, and spasticity in multiple sclerosis, and the results are likely to be available soon. The National Institute on Drug Abuse provided both the active marijuana and the "placebo," a smokable version of the drug from which dronabinol (9-tetrahydrocannabinol, or THC) and certain other active constituents had been removed. "It's like decaf coffee or nicotine-free cigarettes, and it tastes the same [as marijuana]," said Igor Grant, a professor of psychiatry at the University of California, San Diego, and director of the CMCR. He said additional studies of the whole plant, as well as its individual components, are still needed. "It's still the case that we don't know which components of botanical marijuana have beneficial effects, if any," he said.

In an open-label trial, oncologist Donald I. Abrams of the University of California, San Francisco, found evidence of marijuana's effectiveness in the treatment of neuropathic pain among HIV-infected patients and has just finished a placebo-controlled trial that he intends to publish soon. Abrams has also shown that cannabinoids that are smoked or taken orally do not adversely affect drug treatment of HIV, and he is completing a study that compares blood levels of cannabinoids among volunteers who inhaled vaporized marijuana with similar levels among volunteers who smoked the drug. Vaporizers heat the drug to a temperature below that required for combustion, producing vapor that contains the active ingredients without the tar or particulates thought to be responsible for most of the drug's adverse effects on the respiratory tract.

♣ It's A Fact!!

Clinical research on marijuana has been hampered by the fact that the plant, which contains dozens of active substances, is an illegal drug classified as having no legitimate medical use. Researchers wishing to do clinical studies must first get government permission and obtain a supply of the drug from the National Institute on Drug Abuse.

Source: Excerpted from "Medical Marijuana And The Supreme Court." Copyright © 2005 Massachusetts Medical Society. All rights reserved.

Meanwhile, a new marijuana-derived drug is on the Canadian market and may soon be considered for approval by the Food and Drug Administration. Sativex®, a liquid cannabis extract that is sprayed under the tongue, was approved in Canada in June for the treatment of neuropathic pain in multiple sclerosis. Its principal active ingredients are dronabinol and cannabidiol, which are believed to be the primary active components of marijuana. The drug's manufacturer, GW Pharmaceuticals of Britain, is also testing it for cancer pain, rheumatoid arthritis, postoperative pain, and other indications. Marinol®, a synthetic version of dronabinol supplied in capsules, is approved in the United States for chemotherapy-associated nausea and for anorexia and wasting among patients with AIDS.

On the day the Supreme Court ruling was announced, John Walters, President George W. Bush's "drug czar," issued a statement declaring, "Today's decision marks the end of medical marijuana as a political issue. . . . We have a responsibility as a civilized society to ensure that the medicine Americans receive from their doctors is effective, safe, and free from the pro-drug politics that are being promoted in America under the guise of medicine." Nine days later, the House of Representatives, for the third year in a row, defeated a measure that would have prevented the Justice Department from spending money to prosecute medical marijuana cases under federal law.

Nevertheless, marijuana advocates insist that the long-running battle between federal and state governments over the medicinal use of marijuana is far from over. Activists next plan to focus on getting more states to pass laws legalizing medical marijuana, according to Steve Fox, former director of government relations for the Marijuana Policy Project.

It is surprising that the Supreme Court decision does not necessarily spell the end even of Angel Raich's legal case. Raich and another California patient, Diane Monson, who initially sued to prevent the Justice Department from prosecuting them or their suppliers, won a favorable ruling in 2003 from California's Court of Appeals for the Ninth Circuit. The Supreme Court's reversal now sends their case back to that court. Raich said that she, Monson, and their attorneys will ask the appeals court judges to consider other legal arguments, such as whether prosecuting patients who use marijuana to relieve pain violates their right to due process of law. "Previous decisions have established that there is a fundamental right to preserve one's life and avoid needless pain and suffering," explained Boston University's Randy Barnett, a constitutional lawyer who argued the women's case before the Supreme Court. "Federal restriction on accessibility to medical cannabis is an infringement" on that right, he said.

Raich vowed to continue her personal battle. "I'm stubborn as heck, so I don't plan to give it up that easily. I plan to fight until I can't fight anymore," she said.

Chapter 69

An Opposing Point Of View: Against Marijuana Prohibition

Marijuana Prohibition Facts

- Very few Americans had even heard about marijuana when it was first federally prohibited in 1937. Today, between 95 and 100 million Americans admit to having tried it.

- According to government-funded researchers, high school seniors consistently report that marijuana is easily available, despite decades of a nationwide drug war. With little variation, every year about 85% consider marijuana "fairly easy" or "very easy" to obtain. Data from the U.S. Centers for Disease Control and Prevention show that more U.S. high school students currently smoke marijuana, which is completely unregulated, than smoke cigarettes, which are sold by regulated businesses.

- There have been over seven million marijuana arrests in the United States since 1993, including 755,186 arrests in 2003—an all-time record. One person is arrested for marijuana every 42 seconds. About 88% of all marijuana arrests are for possession—not manufacture or distribution.

About This Chapter: "Marijuana Prohibition Facts" is reprinted with permission from the Marijuana Policy Project, Washington, D.C. © 2005 Marijuana Policy Project. All rights reserved. For additional information, visit the Marijuana Policy Project website at http://www.mpp.org.

- Every comprehensive, objective government commission that has examined the marijuana phenomenon throughout the past 100 years has recommended that adults should not be criminalized for using marijuana.

- Cultivation of even one marijuana plant is a federal felony.

- Lengthy mandatory minimum sentences apply to myriad offenses. For example, a person must serve a five-year mandatory minimum sentence if federally convicted of cultivating 100 marijuana plants—including seedlings or bug-infested, sickly plants. This is longer than the average sentences for auto theft and manslaughter.

- A one-year minimum prison sentence is mandated for "distributing" or "manufacturing" controlled substances within 1,000 feet of any school, university, or playground. Most areas in a city fall within these "drug-free zones." An adult who lives three blocks from a university is subject to a one-year mandatory minimum sentence for selling an ounce of marijuana to another adult—or even growing one marijuana plant in his or her basement.

- Approximately 77,000 marijuana offenders are in prison or jail right now.

- A recent study of prisons in four Midwestern states found that approximately one in ten male inmates reported that that they had been raped while in prison. Rates of rape and sexual assault against women prisoners, who are most likely to be abused by male staff members, have been reported to be as high as 27 percent in some institutions.

- Civil forfeiture laws allow police to seize the money and property of suspected marijuana offenders—charges need not even be filed. The claim is against the property, not the defendant. The owner must then prove that the property is "innocent." Enforcement abuses stemming from forfeiture laws abound.

- Marijuana Policy Project (MPP) estimates that the war on marijuana consumers costs taxpayers nearly $12 billion annually.

- Many patients and their doctors find marijuana a useful medicine as part of the treatment for AIDS, cancer, glaucoma, multiple sclerosis, and other ailments. Yet the federal government allows only seven patients in the United States to use marijuana as a medicine, through a program now closed to new applicants. Federal laws treat all other patients currently using medical marijuana as criminals. Doctors are presently allowed to prescribe cocaine and morphine—but not marijuana.

- Organizations that have endorsed medical access to marijuana include: the AIDS Action Council, American Academy of Family Physicians, American Public Health Association, American Academy of HIV Medicine, American Nurses Association, Lymphoma Foundation of America, National Association of People With AIDS, the New England Journal of Medicine, the state medical associations of New York, California, Florida and Rhode Island, and many others.

- A few of the many editorial boards that have endorsed medical access to marijuana include: *Boston Globe, Chicago Tribune, Miami Herald, New York Times, Orange County Register, USA Today, Baltimore's Sun*, and *The Los Angeles Times*.

- Since 1996, a majority of voters in Alaska, Arizona, California, Colorado, the District of Columbia, Maine, Montana, Nevada, Oregon, and Washington state have voted in favor of ballot initiatives to remove criminal penalties for seriously ill people who grow or possess medical marijuana.

- Seventy-two percent of Americans believe that marijuana users should not be jailed. Eighty percent support legal access to medical marijuana for seriously ill adults.

- "Decriminalization" involves the removal of criminal penalties for possession of marijuana for personal use. Small fines may be issued (somewhat similarly to traffic tickets), but there is typically no arrest, incarceration, or criminal record. Marijuana is presently decriminalized in 11 states—California, Colorado, Maine, Minnesota, Mississippi, Nebraska, Nevada, New York, North Carolina, Ohio, and Oregon. In these states, cultivation and distribution remain criminal offenses.

♣ It's A Fact!!

A new report provides strong evidence that state medical marijuana laws have not increased adolescent marijuana use, contradicting claims made by opponents of such laws. The report, co-authored by substance abuse researcher Mitch Earleywine, Ph.D., of the University at Albany, State University of New York, and Marijuana Policy Project Legislative Analyst Karen O'Keefe, Esq., is the first comprehensive analysis of all available data from state and national drug use surveys to determine trends in teen marijuana use in states with medical marijuana laws. The following are among the key findings:

- No state that has passed a medical marijuana law has seen an overall increase in teen marijuana use since the law's passage.

- The decline in teen marijuana use in states with medical marijuana laws slightly exceeds the decline seen nationally.

- California, which passed the first effective medical marijuana law in 1996, has seen particularly large reductions, ranging from 40% to 50% in many categories.

Opponents of medical marijuana laws regularly claim that such measures increase teen marijuana use by "sending the wrong message to young people." Most recently, Rhode Island Gov. Donald Carcieri (R) cited such arguments in June 2005 when he announced his veto of medical marijuana legislation. A vote to override that veto is pending in the Rhode Island House of Representatives.

"While survey data alone cannot prove cause and effect, there is no evidence whatsoever that medical marijuana laws have increased teen marijuana use," Dr. Mitch Earleywine said. "None of the states with medical marijuana laws have seen an overall increase in adolescent marijuana use, and some have had huge reductions."

"Again and again, opponents of medical marijuana laws claim that such proposals are dangerous because they encourage young people to use marijuana," Karen O'Keefe said. "There is now a massive body of data showing that no such effect has happened, and it's time for those who want to continue arresting patients to stop making unsubstantiated claims."

Source: Reprinted with permission from the Marijuana Policy Project, Washington, D.C. © 2004 Marijuana Policy Project. All rights reserved. For additional information, visit the Marijuana Policy Project website at http://www.mpp.org.

- Decriminalization saves a tremendous amount in enforcement costs. California saves $100 million per year.

- A 2001 National Research Council study sponsored by the U.S. government found "little apparent relationship between the severity of sanctions prescribed for drug use and prevalence or frequency of use, and . . . perceived legal risk explains very little in the variance of individual drug use." The primary evidence cited came from comparisons between states that have and have not decriminalized marijuana.

- In the Netherlands, where adult possession and purchase of small amounts of marijuana are allowed under a regulated system, the rate of marijuana use by teenagers is far lower than in the U.S. Under a regulated system, licensed merchants have an incentive to check ID and avoid selling to minors. Such a system also separates marijuana from the trade in hard drugs such as cocaine and heroin.

- "Zero tolerance" policies against "drugged driving" can result in "DUI (driving under the influence)" convictions of drivers who are not intoxicated at all. Trace amounts of THC metabolites—detected by commonly used tests—can linger in blood and urine for weeks after any psychoactive effects have worn off. This is equivalent to convicting someone of "drunk driving" weeks after he or she drank one beer.

- The arbitrary criminalization of tens of millions of Americans who consume marijuana results in a large-scale lack of respect for the law and the entire criminal justice system.

- Marijuana prohibition subjects users to added health hazards such as the following:

  - Adulterants, contaminants, and impurities: Marijuana purchased through criminal markets is not subject to the same quality control standards as are legal consumer goods. Illicit marijuana may be adulterated with much more damaging substances; contaminated with pesticides, herbicides, or fertilizers; and/or infected with molds, fungi, or bacteria.

- Inhalation of hot smoke: One well-established hazard of marijuana consumption is the fact that smoke from burning plant material is bad for the respiratory system. Laws that prohibit the sale or possession of paraphernalia make it difficult to obtain and use devices such as vaporizers, which can reduce these risks.

- Because vigorous enforcement of the marijuana laws forces the toughest, most dangerous criminals to take over marijuana trafficking, prohibition links marijuana sales to violence, predatory crime, and terrorism.

- Prohibition invites corruption within the criminal justice system by giving officials easy, tempting opportunities to accept bribes, steal and sell marijuana, and plant evidence on innocent people.

- Because marijuana is typically used in private, trampling the Bill of Rights is a routine part of marijuana law enforcement—e.g., use of drug dogs, urine tests, phone taps, government informants, curbside garbage searches, military helicopters, and infrared heat detectors.

Part Eight

If You Need More Information

Chapter 70

National Organizations For Drug Information

Federal Agencies

Center for Food Safety and Applied Nutrition

U.S. Food and Drug
Administration
5100 Paint Branch Parkway
College Park, MD 20704-3835
Phone: 301-436-1600
Toll Free: 888-723-3366
Website: http://www.cfsan.fda.gov

Center for Substance Abuse Prevention (CSAP)

Substance Abuse and Mental
Health Services Administration
1 Choke Cherry Road
Rockville, MD 20857
Toll Free: 800-662-HELP (4357)
Toll Free: 800-787-8432 (Spanish)
Phone: 240-276-2420
Fax: 301-443-5447
Website: http://
www.csap.samhsa.gov

About This Chapter: Information in this chapter was excerpted from "What You Can Do about Drug Use in America," Office for Substance Abuse Prevention, U.S. Department of Health and Human Services, DHHS Pub. No. ADM 91-1572 and compiled from other sources deemed accurate. All information was updated and verified in January 2006.

Center for Substance Abuse Treatment (CSAT)
Toll Free: 800-662-HELP (4357)
Toll Free: 800-787-8432 (Spanish)
Website: http://
www.csat.samhsa.gov

Centers for Disease Control and Prevention
1600 Clifton Rd. MS D-31
Atlanta, GA 30333
Toll Free: 800-311-3435
Phone: 404-639-3534
Website: http://www.cdc.gov

Drug Enforcement Administration (DEA)
2401 Jefferson Davis Highway
Alexandria, VA 22301
Phone: 202-307-1000
Website: http://www.dea.gov

National Clearinghouse for Alcohol and Drug Information (NCADI)
P.O. Box 2345
Rockville, MD 20847-2345
Toll Free: 800-729-6686
Phone: 301-468-2600
TDD: 800-487-4889
Fax: 301-468-6433
Linea gratis en Español:
877-767-8432
Website: http://www.health.org
E-mail: info@health.org

National Drug Intelligence Center
319 Washington Street, 5th Floor
Johnstown, PA 15901-1622
Phone: 814-532-4601
Fax: 814-532-4690
Website: http://www.usdoj.gov/
ndic
E-mail: NDIC.Contacts@usdoj.gov

National Institute on Alcohol Abuse and Alcoholism
5635 Fishers Lane, MSC 9304
Bethesda, MD 20892-9304
Website: http://www.niaaa.nih.gov
E-mail: niaaaweb-
r@exchange.nih.gov

National Institute on Drug Abuse (NIDA)
6001 Executive Blvd., Room 5213
Bethesda, MD 20892
Phone: 301-443-1124
Fax: 301-443-7397
Website: http://www.nida.nih.gov
E-mail: information@nida.nih.gov

National Institute of Justice
810 7th Street NW, 7th Floor
Washington, DC 20531
Toll Free: 800-851-3420
Phone: 202-307-2942
Fax: 202-307-6394
Website: http://www.ojp.usdoj.gov/
nij

National Institutes of Health

9000 Rockville Pike
Bethesda, MD 20892
TTY: 888-889-6432
Phone: 301-496-4000
Website: http://www.nih.gov
E-mail: NIHInfo@od.nih.gov

Office of National Drug Control Policy

Drug Policy Information
Clearinghouse
P.O. Box 6000
Rockville, MD 20849-6000
Toll Free: 800-666-3332
Fax: 301-519-5212
Website: http://
www.whitehousedrugpolicy.gov
E-mail: ondcp@ncjrs.gov

Substance Abuse and Mental Health Services Administration (SAMHSA)

1 Choke Cherry Road
Rockville, MD 20857
Phone: 240-276-2130
Fax: 240-276-2135
Website: http://www.samhsa.gov
E-mail: info@samhsa.gov

U.S. Bureau of Alcohol, Tobacco, and Firearms (ATF)

650 Massachusetts Avenue, NW,
Room 8290
Washington, DC 20226
Toll Free: 888-283-2662
Toll Free: 800-ATF-GUNS (To
report illegal firearms activity)
Website: http://www.atf.treas.gov
E-mail: atfmail@atf.gov

U.S. Department of Labor

Frances Perkins Building
200 Constitution Avenue, NW
Washington, DC 20210
Toll Free: 866-4-USA-DOL (866-
487-2365)
TTY: 877-889-5627
Website: http://www.dol.gov

U.S. Food and Drug Administration

5600 Fishers Lane
Rockville, MD 20857
Toll Free: 888-463-6332
Website: http://www.fda.gov

U.S. Indian Health Service

The Reyes Building
801 Thompson Avenue, Suite 400
Rockville, MD 20852-1627
Phone: (alcohol and substance
abuse) 301-443-2038
Website: http://www.ihs.gov

Private Organizations, Civic Groups, And Religious Organizations

Action on Smoking and Health (ASH)
2013 H Street, NW
Washington, DC 20006
Phone: 202-659-4310
Fax: 202-833-2314
Website: http://www.ash.org

Al-Anon/Alateen Family Groups
1600 Corporate Landing Parkway
Virginia Beach, VA 23454-5617
Toll Free: 888-4AL-ANON
Phone: 757-563-1600
Fax: 757-563-1655
Website: http://www.al-anon.org
E-mail: WSO@al-anon.org

Alcoholics Anonymous (AA)
475 Riverside Dr., 11th Floor
New York, NY 10015
Phone: 212-870-3400
Website: http://www.alcoholics-anonymous.org

American Council for Drug Education
164 W. 74th Street
New York, NY 10023
Toll Free: 800-488-DRUG
Website: http://www.acde.org

American Council on Alcoholism
1000 E. Indian School Road
Phoenix, AZ 85014
Toll Free: 800-527-5344
Fax: 602-264-7403
Website: http://www.aca-usa.org
E-mail: info@aca-usa.org

Boys and Girls Clubs of America
1230 West Peachtree Street, NW
Atlanta, GA 30309
Toll Free: 800-854-CLUB
Phone: 404-815-5700
Fax: 404-487-5757
Website: http://www.bgca.org

Campaign for Tobacco-Free Kids
1400 Eye Street, NW, Suite 1200
Washington, DC 20005
Phone: 202-296-5469
Fax: 202-296-5427
Website: http://www.tobaccofreekids.org

CoAnon Family Groups
P.O. Box 12722
Tucson, AZ 85732-2722
Phone: 520-513-5028
Website: http://www.co-anon.org

Cocaine Anonymous (CA)

3740 Overland Avenue, Suite C
Los Angeles, CA 90034
Toll-Free: 800-347-8998
Phone: 310-559-5833
Fax: 310-559-2554
Website: http://www.ca.org
E-mail: cawso@ca.org

Connecticut Clearinghouse

334 Farmington Ave.
Plainville, CT 06062
Toll Free: 800-232-4424
Phone: 860-793-9791
Fax: 860-793-9813
Website: http://
www.ctclearinghouse.org
E-mail: info@ctclearinghouse.org

Do It Now Foundation

P.O. Box 27568
Tempe, AZ 85285-7568
Phone: 480-736-0599
Fax: 480-736-0771
Website: http://www.doitnow.org
E-mail: sara@doitnow.org

Families Anonymous, Inc.

P.O. Box 3475
Culver City, CA 90231-3475
Phone: 800-736-9805
Fax: 310-815-9682
Website: http://
www.familiesanonymous.org
E-mail:
famanon@familiesanonymous.org

Focus Adolescent Services

1113 Woodland Road
Salisbury, MD 21801
Toll Free: 877-362-8727
Phone: 410-341-4342
or 410-341-4216
Website: http://www.focusas.com
E-mail: help@focusas.com

Hazelden Foundation

P.O. Box 11, CO3
Center City, MN 55012-0011
Toll Free: 800-257-7810
Toll Free: 800-I-DO-CARE
Phone: 651-213-4000
Website: http://www.hazelden.org
E-mail: info@hazelden.org

Indiana Prevention Resource Center

Creative Arts Building
2735 E. 10th St., Rm. 110
Bloomington, IN 47408-2606
Toll Free: 800-346-3077 in Indiana
only
Phone: 812-855-1237
Fax: 812-855-4940
Website: http://
www.drugs.indiana.edu
E-mail: drugs@Indiana.edu

Institute on Black Chemical Abuse

African American Family Services
2616 Nicollet Avenue
Minneapolis, MN 55408
Phone: 612-871-7878
Fax: 612-871-2567
Website: http://www.aafs.net
E-mail: contact@aafs.net

Join Together

One Appleton Street, 4th Floor
Boston, MA 02116-5223
Phone: 617-437-1500
Fax: 617-437-9394
Website: http://
www.jointogether.org
E-mail: info@jointogether.org

Minnesota Drug Information Service

Bio-Medical Library
Diehl Hall
University of Minnesota
Minneapolis, MN 55455-0334
Phone: 612-626-5653
Fax: 612-626-2454
Website: http://
biomed.lib.umn.edu/dis/
dismain.html
E-mail: medref@umn.edu

Mothers Against Drunk Driving (MADD)

511 E. John Carpenter Fwy.
Suite 700
Irving, TX 75062
Toll Free: 800-438-6233
Phone: 214-744-6233
Fax: 972-869-2206/7
Website: http://www.madd.org
E-mail: info@madd.org

Nar-Anon Family Group Headquarters, Inc.

22527 Crenshaw Blvd. #200B
Torrance, CA 90505
Toll-Free: 800-477-6291
Phone: 310-534-8188
Fax: 310-534-8688
Website: http://www.nar-anon.org
E-mail:
naranonWSO@hotmail.com

Narcotics Anonymous (NA)

P.O. Box 9999
Van Nuys, CA 91409
Phone: 818-773-9999
Fax: 818-700-0700
Website: http://www.na.org
E-mail: wso@na.org

The National Alliance for Hispanic Health

1501 16th Street, N.W.
Washington, DC 20036
Phone: 202-387-5000
Fax: 202-797-4353
Website: http://
www.hispanichealth.org
E-mail:
alliance@hispanichealth.org

National Asian Pacific American Families Against Drug Abuse

340 East Second Street, Suite 409
Los Angeles, CA 90012
Phone: 213-625-5795
Fax: 213-625-5796
Website: http://www.napafasa.org
E-mail: napafasa@napafasa.org

National Association of State Alcohol and Drug Abuse Directors (NASADAD)

808 17th Street, NW, Suite 410
Washington, DC 20006
Phone: 202-293-0090
Fax: 202-293-1250
Website: http://www.nasadad.org
E-mail: dcoffice@nasadad.org

National Black Alcoholism and Addictions Council (NBAC)

5104 N. Orange Blossom Trail
Suite 111
Orlando, FL 32810
Toll-Free: 877-662-2674
Phone: 404-532-2747
Fax: 407-532-2815
Website: http://www.nbacinc.org
E-mail: mail@nbacinc.org

The National Center on Addiction and Substance Abuse at Columbia University (CASA)

633 Third Avenue, 19th Floor
New York, NY 10017-6706
Phone: 212-841-5200
Fax: 212-956-8020
Website: http://
www.casacolumbia.org

National Council on Alcoholism and Drug Dependence, Inc.

22 Cortlandt Street, Suite 801
New York, NY 10007-3128
Toll Free: 800-NCA-CALL (800-662-2255)
Phone: 212-269-7797
Fax: 212-269-7510
Website: http://www.ncadd.org
E-mail: national@ncadd.org

National Families in Action
2957 Clairmont Road, Suite 150
Atlanta, GA 30329
Phone: 404-248-9676
Fax: 404-248-1312
Website: http://www.emory.edu/
NFIA
E-mail: nfia@nationalfamilies.org

National Family Partnership
2490 Coral Way, Suite 501
Miami, Fl 33145
Toll Free: 800-705-8997
Phone: 305-856-4886
Fax: 305-856-4815
Website: http://www.nfp.org
E-mail: info@informedfamilies.org

National Inhalant Prevention Coalition
322-A Thompson Street
Chattanooga, TN 37405
Toll Free: 800-269-4237
Phone: 423-265-4662
Website: http://www.inhalants.org
E-mail: nipc@io.com

National Latino Council on Alcohol and Tobacco Prevention
1616 P St., NW, Suite 430
Washington, DC 20036
Phone: 202-265-8054
Fax: 202-265-8056
Website: http://www.nlcatp.org
E-mail: lcat@nlcatp.org

National Parents Resource Institute for Drug Education (PRIDE)
PRIDE Youth Program
4 West Oak Street
Fremont, MI 49412
Toll Free: 800-668-9277
Phone: 231-924-1662
Fax: 231-924-5663
Website: http://
www.prideyouthprograms.org

National Prevention Network
NASADAD
808 17th Street NW, Suite 410
Washington, DC 20006
Phone: 202-293-0090
Fax: 202-293-1250
Website: http://www.nasadad.org
E-mail: dcoffice@nasadad.org

Online Drug Policy Library
Web site: http://
www.druglibrary.org

Partnership for a Drug-Free America
405 Lexington Avenue, Suite 1601
New York, NY 10174
Phone: 212-922-1560
Fax: 212-922-1570
Website: http://
www.drugfreeamerica.org

Phoenix House

164 W. 74th Street
New York, NY 10023
Toll Free: 800-DRUG HELP
Phone: 212-595-5810
Fax: 212-496-6035
Website: http://
www.phoenixhouse.org

Project Cork Institute

Office of Alcohol and Drug Abuse
Programs
Department of Health
108 Cherry Street, Box 70
Burlington, VT, 05402
Phone: 802-651-1573
Website: http://
www.projectcork.org/
E-mail: cork@vdh.state.vt.us

Red Ribbon Works

P.O. Box 10203
Greenville, SC 29603
Toll Free: 800-732-4099
Phone: 864-467-4099
Fax: 864-467-4102
Website: http://
www.redribbonworks.org

Students Against Destructive Decisions (SADD)

SADD National
255 Main Street
Marlboro, MA 01752
Toll Free: 877-SADD-INC
Fax: 508-481-5759
Website: http://www.sadd.org
E-mail: info@sadd.org

Resources For Children Of Alcoholics And Other Drug Users

Children of Alcoholics Foundation

164 West 74th Street
New York, NY 10023
Toll Free: 800-488-DRUG
Phone: 646-505-2060
Fax: 212-595-2553
Website: http://www.coaf.org
E-mail: coaf@phoenixhouse.org

National Association for Children of Alcoholics

11426 Rockville Pike, Suite 301
Rockville, MD 20852
Toll Free: 888-55-4COAS
Phone: 301-468-0985
Fax: 301-468-0987
Website: http://www.nacoa.net
E-mail: nacoa@nacoa.org

Chapter 71

Substance Abuse: Where To Go For Help

Sometimes the quickest way to find out what help is available in your local area is to join a group such as Alcoholics Anonymous or Al-Anon. People in these groups often know where help is available in the community. Other sources of help and information are listed below.

Hotlines And Helplines

Alcohol Hotline
1-800-ALCOHOL (800-252-6465)
7 days a week, 24 hours a day

Al-Anon/Alateen Family Group Headquarters
1-800-344-2666
Monday through Friday,
8:00 a.m.–6:00 p.m. EST

American Council on Alcoholism
1-800-527-5344

Cocaine Hotline
1-800-COCAINE (800-262-2463)

Ecstasy Addiction
1-800-468-6933

About This Chapter: Information in this chapter was excerpted from "What You Can Do about Drug Use in America," Office for Substance Abuse Prevention, U.S. Department of Health and Human Services, DHHS Pub. No. ADM 91-1572 and compiled from other sources deemed accurate. All information was updated and verified in January 2006.

Girls and Boys Town National Hotline
1-800-448-3000

Marijuana Anonymous
1-800-766-6779
7 days a week, 24 hours a day

National Clearinghouse for Alcohol and Drug Information
1-800-729-6686
Monday through Friday,
9:00 a.m.–7:00 p.m. EST

National Council on Alcoholism and Drug Dependence
1-800-622-2255
7 days a week, 24 hours a day

National Drug and Alcohol Treatment Referral Service
1-800-662-HELP (4357)
Monday through Friday,
9:00 a.m.–3:00 a.m.

National Hopeline Network
1-800-SUICIDE (800-784-2433)
7 days a week, 24 hours a day

National Mental Health Association Help Line
1-800-950-6264
Monday through Friday, 10:00 a.m.–6:00 p.m. EST

National Runaway Hotline
1-800-231-6946
7 days a week, 24 hours a day

Steroids Hotline
1-800-STEROIDS (800-783-7643)

Victims of Crime Help Line
1-800-FYI-CALL (800-394-2255)
Monday through Friday,
8:30 a.m.–8:30 p.m. EST

Finding Treatment Resources And Support Groups

For information on where to find treatment for alcohol and other drug problems, the best place to look is in the telephone book's Yellow Pages under "Alcoholism Information" or "Drug Abuse and Addiction Information." Usually there is a listing of the nearest Council on Alcoholism (or Council on Alcohol and Drug Abuse). These Councils provide information over the phone on the availability of the nearest alcohol treatment programs. Alcoholics Anonymous (AA) or Narcotics Anonymous (NA) may also be listed. Both offer immeasurable help in enabling people to cope with problems with alcohol and other drugs.

Alcoholics Anonymous (AA)
475 Riverside Drive, 11th Floor
New York, NY 10015
Phone: 212-870-3400
Fax: 212-870-3003
Website: http://www.alcoholics
-anonymous.org

Alcoholics Victorious
1045 Swift Avenue
North Kansas City, MO 64116-4127
Phone: 816-471-8020
24-Hour Hotline: 503-245-9629
Fax: 816-471-3718
Website: http://av.iugm.org

American Council for Drug Education
164 W. 74th Street
New York, NY 10023
Toll Free: 800-488-DRUG (3784)
Website: http://www.acde.org
E-mail: acde@phoenixhouse.org

Chemically Dependent Anonymous
CDA Communications, Inc.
P.O. Box 423
Severna Park, MD 21146-0423
Toll Free: 888-CDA-HOPE
Website: http://www.cdaweb.org

Christian Recovery International
P.O. Box 215
Brea, CA 92822
Phone: 714-529-6227
Fax: 714-529-1120
Website: http://
www.christianrecovery.com

Co-Anon Family Groups World Services
P.O. Box 12722
Tuscon, AZ 85732-2722
Toll-Free: 800-898-9985
Phone: 520-513-5028
Website: http://www.co-anon.org
E-mail: info@co-anon.org

Cocaine Anonymous (CA)
3740 Overland Avenue, Suite C
Los Angeles, CA 90034
Phone: 310-559-5833
Toll Free: 800-347-8998
Website: http://www.ca.org
E-mail: cawso@ca.org

Crystal Meth Anonymous
8205 Santa Monica Blvd., PMB 1-114
West Hollywood, CA 90046-5977
Phone: 213-488-4455 (24 hour information line)
Website: http://www.crystalmeth.org
E-mail:
generalservice@crystalmeth.org

JACS (Jewish Alcoholics, Chemically Dependent Persons, and Significant Others)
850 Seventh Avenue
New York, NY 10019
Phone: 212-397-4197
Fax: 212-399-3525
Website: http://www.jacsweb.org
E-mail: jacs@jacsweb.org

Marijuana Anonymous World Services
P.O. Box 2912
Van Nuys, CA 91404
Toll Free: 800-766-6779
Website: http://www.marijuana
-anonymous.org
E-mail: office@marijuana
-anonymous.org

Narcotics Anonymous (NA)
P.O. Box 9999
Van Nuys, CA 91409
Phone: 818-733-9999
Fax: 818-700-0700
Website: http://www.na.org
E-mail: wso@na.org

National Association of State Alcohol and Drug Abuse Directors (NASADAD)
808 17th Street NW, Suite 410
Washington, DC 20006
Phone: 202-293-0090
Fax: 202-293-1250
Website: http://www.nasadad.org
E-mail: dcoffice@nasadad.org

National Clearinghouse for Alcohol and Drug Information (NCADI)
P.O. Box 2345
Rockville, MD 20847-2345
Phone: 301-468-2600
Toll Free: 800-729-6686
Español: (877) 767-8432
TDD: 800-487-4889
Fax: 301-468-6433
Website: http://www.health.org
E-mail: info@health.org

National Council on Alcoholism and Drug Dependence, Inc.
22 Cortlandt Street, Suite 801
New York, NY 10007-3128
Phone: 212-269-7797
Toll Free: 800-NCA-CALL (800-662-2255)
Fax: 212-269-7510
Website: http://www.ncadd.org
E-mail: national@ncadd.org

Nicotine Anonymous World Services

419 Main Street, PMB #370
Huntington Beach, CA 92648
Phone: 415-750-0328
Website: http://nicotine
-anonymous.org
E-mail: info@nicotine
-anonymous.org

Overcomers Outreach

P.O. Box 922950
Sylmar, CA 91392-2950
Toll Free: 800-310-3001
Website: http://
www.overcomersoutreach.org
E-mail:
info@overcomersoutreach.org

SMART Recovery®

7537 Mentor Avenue, Suite #306
Mentor, OH 44060
Toll-Free: 866-951-5357
Phone: 440-951-5357
Fax: 440-951-5358
Website: http://
www.smartrecovery.org
E-mail: SRMail1@aol.com

Women for Sobriety

P.O. Box 618
Quakertown, PA 18951-0618
Phone: 215-536-8026
Fax: 215-538-9026
Website: http://
www.womenforsobriety.org
E-mail: newlife@nni.com

Chapter 72

State-By-State List Of Alcohol And Drug Referral Phone Numbers

For each of the 50 states, this chapter lists the appropriate agency to contact for referrals to local drug-treatment and information resources.

National Information

National Association of State Alcohol and Drug Abuse Directors (NASADAD)
808 17th Street NW, Suite 410
Washington, DC 20006
Phone: 202-293-0090
Fax: 202-293-1250
Web site: http://www.nasadad.org
E-mail: dcoffice@nasadad.org

States

Alabama
Division of Mental Health Illness and Substance Abuse Community Programs
Department of Mental Health
100 N. Union Street
Montgomery, AL 36130
Toll-Free: 800-367-0955
Phone: 334-242-3174
Website: http://www.mh.state.al.us

About This Chapter: Information in this chapter was excerpted from "What You Can Do about Drug Use in America," Office for Substance Abuse Prevention, U.S. Department of Health and Human Services, DHHS Pub. No. ADM 91-1572. All information was updated and verified in January 2006.

Alaska

Office of Alcoholism and Drug
Abuse
Department of Health and Social
Services
249 Main Street
P.O. Box 110608
Juneau, AK 99811-0608
Toll Free: 888-464-8920
Phone: 907-465-8920
Fax: 907-465-4410
Website: http://
www.hss.state.ak.us/dbh

Arizona

Alcoholism and Drug Abuse
Office of Community Behavior
Health
Department of Health Services
150 North 18th Avenue
Phoenix, AZ 85007
Phone: 602-542-1000
Fax: 602-542-0883
Web site: http://www.azdhs.gov

Arkansas

Office on Alcohol and Drug Abuse
Prevention
4313 West Markham
3rd Floor, Administration, Room 303
Little Rock, AR 72205
Phone: 501-686-9866
Web site: http://www.state.ar.us/
dhs/dmhs

California

Department of Alcohol and Drug
Programs
1700 K Street
Sacramento, CA 95814
Toll Free: 800-879-2772
Phone: 916-445-0834
Web site: http://www.adp.ca.gov

Colorado

Alcohol and Drug Abuse Division
Department of Health
4055 S. Lowell Blvd.
Denver, CO 80236
Phone: 303-866-7480
Fax: 303-866-7481
Web site: http://
www.cdhs.state.co.us/ohr/adad/
index.html

Connecticut

Department of Mental Health and
Addiction Services
410 Capitol Avenue
P.O. Box 341431
Hartford, CT 06134
Toll Free: 800-446-7348
Phone: 860-418-7000
TDD Toll Free: 888-621-3551
TDD: 860-418-6707
Web site: http://
www.dmhas.state.ct.us

Delaware

Delaware Division of Substance
Abuse and Mental Health
1901 North DuPont Highway,
Main Bldg.
Newcastle, DE 19720
Toll Free Helpline: 800-464-HELP
Phone: 302-255-9399
Fax: 302-255-4428
Web site: http://www.state.de.us/
dhss/dsamh
E-mail: dhssinfo@state.de.us

District of Columbia

Addiction Prevention and Recovery
Administration
825 North Capitol Street, NE
Washington, DC 20002
24 Hour Hotline: 888-7WE-HELP
Phone: 202-698-6080
Website: http://dchealth.dc.gov

Florida

Alcohol and Drug Abuse Program
Department of Health and
Rehabilitative Services
1317 Winewood Blvd., Bldg. 6,
Room 300
Tallahassee, FL 32399-0700
Phone: 850-487-2920
Fax: 850-414-7474
Web site: http://
www.dcf.state.fl.us/mentalhealth/sa

Georgia

MHDDAD
Two Peachtree Street, NW
22nd Floor
Atlanta, GA 30303
Toll Free Helpline: 800-338-6745
Phone: 404-657-5737
Web site: http://
www.mhddad.dhr.georgia.gov

Hawaii

Alcohol and Drug Abuse Division
Department of Health
601 Kamokila Blvd.
Room 360
Kapolei, HI 96707
Phone: 808-692-7506
Website: www.hawaii.gov/health/
substance-abuse

Idaho

Department of Health and Welfare
Family and Children's Services
Drug and Alcohol Abuse Division
450 West State Street, 5th Floor
Boise, ID 83720
Toll Free Idaho CareLine:
800-926-2588
Phone: 208-334-5500
TDD: 208-332-7205
Fax: 208-334-6558
Web site: http://
www.healthandwelfare.idaho.gov

Illinois

Department of Alcoholism and
Substance Abuse
Phone: 800-843-6154
TTY: 800-447-6404
Website: http://www.dhs.state.il.us

Indiana

Division of Addiction Services
Department of Mental Health
Indiana Government Center
3rd Floor South, Room W353
Indianapolis, IN 46204
Phone: 317-232-7800
Fax: 317-233-3472
Web site: http://www.in.gov/fssa/
servicemental

Iowa

Department of Public Health
Division of Substance Abuse and
Health Promotion
Lucas State Office Building
321 East 12th Street, 6th Floor
Des Moines, IA 50319-0075
Phone: 515-281-4417
Website: http://
www.idph.state.ia.us

Kansas

Alcohol and Drug Abuse
Prevention, Treatment, and
Recovery
Docking State Office Building
915 SW Harrison, 10th Floor N.
Topeka, KS 66612-1570
Phone: 785-296-6807
Fax: 785-296-7275
Website: http://www.srskansas.org/
hcp/aaps/AAPSTreatment.htm

Kentucky

Division of Substance Abuse
Department for Mental Health and
Mental Retardation Services
100 Fair Oaks Lane, 4th Floor
Frankfort, KY 40621
Phone: 502-564-2880
Fax: 502-564-7152
Web site: http://www.mhmr.ky.gov/
kdmhmrs

Louisiana

Office of Human Services
Office for Addictive Disorders
1201 Capitol Access Road
P.O. Box 2790, Bin 18
Baton Rouge, LA 70821-2790
Phone: 225-342-6717
Fax: 225-342-3875
Website: http://
www.dhh.louisiana.gov/offices/
?ID=23

Maine

Office of Substance Abuse
AMHI Marquardt, 3rd Floor
11 State House Station
Augusta, ME 04333-0011
Toll Free: 800-499-0027 (Maine
only)
Phone: 207-287-2595
TTY: 207-287-4475
Fax: 207-287-8910
Web site: http://www.maine.gov/
dhhs/bds/osa

Maryland

Maryland State Alcohol and Drug
Abuse Administration
55 Wade Avenue
Catonsville, MD 21228
Phone: 410-402-8600
Fax: 410-402-8601
TTY: 410-528-2258
Web site: http://maryland-adaa.org
E-mail:
addainfo@dhmh.state.md.us

Massachusetts

Division of Substance Abuse
Services
250 Washington Street, 3rd Floor
Boston, MA 02108-4619
Phone: 617-624-5111
Fax: 617-624-5185
Website: http://www.mass.gov/
dph/bsas

Michigan

Office of Substance Abuse Services
Department of Public Health
320 South Walnut
Lansing, MI 48913
Phone: 517-373-4700
Website: http://www.michigan.gov/
mdch

Minnesota

Chemical Dependency Program
Division
Department of Human Services
P.O. Box 64977
St. Paul, MN 55164-0977
Phone: 651-431-2460
Fax: 651-4314-7449
Website: http://
www.dhs.state.mn.us

Mississippi Department of Mental Health

Division of Alcohol and Drug
Abuse
239 North Lamar Street
1101 Robert E. Lee Building
Suite 901
Jackson, MS 39201
Phone: 601-359-6220
Fax: 601-576-4040
Website: http://
www.dmh.state.ms.us/
substance_abuse_services.html

Missouri

Division of Alcohol and Drug
Abuse
Department of Mental Health
1706 East Elm Street
P.O. Box 687
Jefferson City, MO 65102
Toll-Free: 800-364-9687
Phone: 573-751-4942
Fax: 573-751-8224
Website: http://
www.dmh.missouri.gov

Montana

Addictive and Mental Disorders
Division
Department of Institutions
555 Fuller
Helena, MT 59620
Phone: 406-444-3964
Fax: 406-444-4435
Website: http://www.dphhs.mt.gov

Nebraska

Health and Human Services
Division of Behavioral Health
P.O. Box 98925
Lincoln, NE 68509
Phone: 402-479-5117
Fax: 402-479-5162
Web site: http://
www.hhs.state.ne.us/beh/mhsa.htm

Nevada

Alcohol & Drug Abuse Bureau
Department of Human Resources
505 East King Street, Room 500
Carson City, NV 89710
Phone: 775-684-4190
Fax: 775-684-4185
Web site: http://
health2k.state.nv.us/bada

New Hampshire

Office of Alcohol and Drug Abuse
Prevention
State Office Park South
105 Pleasant Street
Concord, NH 03301
Toll Free: 800-804-0909
Phone: 603-271-6110
Fax: 603-271-6105
Web site: http://
www.dhhs.state.nh.us

New Jersey

Department of Health
Addiction Services
120 South Stockton Street
PO Box 362
Trenton, NJ 08625-0362
Toll Free: 800-322-5525 (New
Jersey only)
Phone: 609-292-7232
Web site: http://www.state.nj.us/
humanservices/das

New Mexico

Behavioral Health Services
Division
1190 St. Francis Drive
Room 3300 North
P.O. Box 26110
Santa Fe, NM 87502
Toll Free: 800-962-8936 (outside
Albuquerque)
Phone: 505-827-2658
Fax: 505-827-0097
Website: http://
www.health.state.nm.us

New York

Division of Alcoholism and
Substance Abuse Services
1450 Western Avenue
Albany, NY 12203
Phone: 518-485-1768
Fax: 518-485-2142
Web site: http://
www.oasas.state.ny.us

North Carolina

Alcohol and Drug Abuse Section
Division of Mental Health and
Mental Retardation Services
325 North Salisbury Street
Raleigh, NC 27603
Phone: 919-733-4670
Fax: 919-733-4556
Web site: http://
www.dhhs.state.nc.us/mhddsas

North Dakota

Division of Mental Health &
Substance Abuse Services
1237 W Divide Ave, Suite C
Bismark, ND 58501-1208
Toll-Free: 800-755-2719
Phone: 701-328-8920
Fax: 701-328-8969
Website: http://www.nd.gov/
humanservices/services/
mentalhealth
E-mail: dhsmhsas@state.nd.us

Ohio

Bureau on Alcohol Abuse and
Recovery
Ohio Department of Health
Two Nationwide Plaza
280 North High Street, 12th Floor
Columbus, OH 43215
Phone: 614-466-3445
Fax: 614-752-8645
Web site: http://
www.odadas.state.oh.us

Oklahoma

ODMHSAS
1200 NE 13th Street
P.O. Box 53277
Capitol Station
Oklahoma City, OK 73152-3277
Toll-Free Teenline: 800-522-8336
Toll Free: 800-522-9054
Phone: 405-522-3908
Fax: 405-522-3650
Web site: http://www.odmhsas.org

Oregon
Office of Mental Health and
Addiction
500 Summer St., NE, E86
Salem, OR 97301-1118
Phone: 503-945-5763
Fax: 503-378-8467
TTY: 503-945-5895
Web site: http://www.oregon.gov/
DHS
E-mail: omhas.web@state.or.us

Pennsylvania
Drug and Alcohol Programs
Department of Health
02 Kline Plaza
Harrisburg, PA 17104
Toll Free: 800-582-7746
Phone: 717-787-2712
Fax: 717-787-6285
Website: http://
www.health.state.pa.us/bdap

Rhode Island
Council on Alcoholism
Department of Mental Health,
Retardation and Hospitals
500 Prospect St.
Pawtucket, RI 02860
Toll Free: 866-252-3784
Phone: 401-725-0410
Fax: 401-725-0768
Web site: http://
www.mhrh.state.ri.us

South Carolina
South Carolina Commission on
Alcohol and Drug Abuse
101 Executive Center Drive
Suite 215
Columbia, SC 29210
Phone: 803-896-5555
Fax: 803-896-5557
Web site: http://
www.daodas.state.sc.us/web

South Dakota
Division of Alcohol and Drug
Abuse
E. Hwy. 34, Hillsview Plaza
c/o 500 E. Capital Avenue
Pierre, SD 57501
Toll-Free: 800-265-9684
Phone: 605-773-3123
Fax: 605-773-7076
Web site: http://www.state.sd.us/
dhs/ADA

Tennessee
Alcohol and Drug Abuse Services
William R. Snodgrass Tennessee
Tower, 26th Floor
312 8th Avenue North
Nashville, TN 37247-4401
Phone: 615-741-1921
Fax: 615-532-2419
Web site: http://www2.state.tn.us/
health/A&D

Texas

Texas Commission on Alcohol and
Drug Abuse
909 West 45th Street
Austin, TX 78758
Toll Free: 800-832-9623
Web site: http://
www.tcada.state.tx.us

Utah

Department of Human Services
Division of Substance Abuse and
Mental Health
Department of Social Services
120 North 200 West, Room 209
Salt Lake City, UT 84103
Toll Free Hotline: 888-633-4673
Phone: 801-538-3939
Fax: 801-538-9892
Web site: http://
www.hsdsa.utah.gov

Vermont

Office of Alcohol and Drug Abuse
Programs
108 Cherry Street
P.O. Box 70
Burlington, VT 05402-0070
Toll-Free: 800-464-4343
Phone: 802-651-1550
Fax: 802-651-1573
Web site: http://www.state.vt.us/
adap

Virginia

Office of Substance Abuse Services
Department of Mental Health,
Mental Retardation and Substance
Abuse
Ninth Street Office Building
202 North Ninth Street, 4th Floor
Richmond, VA 23219
Phone: 804-786-9072
Fax: 804-786-1807
Web site: http://
www.gosap.state.va.us
E-mail: gosap@gov.virginia.gov

Washington

Bureau of Alcoholism and
Substance Abuse
P.O. Box 45330
Olympia, WA 98504-5330
Toll Free: 877-301-4557
Phone: 360-725-3700
Fax: 360-438-8057
Website: http://www1.dshs.wa.gov/
dasa

West Virginia

Bureau for Behavioral Health and
Health Facilities
Division on Alcoholism and Drug
Abuse
350 Capitol Street, Room 350
Charleston, WV 25301-3702
Phone: 304-558-2276
Fax: 304-558-3275
Web site: http://www.wvdhhr.org/
bhhf/ada.asp

Wisconsin
Office of Alcohol and Other Drug
Abuse
1 West Wilson Street, Room 434
Madison, WI 53702
Phone: 608-266-2717
Fax: 608-266-1533
Website: http://
www.dhfs.state.wi.us/substabuse

Wyoming
Department of Health
Substance Abuse Division
6101 Yellowstone Road, Suite 220
Cheyenne, WY 82002
Toll Free: 800-535-4006
Phone: 307-777-6494
Fax: 307-777-5849
Web site: http://wdh.state.wy.us/SAD
E-mail: substanceabuse@state.wy.us

Chapter 73

Additional Reading About Drugs And Addiction

Books

Addict in the Family: Stories of Loss, Hope, and Recovery
Beverly Conyers; Hazelden, Center City, MN; August 2003
ISBN: 156838999X

Addiction and Recovery for Dummies
Brian F. Shaw, Paul Ritvo, Jane Irvine; Wiley Publishing, Inc., Hoboken, NJ; January 2005
ISBN: 0764576259

Alcohol Information for Teens
Joyce Brennfleck Shannon; Omnigraphics, Inc., Detroit, MI; January 2005
ISBN: 0780807413

About This Chapter: This chapter includes a compilation of various resources from many sources deemed reliable. It serves as a starting point for further research and is not intended to be comprehensive. Inclusion does not constitute endorsement. Resources in this chapter are categorized by type and, under each type, they are listed alphabetically by title to make topics easier to identify.

Clearing the Haze: A Teen's Guide to Smoking-Related Health Issues

Joan Esherick; Mason Crest Publishers, Broomall, PA; December 2004
ISBN: 1590848446

Drugs 101: An Overview for Teens

Margaret O. Hyde, John F. Setaro, M.D.; 21st Century, Kirkland, WA;
January 2003
ISBN: 0761326081

Dying for Acceptance: A Teen's Guide to Drug- and Alcohol-Related Health Issues

Joan Esherick; Mason Crest Publishers, Broomall, PA; December 2004
ISBN: 1590848470

Illegal Drugs: A Complete Guide to Their History, Chemistry, Use, and Abuse

Paul Gahlinger, M.D., Ph.D.; Penguin Group (USA) Inc., New York, NY;
January 2004
ISBN: 0452285054

Quitting Smoking for Dummies

David Brizer, M.D.; Wiley Publishing, Inc., Hoboken, NJ; September 2003
ISBN: 0764526294

Smoking 101: An Overview for Teens

Margaret O. Hyde, John F. Setaro, M.D.; 21st Century, Kirkland, WA;
July 2005
ISBN: 0761328351

Teen Addiction

Linda Theresa Raczek; Thomson Gale, Farmington Hills, MI; December 2003
ISBN: 1560067799

Teen Alcoholism

Barbara Sheen; Thomson Gale, Farmington Hills, MI; January 2004
ISBN: 1590185013

Articles

"Abuse of Inhalants and Prescription Drugs: Real Dangers for Teens," *Junior Scholastic*, April 11, 2005, p. S1(4).

"Brain Change: Two Very Different Ways," by Laura D'Angelo, *Science World*, April 26, 2004, p. 20(1).

"Buff Enough? More Teens are Using Steroids to Look Pumped and Do Better at Sports," by Scott Ingram, *Current Science*, September 24, 2004, p. 4(5).

"Clean Teens: What Do You Call a Teen Who Doesn't Drink or Do Drugs? One of the Crowd," by Melissa Daly, *Current Health 2*, April-May 2005, p. 20(3).

"The Downward Spiral Caused by a Drug Called Heroin: This Teen's Abuse of Heroin Led Him Down a Path of Illness, Addiction, and Crime that He's Just Beginning to Recover From," by Alexia Lewnes, *Scholastic Choices*, November-December 2004, p. 10(8).

"Gasping for Oxygen: Kids Are Putting Their Lives at Risk by Huffing Toxic Chemicals," by Sean McCollum, *Scholastic Choices*, April-May 2005, p. 18(7).

"Getting Help: Two Teens in Treatment Get Real about What It's Like to Smoke Pot," *Current Health 2*, March 2005, p. 13(1).

"How Alcohol Ads Target Teens: They're Cute. They're Funny. But Did You Ever Think that Those Funny, Sometimes Annoying Frogs Croaking the Name of a Beer Could Be Dangerous to You?" by Nina Riccio, *Current Health 2*, September 2002, p. 14(4).

"Huffing: Will Your Next Breath Be Your Last?" by Lori Leibovich, *Teen People*, March 1, 2003, p. 110.

"Knocking on Death's Door: Club Drugs Leave Teens High and Dry. Some Kids Die," by Jennifer L. Peters, *Know Your World Extra*, April 25, 2003, p. 4(3).

"Over the Counter Killer: It's Cheap, It's Legal, and It's Available at Any Drugstore. DXM, a Cough Medicine Ingredient, is the Latest Craze for Teens Who Want to Get High or Die Trying," by Thomas Fields-Meyer and Melinda Janiszewski, *People Weekly*, February 2, 2004, p. 48.

"The Party's Over: Teens are Drawn to Club Drugs like GHB, Ecstasy, and Ketamine, but the Drugs are Extremely Dangerous," by Denise Rinaldo, *Scholastic Choices*, January 2004, p. 10(7).

"Performance-Enhancing Drugs: The Truth behind the Hype: Real Winners Resist the Temptation to Take Performance-Enhancing Drugs," by Kathiann M. Kowalski, *Current Health 2*, February 2003, p. 6(6).

"Prescription Drugs: More Teens are Popping Pills for an Easy High, but Nicole's Story Will Make You Put the Medicine Back in the Cabinet," by Larry Smith, *Teen People*, May 1, 2003, p. 134.

"Rave Realities: The Truth about Club Drugs," *Science World*, January 12, 2004, p. S8(1).

"Rx for Trouble: Abusing Legal Drugs Can Destroy Lives," by Melissa Klein, *Current Health 2*, January 2006, p. 22(4).

"The Scariest Drug Epidemic You've Never Heard Of," by Jason Bane, *Teen People*, December 1, 2003, p. 136.

"Smoke Screen: Why Do Tobacco Ads Look Glamorous and Sexy when Everyone Knows Smoking is Gross? Here's How to See through the Advertising Haze," by John DiConsiglio, *Scholastic Choices*, February-March 2005, p. 10(6).

"Teens, Drug Abuse and AIDS: The Deadly Connection," *Science World*, March 7, 2005, p. S1(8).

"Wasted: Life's No Party for Teens Who Drink Too Much, Too Fast," by Julie Mehta, *Current Health 2*, February 2005, p. 15(6).

"Your Top 10 Questions about Pot," by Larry Smith, *Teen People*, April 1, 2003, p. 136.

"The X Files: Experts Answer Your Top Questions about Ecstasy," by Larry Smith, *Teen People*, August 1, 2003, p. 240.

Web Page Documents

Alcohol: What You Don't Know Can Harm You
National Institute on Alcohol Abuse and Alcoholism
http://pubs.niaaa.nih.gov/publications/WhatUDontKnow_HTML/
dontknow.htm

Cigarettes and Other Nicotine Products
The National Institute on Drug Abuse
http://www.drugabuse.gov/Infofacts/tobacco.html

Coping with an Alcoholic Parent
The Nemours Foundation
http://www.teenshealth.org/teen/drug_alcohol/alcohol/
coping_alcoholic.html

Date Rape Is a Crime
Community Crisis Center, Inc.
http://www.crisiscenter.org/date_rape.htm

Drug Abuse and AIDS
The National Institute on Drug Abuse
http://www.drugabuse.gov/Infofacts/DrugAbuse.html

Drugged Driving
 The National Institute on Drug Abuse
http://www.drugabuse.gov/Infofacts/driving.html

Drugs, Alcohol and Smoking—Straight Talk
The National Women's Health Information Center
http://www.4girls.gov/substance/tobacco.htm

Heads Up: Real News about Drugs and Your Body
Scholastic and the Scientists of The National Institute on Drug Abuse
http://www.drugabuse.gov/PDF/Scholastic/HeadsUp-SkillsBook-Yr2.pdf

Inhalants
National Institute on Drug Abuse
http://www.nida.nih.gov/Infofacts/Inhalants.html

The Interaction between Substance Abuse and Specific Mental Health Disorders
Office of National Drug Control Policy
http://www.drugstory.org/pdfs/SubstanceAbuse_MentalHealth.pdf

Marijuana
The National Institute on Drug Abuse
http://www.drugabuse.gov/Infofacts/marijuana.html

Muscle Madness: The Ugly Connection between Body Image and Steroid Abuse
Office of National Drug Control Policy
http://www.drugstory.org/pdfs/musclemadness2.pdf

Prescription Drug Abuse
The Nemours Foundation
http://www.teenshealth.org/teen/drug_alcohol/drugs/prescription_drug_abuse.html

Sex, Drugs and Teens Fact Sheet
Office of National Drug Control Policy
http://www.drugstory.org/pdfs/sex_and_drugs_factsheet.pdf

Tobacco Use and the Health of Young People
Centers for Disease Control and Prevention
http://www.cdc.gov/HealthyYouth/tobacco/facts.htm

Types of Help for Alcohol and Drug Abuse
Bowles Center for Alcohol Studies, University of North Carolina at Chapel Hill
http://www.med.unc.edu/alcohol/prevention/helptypes.html

Understanding Drug Abuse and Addiction
The National Institute on Drug Abuse
http://www.drugabuse.gov/Infofacts/understand.html

Index

Index

Page numbers that appear in *Italics* refer to illustrations. Page numbers that have a small 'n' after the page number refer to information shown as Notes at the beginning of each chapter. Page numbers that appear in **Bold** refer to information contained in boxes on that page (except Notes information at the beginning of each chapter).